LETTERS ON OCCULT MEDITATION

BOOKS BY ALICE A. BAILEY

Letters On Occult Meditation

Received and Edited by

ALICE A. BAILEY

LUCIS PUBLISHING COMPANY

New York

LUCIS PRESS, LTD.

London

First printing, 1922
Tenth Printing, 1972 (1st Paperback Edition)
Fifteenth Printing, 1993

ISBN No. 0-85330-111-5

Library of Congress Card Catalog Number: 26-8569

The publication of this book is financed by the Tibetan Book Fund which is established for the perpetuation of the teachings of the Tibetan and Alice A. Bailey.

This Fund is controlled by the Lucis Trust, a tax-exempt, religious, educational corporation.

The Lucis Publishing Company is a non-profit organisation owned by the Lucis Trust. No royalties are paid on this book.

This title is also available in a
clothbound edition.

It has been translated into Dutch, Spanish, French, German, Italian, Greek, Icelandic, Portuguese, Japanese and Swedish. Translation into other languages is proceeding.

LUCIS PUBLISHING COMPANY
113 University Place, 11th Fl.
P.O. Box 722, Cooper Station
New York, NY 10276

LUCIS PRESS, LTD.
Suite 54
3 Whitehall Court
London SW1A 2EF

MANUFACTURED IN THE UNITED STATES OF AMERICA
By Fort Orange Press, Inc., Albany, N.Y.

DEDICATED

TO

THE TIBETAN TEACHER

WHO

WROTE THESE LETTERS

AND

AUTHORISED THEIR PUBLICATION

FOREWORD

The following letters were received during the period included within the dates, May 16th, 1920, and October 20th, 1920, with the exception of the two letters which were received in 1919. With the consent of their author they have been gathered together for publication.

They are published in full as received, with the exception of certain parts which have a purely personal application, those having reference to a certain occult school, and those of a prophetic or esoteric nature, which may not now be communicated.

It is hoped that those who read these letters will endeavour to do two things:

1. Read always with an open mind, remembering that the truth is a many-sided diamond, and that its different aspects will appear at different times, as those who guide the race see a need which must be met. Many books on meditation have been written, some too abstruse and some too superficial to satisfy the average educated man. The writer of these letters has apparently attempted to supply the need of a brief yet scientific exposition of a rationale of meditation, emphasising the goal immediately ahead and the intermediate stages.

2. Judge of the letters on their merits and not upon claims put forth on behalf of the writer. For this reason he has chosen to preserve his anonymity and has requested the recipient of the letters to publish them under his pseudonym.

If the subject matter of the letters is of value it will call forth a response from the readers and serve to help some onward towards the goal, and prove to many the inspiration and aid it already has to a few.

ALICE A. BAILEY.

New York, 1922.

EXTRACT FROM A STATEMENT BY THE TIBETAN

PUBLISHED AUGUST 1934

Suffice it to say, that I am a Tibetan disciple of a certain degree, and this tells you but little, for all are disciples from the humblest aspirant up to, and beyond, the Christ Himself. I live in a physical body like other men, on the borders of Tibet, and at times (from the exoteric standpoint) preside over a large group of Tibetan lamas, when my other duties permit. It is this fact that has caused it to be reported that I am an abbot of this particular lamasery. Those associated with me in the work of the Hierarchy (and all true disciples are associated in this work) know me by still another name and office. A.A.B. knows who I am and recognises me by two of my names.

I am a brother of yours, who has travelled a little longer upon the Path than has the average student, and has therefore incurred greater responsibilities. I am one who has wrestled and fought his way into a greater measure of light than has the aspirant who will read this article, and I must therefore act as a transmitter of the light, no matter what the cost. I am not an old man, as age counts among the teachers, yet I am not young or inexperienced. My work is to teach and spread the knowledge of the Ageless Wisdom wherever I can find a response, and I have been doing this for many years. I seek also to help the Master M. and the Master K.H. whenever opportunity offers, for I have been long connected with Them and with Their work. In all the above, I have told you much; yet at the same time I have told you nothing which would lead you to offer me that blind obedience and the foolish devotion which the emotional aspirant offers to the Guru and Master whom he is as yet unable to contact. Nor will he make that desired contact until he has transmuted emotional devotion into unselfish service to humanity —not to the Master.

The books that I have written are sent out with no claim for their acceptance. They may, or may not, be correct, true and useful. It is for you to ascertain their truth by right practice and by the exercise of the intuition. Neither I nor A.A.B. is the least interested in having them acclaimed as inspired writings, or in having anyone speak of them (with bated breath) as being the work of one of the Masters. If they present truth in such a way that it follows sequentially upon that already offered in the world teachings, if the information given raises the aspiration and the will-to-serve from the plane of the emotions to that of the mind (the plane whereon the Masters *can* be found) then they will have served their purpose. If the teaching conveyed calls forth a response from the illumined mind of the worker in the world, and brings a flashing forth of his intuition, then let that teaching be accepted. But not otherwise. If the statements meet with eventual corroboration, or are deemed true under the test of the Law of Correspondences, then that is well and good. But should this not be so, let not the student accept what is said.

SYNOPSIS OF "LETTERS ON OCCULT MEDITATION"

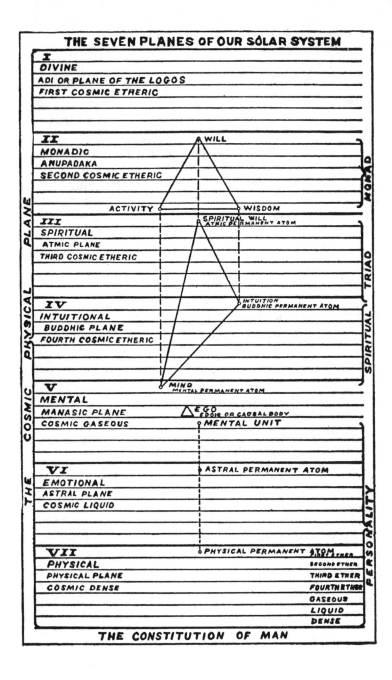

THE SEVEN PLANES OF OUR SOLAR SYSTEM

I
DIVINE
ADI OR PLANE OF THE LOGOS
FIRST COSMIC ETHERIC

II
MONADIC
ANUPADAKA
SECOND COSMIC ETHERIC

WILL

ACTIVITY — WISDOM

III
SPIRITUAL
ATMIC PLANE
THIRD COSMIC ETHERIC

SPIRITUAL WILL
ATMIC PERMANENT ATOM

IV
INTUITIONAL
BUDDHIC PLANE
FOURTH COSMIC ETHERIC

INTUITION
BUDDHIC PERMANENT ATOM

V
MENTAL
MANASIC PLANE
COSMIC GASEOUS

MIND
MENTAL PERMANENT ATOM
EGO
EGOIC OR CAUSAL BODY
MENTAL UNIT

VI
EMOTIONAL
ASTRAL PLANE
COSMIC LIQUID

ASTRAL PERMANENT ATOM

VII
PHYSICAL
PHYSICAL PLANE
COSMIC DENSE

PHYSICAL PERMANENT ATOM FIRST ETHER
SECOND ETHER
THIRD ETHER
FOURTH ETHER
GASEOUS
LIQUID
DENSE

Left margin: THE COSMIC PHYSICAL PLANE

Right margin: MONAD · TRIAD · SPIRITUAL · PERSONALITY

THE CONSTITUTION OF MAN

The constitution of man, as considered in the following pages, is basically threefold, as follows:—

I. The Monad, or pure Spirit, the Father in Heaven.

This aspect reflects the three aspects of the Godhead:
1. Will or Power..................The Father
2. Love-Wisdom.....................The Son
3. Active Intelligence...........The Holy Spirit

and is only contacted at the final initiations, when man is nearing the end of his journey and is perfected.

The Monad reflects itself again in

II. The Ego, Higher Self, or Individuality.
This aspect is potentially:—
1. Spiritual Will ....Atma
2. Intuition ....Buddhi, Love-Wisdom, the Christ principle.
3. Higher or abstract Mind.......Higher Manas.

The Ego begins to make its power felt in advanced men, and increasingly on the Probationary Path until by the third initiation the control of the lower self by the higher is perfected, and the highest aspect begins to make its energy felt.

The Ego reflects itself in

III. The Personality, or lower self, physical plane man.
This aspect is also threefold:—
1. A mental body.................lower manas.
2. An emotional body..............astral body.
3. A physical body........the dense physical and the etheric body.

The aim of meditation is therefore to bring man to the realisation of the Egoic aspect and to bring the lower nature under its control. This is the immediate goal for the average man.

LETTER I

THE ALIGNMENT OF THE EGO WITH THE PERSONALITY.

1—The Aligning of the three lower bodies.
2—Aligning with the Causal Body.
3—The Method of Alignment.
4—Macrocosmic and Microcosmic Alignment.

LETTERS ON
OCCULT MEDITATION.

LETTER I
ALIGNMENT OF THE EGO WITH THE PERSONALITY.

Sunday, May 16, 1920.

It is in the aligning of the three vehicles, the physical, the emotional, and the lower mind body, within the causal periphery, and their stabilising there by an effort of the will, that the real work of the Ego or Higher Self in any particular incarnation can be accomplished. The great thinkers of the race, the true exponents of lower mind, are fundamentally those whose three lower bodies are aligned; that is to say, those whose mental body holds the other two in circumspect alignment. The mental body, then, is in direct communication, unobstructed and free from interference, straight through to the physical brain.

When the alignment is fourfold and when the three above-mentioned bodies are aligned with the body of the Higher Self, the causal or egoic body, and held steady within its circumference, then the great leaders of the race,—those who emotionally and intellectually sway mankind,—can be seen working; then the inspirational writers and dreamers can bring down their inspirations and dreams; and then the synthetic and abstract thinkers can transfer their conceptions to the world of form. It is, right through, a question of an unimpeded channel. Study, therefore, in this connection and when time permits, physical co-ordination; then to physical co-ordination add emotional stability, and you have the two vehicles functioning as one. When the co-ordination extends to the mental body, the threefold lower man is reaching his apotheosis, and has rung most of the changes in the world of form.

Later comes co-ordination perfected with the Higher Self, the channel of communication reaching in line direct, —via an unimpeded funnel, if so I might express it,—to the physical brain consciousness. Heretofore it has only been direct at rare intervals. The four lesser brain centres are functioning at high vibration in the man of a highly co-ordinated personality; when the Ego is nearing alignment with the lower bodies, the pineal gland and the pituitary body are in process of development; and when they are functioning with correlation (which eventuates by the time the third Initiation is taken), then the third, or alta major centre, intensifies its hitherto gentle vibration. When the fifth Initiation is taken, the interplay between the three centres is perfected, and the alignment of the bodies is geometrically rectified; you have then the perfected fivefold superman.

For the average man, then, this alignment occurs only at intervals,—in moments of stress, in hours of needed humanitarian effort and in times of intensest aspiration. Abstraction of a more or less degree has to enter in before the Ego takes continued notice of the personality or lower self. When that abstraction involves the emotions, is based in the mentality and contacts the physical brain, then alignment is commencing.

Hence the work of meditation, for it tends to abstraction and seeks to awaken to abstract consciousness both the emotions and the mentality.

Alignment and Vibration.

Forget not either that it is largely a question of matter and vibration. The abstract levels of the mental plane consist of the three higher levels, the first being that termed the third subplane. As I have explained to you before, each subplane has its correlations on the major planes. When, therefore, you have built into your bodies, —physical, emotional and mental,—matter of the third subplane of each of those planes, then the Higher Self commences consciously and ever more continuously to function through the aligning Personality. Perhaps we might reverse the idea and state that it is only when third subplane matter of a certain percentage (which percentage is one of the secrets of Initiation) is contained in the vehicles, that the Personality as a conscious whole recognises and obeys that Higher Self. After such a percentage is attained, it is then necessary to build in matter of the two higher subplanes on the physical and emotional planes; hence the struggle for the aspirant to purify and discipline the physical body and to subdue the emotional. *Purification* and *subjugation* describe the work to be done on the two planes. This involves the use of lower mind, and the three lower vehicles thus become aligned.

The vibrations of the abstract levels can then begin to be felt. You need to remember that they come via the causal body, the vehicle of the Higher Self, and the average causal body is on the third subplane of the mental plane. This is a point not sufficiently recognised. Ponder on it. Real abstract thought becomes possible only when the Personality has, by vibration reciprocal to that of the

Ego, aligned itself sufficiently to form a fairly unimpeded channel. Then at intervals, rare at first but of increasing frequency, will abstract ideas begin to filter down, to be followed in due time by flashes of real illumination or intuition from the Spiritual Triad or the true threefold Ego itself.

The Chord of the Ego.

When I use the term "reciprocal vibration," what do I mean? I mean the adaptation of the Personality or Lower Self, to the Ego, or Higher Self, the dominating of the Personality ray by the ray of the Ego and the combining of their tones. I mean the blending of the primary colour of the Higher Self with the secondary hue of the Lower Self until beauty is achieved. At first, there is dissonance and discord, a clashing of the colours, and a fight between the Higher and the Lower. But as time progresses, and later with the aid of the Master, harmony of colour and tone is produced (a synonymous matter), until eventually you will have the basic note of matter, the major third of the aligned Personality, the dominant fifth of the Ego, followed by the full chord of the Monad or Spirit.

It is the dominant we seek at adeptship, and earlier the perfected third of the Personality. During our various incarnations we strike and ring the changes on all the intervening notes, and sometimes our lives are major and sometimes minor, but always they tend to flexibility and greater beauty. In due time, each note fits into its chord, the chord of the Spirit; each chord forms part of a phrase, the phrase or group to which the chord belongs; and the phrase goes to the completion of one seventh of the whole. The entire seven sections, then, complete the sonata of this solar system,—a part of the threefold masterpiece of the Logos or God, the Master-Musician.

June 2, 1920.

Microcosmic and Macrocosmic Alignment.

This morning, I would touch on the matter of egoic alignment again, showing you, under the Law of Correspondences, the universal application. It lies based in geometry, or in figures and numbers.

The aim of the evolution of man in the three worlds—the physical, emotional and mental planes—is the alignment of his threefold Personality with the body egoic, till the one straight line is achieved and the man becomes the One.

Each life that the Personality leads is, at the close, represented by some geometrical figure, some utilisation of the lines of the cube, and their demonstration in a *form* of some kind. Intricate and uncertain in outline and crude in design are the forms of the earlier lives; definite and clear in outline are the forms built by the average advanced man of this generation. But when he steps upon the Path of Discipleship, the purpose consists in merging all these many lines into one line, and gradually this consummation is achieved. The Master is He Who has blended all the lines of fivefold development first into the three, and then into the one. The six-pointed star becomes the five-pointed star, the cube becomes the triangle, and the triangle becomes the one; whilst the one (at the end of the greater cycle) becomes the point in the circle of manifestation.

Hence the effort made to teach all devotees simplicity, based on a trinity of foundation truths, and the inculcation of one-pointedness.

Each life tends to greater stability but seldom is the three-fold Personality yet to be found lined up, if so I may put it, with the causal consciousness. Temporary moments occur when this is the case and when (in moments of highest aspiration and for purposes of unselfish endeavor) the higher and the lower form a line direct. Usually the emotional body, through violent emotion and vibration, or a fluctuating restlessness, is continuously out of alignment. Where the emotional body may be momentarily aligned, then the mental body acts as an obstruction, preventing the percolation down from the higher to the lower, and so to the physical brain. It takes many lives of strenuous endeavor before the emotional body can be stilled and a mental body built that will act as a filter and not as an impediment. Even when this has been somewhat accomplished and the emotional body is stabilised and a pure reflector, and the mental body serves the purpose of a sensitive plate and discriminator, and the intelligent explainer of the higher imparted truth,—even then, I say, it takes much discipline and many lives of effort to align the two *at the same time*. When that is done, the control of the physical brain and its final alignment remain to be effected, so that it may act as a direct receiver and transmitter of the imparted teaching, and may reflect with accuracy the higher consciousness.

Wherein, therefore, lies the macrocosmic correspondence? Where is the analogy in the Solar System? An indication I give here. In the direct alignment of certain planets in the process of systemic evolution, with each other and with the Sun comes Logoic or divine alignment. Think this out, but one word of warning I give. Seek not to work out hypotheses of alignment based on the physical planets. The truth lies not there. Only three of the physical planets (and those three in etheric matter) enter into the final alignment that marks the attainment by the Logos of the cosmic egoic consciousness, which is His goal of attainment. Of these three, the earth is not one, but Venus has her place corresponding to the emotional permanent atom.

Further still the alignment may be progressed:—in the alignment of our entire solar system with the system of Sirius lies a still more remote goal. It is a point far ahead in time, but holds hid the secret of the greater cycle.

LETTER II

THE IMPORTANCE OF MEDITATION.

1—It results in egoic contact and alignment.
2—It brings about a state of equilibrium.
3—It stabilises vibration.
4—It assists in a transference of polarisation.

THE IMPORTANCE OF MEDITATION.

June 3, 1920.

Let me this morning give you some more thoughts on the subject of meditation; they will bear somewhat on the matter given yesterday, and on the 16th ultimo.

Fundamentally, meditation is to assist alignment and so permit of contact with the Higher Self; hence its institution. I would, in order duly to elucidate, take up the study of this topic under the following heads:

The Importance of Meditation.
Points considered when assigning a Meditation.
The use of the Sacred Word in Meditation.
Dangers to be avoided in Meditation.
The use of Form in Meditation.
The use of Colour and Sound in Meditation.
Access to the Masters through Meditation.
Future Schools of Meditation.
Purification of the Vehicles.
The Exoteric Life of Service.

Let us today take up the consideration of the first point:—What makes Meditation of importance?

The emphasis upon the importance of meditation follows naturally upon the realisation by the student of the absolute necessity for the domination of the Personality by the Ego.

Man at this time is engaged in many pursuits and through the force of circumstances he is polarised entirely in the lower self, that polarisation being in either the emotional or mental body. One point of interest I would indicate:—as long as the polarisation is purely physical or purely emotional, no need for meditation is ever felt. Even when the mental body is active, no urge arises until the man has run through many changes and many lives, has tasted the cup of pleasure and of pain through many incarnations, has sounded the depths of the life lived entirely for the lower self and found it unsatisfying. Then he begins to turn his thought to other things, to aspire to that which is unknown, to realize and sense within himself the pairs of opposites, and to contact within his consciousness possibilities and ideals undreamt of hitherto. He has come to a point where success, popularity and diverse gifts are his, and yet from their use he derives no content; always the urge within persists until the pain is so severe that the desire to reach out and up, to ascertain something and someone beyond, overcomes all obstacles. The man begins to turn within and to seek the source from whence he came. Then he begins to meditate, to ponder, to intensify vibration until in process of time he garners the fruits of meditation.

Four things meditation does:

1—It enables a man to contact the Ego and to align the three lower bodies.

2—It puts a man into an attitude of equilibrium, neither utterly receptive and negative, nor utterly positive, but at the point of balance. Thus is afforded opportunity to the Ego, and later to the Master, to disturb that equilibrium and tune the quiescent vibration to a higher note than heretofore; to cause the consciousness to vibrate to a newer and higher measure, and to swing (if so I may express it) into the periphery of the threefold Spirit. By the constant practice of this, the whole point of equilibrium is gradually shifted higher and higher, until the time comes when the lower point of attraction in the swinging and adjustment, is not the physical, touches not the emotional, contacts not the mental (the causal body even escaping) and the man is polarised in the spiritual consciousness from thenceforth.

This marks the fourth Initiation; after that Initiation, the Adept makes for Himself a body of manifestation, a free creation,—there is nothing in Him to call into objectivity a body for use in the three worlds and evolved under the Law of Causes.

3—It stabilises the lower vibrations on the subplanes of the emotional and mental planes. It commences the work of attuning the self to the vibration of the third subplane on each of the three lower planes, until that subplane is dominated. The second subplane is then the next to be synchronised.

A man reaches the point of personality attainment in this cycle when he has the capacity to vibrate and move consciously on the fourth subplane. We might term the fourth subplane on the physical, emotional and mental planes (when dominated, aligned and functioning simultaneously in the same incarnation) the *plane of perfected personality* in the concrete sense of the word, and from the lower vision. That particular incarnation will be one in which the man achieves the fullest expression of his lower self,—physically perfect, emotionally vibrant, and mentally colossal. Then succeeding that, begins the transference to a higher vibration, the keying up to the Higher Self, and the attuning of the Personality, or the major third, to the dominant fifth of the Ego.

4—It assists in the transference of the polarisation from one of the permanent atoms of the Personality into the corresponding atom in the spiritual Triad. Later I will elucidate this further.

Hence may easily be seen the essential nature of Meditation and its wise, diligent and serious following.

Early in experience, after the attainment of the highest the lower nature has to offer, man begins to meditate. Disorderly at first are his attempts, and sometimes several incarnations may go by in which the Higher Self only forces the man to think and seriously to meditate at rare and separated intervals. More frequently come the occasions of withdrawing within, until there arises for the man several lives given to mystic meditation and aspiration, culminating usually in a life given entirely to it. It marks the point of the highest emotional aspiration, apart from the scientific application of the law, via the mental body. These laws are those governing the true occult meditation.

Behind each of you who are working definitely under one of the Masters, lie two lives of culmination:—the life of worldly apotheosis and the life of intensest meditation along the mystic or emotional-intuitional line. This meditative life was taken either in a monastery or nunnery in middle Europe by those linked with the Master Jesus and His disciples, or in India, Tibet or China by the pupils of the Master M. or the Master K. H.

Now comes to all of you the most important series of lives to which the previous points of culmination were but stepping stones. In the lives immediately ahead of those upon the Path will come final achievement through the instrumentality of the ordered occult meditation, based on law. For some few may come attainment in this life or the next; for others, shortly in other lives. For a few there lies ahead the attainment of the mystic method, to be the basis later on of the occult or mental method.

LETTER III

POINTS CONSIDERED WHEN ASSIGNING MEDITATION.

1—The Ray of the Ego or Higher Self.
2—The Ray of the Personality or Lower Self.
3—Karmic condition of the threefold man.
4—The condition of the Causal Body.
5—The need of the period and the man's availability.
6—The groups, inner and outer, with which he is affiliated.

LETTER III

POINTS CONSIDERED WHEN ASSIGNING MEDITATION.

June 4, 1920.

We have dealt with the importance of meditation, and I have suggested for your consideration four reasons out of the many why the practice should be followed. At this period when meditation is followed by many of you without the guidance of a teacher who is personally acquainted with you on the physical plane, it has been impossible to do more than formulate a plan for practice that carries in it the elements of safety and of universality.

When a teacher is on the spot, differentiated practice may be carried on suited to the temperament of the pupil, and having certain attributes that make that particular meditation the line of least resistance from the physical brain of the personality to the causal body.

In formulating methods of meditation certain factors must be taken into consideration. These factors I will now enumerate. I seek not to give you outlines and methods to be followed. I but indicate the underlying principles that guide the teacher in the choice of method suitable for the pupil. Later, when the teacher comes and the scientific application of the method to the individual is being demonstrated, you can then see if the rules laid down here are fundamentals or not. These fundamentals and principles are all I seek to give. Method and detail must be worked out through the use of discrimination, experience, courage and perseverance.

The factors that must be considered by a teacher when assigning a meditation are six in number, if we deal only with the principal ones. They are as follows:

1—The Ray of the pupil's Ego, or Higher Self.

2—The Ray of his Personality or Lower Self.

3—The Karmic condition of his threefold lower nature.

4—The condition of his Causal Body.

5—The immediate need of the period and his availability.

6—The groups, inner and outer, with which he may be affiliated.

We will now take them up and consider them one by one.

1—The Ray of the Higher Self.

The ray on which a man's causal body is found, the egoic ray, should determine the type of meditation. Each ray necessitates a different method of approach, for the aim of all meditation is union with the divine. At this stage, it is union with the spiritual Triad, that has its lowest reflection on the mental plane. Let me illustrate briefly:

When the egoic ray is what is termed the *Power Ray*, the method of approach has to be by the application of the will in a dynamic form to the lower vehicles; it is largely what we term achievement by an intense focusing, a terrific one-pointedness, that inhibits all hindrances and literally forces a channel, thus driving itself into the Triad.

When the egoic ray is the *second or the Love-Wisdom Ray*, the path of least resistance lies along the line of expansion, of a gradual inclusion. It is not so much a driving forward as it is a gradual expanding from an inner centre to include the entourage, the environment, the allied souls, and the affiliated groups of pupils under some one Master, until all are included in the consciousness. Carried to the point of achievement, this expansion results in the final shattering of the causal body at the fourth Initiation. In the first instance—achievement via the Power Ray—the driving forward and the forcing upward had a like result; the opened channel admitted the downflow of force or fire from the Spirit and the causal body in time is equally destroyed.

When the egoic ray is the *third or Activity-adaptability Ray*, the method is somewhat different. Not so much the driving forward, not so much the gradual expansion as the systematic adaptation of all knowledge and of all means to the end in view. It is in fact the process of the utilisation of the many for the use of the one; it is more the accumulation of needed material and quality for the helping of the world, and the amassing of information through love and discrimination that eventually causes the shattering of the causal body. In these "Rays of Aspect" or of divine expression, if so I may call them, the shattering is brought about by the widening of the channel, due to the driving power of will in the first case; by the expansion of the lower auric egg, the causal body, in the second case, due to the inclusiveness of the synthetic Ray of Love and Wisdom; and by the breaking of the periphery of the causal body in the third case, due to the accumulative faculty and systematic absorption of the Adaptability Ray.

All these three different methods have the same result, and are fundamentally all forms of the one great method employed in the evolution of love or wisdom,—the goal of endeavour in this present solar system.

You have *the will* driving a man on to perfection, through realisation of the Higher, and resulting in the service of power through love in activity.

You have *the wisdom or love* aspect driving a man on to perfection through the realisation of his oneness with all that breathes, resulting in the service of love through love in activity.

You have the *activity* aspect driving a man on to perfection through the utilisation of all in the service of man; first by the utilisation of all for himself, then by the graded steps of the utilisation of all for the family, of all for those he personally loves, of all for his environing associates, and thus on and up till all is utilised in the service of humanity.

When the egoic ray is the attributive *Ray of Harmony*, the fourth ray, the method will be along the line of the inner realisation of beauty and harmony; it causes the shattering of the causal body by the knowledge of Sound and Colour and the shattering effect of Sound. It is the process that leads to the realisation of the notes and tones of the solar system, the note and tone of individuals, and the endeavor to harmonise the egoic note with that of others. When the egoic note is sounded in harmony with other egos, the result is the shattering of the causal body, dissociation from the lower and the attainment of perfection. Its exponents develop along the line of music, rhythm and painting. They withdraw within in order to comprehend the life side of the form. The outer manifestation of that life side in the world is through that which we call art. The great painters and the superlative musicians are in many cases reaching their goal that way.

When the fifth ray, the *Ray of Concrete Science or Knowledge* is a man's ray, the method is very interesting. It takes the form of the intense application of the concrete mind to some problem for the helping of the race; it is the bending of every mental quality and the controlling of the lower nature so that one supreme endeavor is made to pierce through that which hinders the downflow of the higher knowledge. It involves also the will element (as might be expected) and results in the wresting of the desired information from the source of all knowledge.

As the process is continued, the piercing of the periphery of the causal body becomes so frequent that in the end disintegration is produced and a man is set free. It is mentality driving a man on to perfection and forcing him to utilise all knowledge in the loving service of his race.

The Ray of Devotion is pre-eminently the ray of sacrifice. When it is the egoic ray the method of approach through meditation takes the form of one-pointed application, through love of some individual or ideal. A man learns to *include* through love of person or ideal; he bends every faculty and every effort to the contemplation of what is required, and in sacrifice for that person or ideal lays even his causal body on the flames of the altar. It is the method of divine fanaticism that counts all lost apart from the vision, and that eventually sacrifices joyously the entire personality. The causal body is destroyed through fire, and the liberated life streams upward to the Spirit in divine beatification.

When the egoic ray is the seventh or *Ray of Ceremonial Law or Magic*, the method is that of the glorification and comprehension of form in approach. As said earlier, the goal of all the meditation practices is approach to the divine within each one, and, through that, approach to the Deity Himself.

The method, therefore, is the bringing under law, order and rule, of every act of the life in all the three bodies, and the building within the causal body of an expanding form that results in the shattering of that body. It is the building of the Shrine under certain rules into a dwelling place for the Shekinah, and when the spiritual light flames forth, the Temple of Solomon rocks, reels and disintegrates. It is the study of the law and the consequent comprehension by the man of how that law is wielded and why; it is then the definite application of that law to the body of causes so as to render it needless and thus effect its shattering. Emancipation is the result, and the man frees himself from the three worlds. Many occultists are coming in on this ray at this time to continue the liberating process. It is the method that leads a man to liberation through the understanding and the intelligent application of the law to his own life, and to the ameliorating of conditions in the body of humanity, thus making the man a server of his race.

This suffices for today.

June 5, 1920.

2—*The Ray of the Personality.*

We have somewhat dealt with the first factor, the egoic ray, in determining the method of meditation. Today we might take up the function of the personality ray in determining this method. As you know, the personality ray is ever a sub-ray of the spiritual ray and varies with greater frequency than the egoic ray. With evolved egos such as may be contacted among the thinkers of the race and among the prominent workers in all departments of world work everywhere, the personality ray may vary from life to life, each life being based on a different note and demonstrating a different colour. In this way the causal body is more rapidly equipped. When the reincarnating unit has reached a point where he can consciously choose his mode of expression, he will first review his past lives, and from the knowledge gained thereby, he will guide his choice for the next. Prior to incarnation he will sound his egoic note and will note the lack of fullness or the discord it may contain; he will then decide upon which note he will base his coming personality vibration.

The whole life, therefore, may be given over to the sounding of a particular note and to the stabilising of one particular vibration. This note must be sounded and this vibration stabilised in diversity of circumstances. Hence the necessity in the life of the aspirant or disciple for frequent change, and the explanation of the obvious condition of variety and apparent chaos in which these lives are spent.

When the discord has been corrected and when the vibration becomes steady and is not subject to change, then the needed work is done. The Ego can call in again his forces, prior to continuing the work of perfecting the causal body and carrying to perfect accuracy and clarity of tone the desired chord. See then the necessity of adapting the method of meditation to the need of the personality, and of synchronising it at the same time with the first factor, involving the ray of the Ego.

A practical illustration.

Let me illustrate, if in any way I can elucidate the matter; accuracy of comprehension is desired.

We will assume that the egoic ray of *A* is that of the Love or Wisdom Ray, whilst the ray of his lower self is that of the fifth or the Ray of Concrete Knowledge. *A* in past lives has demonstrated love and has made real progress in the method of the synthetic ray, that of expansion. He loves much and expands with fair facility his consciousness to include a just part of his environing circumstances. But, though of average intelligence, he lacks the stabilising vibration that attaches to the fifth ray. He has not that concentration that forces results, and he needs the basic foundation of *facts* before he can wisely and safely proceed much further. The wise teacher, in apprehending this necessity, uses the method of expansion inherent in the egoic ray and applies it to the expansion of the mental body. By a wisely adjudicated method, he will apply the faculty of expansion (hitherto used only to include others through love) to the one-pointed effort likewise to expand for the purpose of apprehending knowledge. When this is done, every effort of the personal life may apparently (in one particular incarnation) be given to the acquirement of scientific position and to the development of mind. Intellectual progress may seem of too paramount importance to the uninstructed onlooker; yet, after all, the work proceeds as desired by the inner guide, and only the life succeeding will demonstrate the wisdom of the egoic choice.

Intellectual expansion by the combination of second ray methods with fifth ray application will be achieved. Have I made this matter clear? I write for clarity, for this question of meditation is of much vital importance to many.

It will, therefore, be clear to you on careful perusal, that as one knows more, one judges less. A person may be well-developed on the love side, yet in some particular incarnation that side may be in abeyance, and the line of development most apparent may be the purely intellectual. Reservation of opinion is the best line for the wise onlooker to take, for he has not yet the inner vision that sees the colour, nor the occult hearing that recognises the note.

June 7, 1920.

3—The Karmic Condition of the Threefold Man.

Today the karmic condition of the threefold man and his place in evolution comes up for consideration under our discussion of "Methods of Meditation." It is our third point and of real moment in deciding wisely upon a method suitable for the individual. We have up till now considered first the importance of meditation; then we touched briefly upon the part the egoic ray plays in deciding upon that method, incidentally bringing out a point not much emphasized hitherto that the real goal of meditation is the gradual fracturing, breaking and shattering of the egoic body. Each ray necessitated, we saw, a different process. Then we took up the function of the personality ray in combination with the egoic ray, and saw how in wise consideration of the two factors a method could wisely be apportioned.

Now we take up more specifically the factor of time. Karma and time are more synonymous terms than is oft realised. Occult meditation and the definite commencement of the work of liberating the individual from the periphery of the causal body can only be begun when a certain point in evolution has been attained, and when (through its content) the causal body is of a certain specific gravity, and when the circumference of that body measures up to certain requirements. The whole process is one of Law and not, as is so oft considered, one purely of aspiration and lofty desire. Consider wisely this sentence I have just written upon the karmic condition of the threefold man and his place on the ladder of evolution. What have I specified? Three factors for your consideration:

a—The point in evolution.

b—The specific gravity of the causal body.

c—The size and circumference of the causal body.

Later I intend definitely taking up with you the question of the mental plane and its three higher subplanes, which are the planes of the Ego. We will deal with the position of the causal body on these planes and with the relationship of the causal body to other bodies on the same plane. In this letter I deal only with the three above-mentioned points. I deal, therefore, with the causal body itself, with the egoic consciousness and its relationship to the lower self. Later I will deal with the same consciousness on its own plane and its relationship to other egos and to the Hierarchy. Keep this clearly in mind:—the development of the egoic consciousness *within the Personality* is my main theme at this time. Do not confuse the two. We might word it otherwise:— I will deal with the relationship of the Higher Self to the threefold lower man, and the gradually increasing strength of that relationship through meditation. This increase is coincident with the three factors above named. Let us take them in order.

The Point in Evolution.

The life of the evolving personality might be divided into five divisions. Ours is, after all, a fivefold evolution, and the life of the man (as a human being and prior to taking the fifth Initiation) may be considered as a series of five gradual steps, each step being gauged by the condition of the indwelling Flame of Spirit. From the standpoint of our occult planetary Hierarchy, as before I have told you, *we are measured by our light.*

The first division of progress might be measured from the moment when animal-man became a thinking entity, a human being, to that of the conscious functioning of the emotional body or to the point where the emotions are very largely paramount. It corresponds to the period covered by the Lemurian and early Atlantean days. During this period, the man is polarised in his physical body and is learning to be controlled by his desire body, the body of feeling or of emotion. He has no aspirations save such as pander to the pleasures of the body; he lives for his physical nature, and has no thought for aught that may be higher. This period parallels that of the child from one to seven years. At this time the watching Teachers of the race see the indwelling Flame as a tiny pin-point, and the permanent atom of the physical plane holds the polarisation. No attention is called for from the Teachers, for the instinctive force inherent in the Higher Self does the work, and the driving force of evolution carries all on to perfection.

The second period covers a point in development when the polarisation is largely in the emotional body and when lower mind desire is being developed. Later Atlantean days hold the analogy hid. The desires are not so purely physical, for mind is beginning to permeate, much as yeast causes a movement and a rising in a mass of dough. The man is conscious of vague desires not associated with his physical body; he is capable of a deep love for teachers and guides wiser than himself, of a wild unreasoning devotion for his environing associates, and of an equally wild and unreasoning hatred, for the equilibrium that mind achieves, and the balance that is the result of mental action, is wanting in his make-up. He suffers from extremes.

The polarisation lies now in the emotional permanent atom but, (when this point of development is reached) a light plays between the two atoms that have known polarisation—the emotional and the physical. What I am seeking to bring out at this stage is that the mental unit has not known the force of polarisation, the emotional is holding it, and the result is an integral difference within the periphery of the atom itself. The electronic combinations that compose the atom which has suffered polarisation are grouped in a different geometrical form to those which have not yet experienced the process. It is the effect of the life of the Ego, playing on the matter of the atom and causing various approximations and differentiations unseen in a non-polarised atom. The matter is abstruse and complex.

This period is an analogous one to that in the life of a child from seven to fourteen years, or that period when adolescence is traversed and the child is maturing. This maturity is the product of emotional and physical polarisation in alignment. Alignment is now easily achieved between the physical and emotional bodies. The problem is to bring both under alignment with the mental and later with the egoic bodies.

To the watching Guides of the race, the indwelling Flame or Light can be seen slightly more enlarged, but still so small as to be inappreciable. But, if I can in any way make clear without misleading by the use of words—whereas in the first period the physical atom could be seen illuminated, now in the second period the emotional atom is similarly lit up, a signal to the Teachers that the work progresses. All this covers a vast period of time, for progress at this period is inexpressibly slow. My allusion to the Atlantean and Lemurian races was but to trace analogy in object, and not analogy in time.

Now, on entering *the third period*, comes the most vital point in the development of the man, that in which mind is developing and the polarising life shifts to the mental unit. Speaking in terms of the solar system and viewing humanity as a unit, all of whose permanent atoms form the molecules in a corresponding cosmic atom, the work has progressed from physical to emotional polarisation and remains there. Not till the seventh cycle of the greater cycle, not till the calling of the system into obscuration and out of manifestation will the cosmic mental atom in the body of the Logos achieve polarisation. Here and there individuals are, as units, accomplishing the work and demonstrating therefore the hope for all.

This period corresponds to that between the ages fourteen and twenty-eight. The period here is longer for there is much to be done. Two atoms have felt polarisation, and one is receiving the shifting. It is the middle point. At this time the light plays between the three atoms (outlining the personality triangle). But the focal point is gradually shifting more and more into the mental unit, and the egoic body is becoming gradually more rounded out, and assuming its proportions.

The man has control of the physical body and each life he builds a better; he has a desire body of more refined requirements (note the occult significance of that word); he realizes the joys of intellect and strives ever for a mental body of greater adequacy; his desires turn upward instead of downward, and become transmuted into aspiration,—at first aspiration towards the things of mind, and later towards that which is more abstract and synthetic. The indwelling egoic Flame or Light now radiates from an inner centre to the periphery, lighting the causal body and giving indication of burning. To the on-looking Hierarchy it is apparent that the divine fire is permeating and warming and radiating throughout the causal body, and that the Ego is becoming ever more conscious on his own plane, and ever more interested—*via the permanent atoms,*—in the life of the Personality. The physical brain of the Personality is not yet aware of the difference between inherent mental capacity and the directed impress of the indwelling Ego, but the time is becoming ripe for a change of some kind, and evolution is moving with rapidity. The fourth period approaches. I would here sound a warning. All this proceeds not in ordered sections, if so I may term it. It proceeds as proceeds the greater system, with constant overlapping, and with parallelism, due to the inherent ray of the Spirit or Monad, to cyclic changes, to diversity of forces playing astrologically and oft from unknown cosmic centres upon the palpitating life within the atoms. . . .

The fourth period is that within which co-ordination of the Personality is completed, and that wherein the man comes to himself (as did the prodigal in the far country) and says: "I will arise and go to my Father." This is the result of the first meditation. The three permanent atoms are functioning and the man is an active, feeling, thinking entity. He reaches the consummation of the personality life and he begins to shift *consciously* his polarisation from the personality life to the egoic. He stands upon the Path of Discipleship or Probation, or is close to it. He commences the work of transmutation; he laboriously, painfully and carefully, forces his consciousness higher and to expand at will; at any cost he determines to dominate and function in full liberation on the three lower planes; he realises that the Ego must have perfect expression,—physical, emotional and mental,—and he makes, therefore, at infinite cost, the necessary channel. He attracts the attention of the Teachers.

In what way does he do this? The causal body begins to radiate the indwelling Light. It has been constructed to a point where it is fine enough to act as a transparency and, where the contact of the Ego is made with the Triad, a point of Flame appears. . . . The light is no longer under the bushel, but suddenly flames forth, and catches the eager eye of the Master.

This marks the period between twenty-eight and thirty-five in the life of the adult. It is the period wherein a man finds himself, discovers what his line of activity may be, what he can accomplish, and from the worldly standpoint, comes into his own.

During *the fifth period,* the Flame gradually breaks through the periphery of the causal body, and the "path of the just shineth ever more and more unto the perfect day." It is in the fourth period that meditation commences,—the mystic meditation that leads, in the fifth period, to that occult meditation that brings about results, being under the law and hence following the line of the ray. It is by meditation that the man—as a Personality—feels out the vibration of the Ego, and seeks to reach up to the Ego and bring the egoic consciousness ever more and more down, so as to include consciously the physical plane. It is by meditation or by retreating within that the man learns the significance of Fire, and applies that fire to all the bodies, till naught is left save the fire itself. It is by meditation, or the reaching from the concrete to the abstract, that the causal consciousness is entered, and man—during this final period—becomes the Higher Self and not the Personality.

The polarisation shifts during the fifth period (the period of the Path of Initiation) entirely from the Personality to the Ego, until, at the close of that period, liberation is complete, and the man is set free. Even the causal body is known as a limitation and the emancipation is completed. The polarisation then shifts higher into the Triad—the shifting beginning at the third Initiation. The physical permanent atom goes and the polarisation becomes higher mental; the emotional permanent atom goes and the polarisation becomes intuitional; the mental unit goes and the polarisation becomes spiritual. The man then becomes a Master of the Wisdom and is of the symbolic age of forty-two, the point of perfected maturity in the solar system.

A still later period comes, corresponding to the ages forty-two to forty-nine, wherein the sixth and seventh Initiations may be taken, but this period concerns not the readers of these letters. . . .

June 9, 1920.

The Specific Gravity and Content of the Causal Body.

This subject, anent the causal body, opens up for the thinker much food for speculation. The literal figures and the dimensional lines cannot be given. They form one of the secrets of initiation but certain ideas may be suggested and submitted to the consideration of all interested.

Just what do you mean when you speak of the causal body? Say not glibly, the body of causes, for words thus spoken are oft but nebulous and vague. Let us now consider the causal body and find out its component parts.

On the involutionary path you have what is termed the Group Soul, aptly described (as far as earth words permit) as a collection of triads, enclosed in a triple envelop of monadic essence. On the evolutionary path, groups of causal bodies correspond and are similarly composed, three factors entering in.

The causal body is a collection of permanent atoms, three in all, enclosed in an envelop of mental essence. . . . What happens at the moment when animal-man becomes a thinking entity, a human being? The approximation of the self and the not-self by means of mind, for man is "that being in whom highest spirit and lowest matter are linked together by intelligence." What do I mean by this phrase? Just this: that when animal-man had reached a point of adequacy; when his physical body was sufficiently co-ordinated, when he had an emotional or desire nature sufficiently strong to form a basis for existence, and to guide it by means of instinct, and when the germ of mentality was sufficiently implanted to have donated the instinctive memory and correlation of ideas that can be seen in the average domesticated animal, then the descending Spirit (which had taken to itself an atom on the mental plane) judged the time ripe for taking possession of the lower vehicles. The Lords of the Flame were called in and they effected the transfer of polarisation from the lower atom of the Triad to the lowest atom of the Personality. Even then, the indwelling Flame could come no lower than the third subplane of the mental plane. There the two met and became one and the causal body was formed. All in nature is interdependent, and the indwelling Thinker cannot control in the three lower worlds without the aid of the lower self. *The life of the first Logos must be blended with that of the second Logos and based on the activity of the third Logos.*

Therefore, you have at the moment of individualisation, which is the term used to express this hour of contact, on the third subplane of the mental plane a point of light, enclosing three atoms, and itself enclosed in a sheath of mental matter. The work then to be done consists of:

1. Causing that point of light to become a flame, by steadily fanning the spark and feeding the fire.

2. Causing the causal body to grow and expand from being a colourless ovoid, holding the Ego like a yolk within the egg-shell, to a thing of rare beauty, containing within itself all the colour of the rainbow. This is an occult fact. The causal body will palpitate in due course of time with an inner irradiation, and an inner glowing flame that will gradually work its way from the centre to the periphery. It will then pierce through that periphery, using the body (that product of millennia of lives of pain and endeavour) as fuel for its flames. It will burn all up, it will mount upward to the Triad, and (becoming one with that Triad) will be re-absorbed into the spiritual consciousness,—will carry with it—using heat as the symbol—an intensity of heat or quality of colour or vibration that before were lacking.

Therefore the work of the Personality—for we have to view all from that angle until egoic vision may be ours,—is first to beautify, build and expand the causal body; secondly to withdraw within it the life of the Personality, sucking the good out of the personal life and storing it in the body of the Ego. We might term this the Divine Vampirism, for always evil is but the other side of good. Then, having accomplished this, comes the application of the flame to the causal body itself and the joyous standing by whilst the work of destruction goes on, and the Flame—the live inner man and the spirit of divine life—is set free and mounts to its source.

The specific gravity of the causal body fixes the moment of emancipation and marks the time when the work of beautifying and building is completed, when the

Temple of Solomon is erected, and when the *weight* (occultly understood) of the causal body measures up to the standard looked for by the Hierarchy. Then the work of destruction supervenes and liberation approaches. Spring has been experienced, the full verdure of summer has succeeded, now must be felt the disintegrating force of autumn,—only this time it is felt and applied on mental levels and not on physical. The axe is laid to the root of the tree, but the life essence is garnered into the divine storehouse.

The content of the causal body is the accumulation by slow and gradual process of the good in each life. The building proceeds slowly at first, but towards the end of incarnation,—on the Probationary Path and on the Path of Initiation—the work proceeds rapidly. The structure has been reared, and each stone quarried in the personal life. On the Path, in each of its two divisions, the work of completing and beautifying the Temple proceeds with greater rapidity. . . .

Briefly and in conclusion of this matter, I would seek to point out that the circumference of the causal body varies according to type and ray. Some egoic bodies are of a form more circular than others; some are more ovoid, and others more elongated in shape. It is the content and the pliability that matter, and above all the occult permeability of the lower auric egg that permits of contact with other egos, yet retains identity; that merges itself with its fellows, yet preserves individuality; and that absorbs all that is desirable, yet keeps ever its own shape.

June 16, 1920.

4—*Condition of the Causal Body.*

The fourth factor underlying the choice of a method

of meditation is our subject today and consists of the condition of the causal body.

We have dealt with the causal body in its relationship to the Personality or lower self, showing the interplay between the two and their interdependence. Through steady application to occult meditation, and through the gradual stilling of the lower mind, through concentration and the wise following of the egoic ray meditation, balanced by the personality ray mediation, we found that the relationship of the causal body to the Personality became ever closer and the channel connecting the two became ever more clear and adequate. This resulted eventually, we saw, in a shifting of polarisation from the lower to the higher and later to complete emancipation from both,—centralisation ensuing then in the spiritual consciousness. We dealt with the matter from the lower point of view, seeing it from the standpoint of a man in the three worlds.

Today we will deal with the matter from the standpoint of the Higher Self, from the egoic level, and consider the relationship of that Self to the Hierarchy, to surrounding egos, and to the Spirit. It will be difficult to do more than give some few hints, for much that I could say would be little comprehended, and much be too occult and dangerous for general communication.

Three things may be imparted, which—when wisely meditated upon—may lead to illumination:

The Ego on its own plane, realises *consciously* its relationship to the Master, and seeks to transmit that consciousness to the Personality.

The Higher Self on its own plane, is not trammelled by time and space, and (knowing the future as well as that which is past) seeks to bring the desired end nearer and make it more rapidly a fact.

The Higher Self or Ego on its own plane has direct relationship with other egos on the same ray, and on a corresponding concrete or abstract ray, and—realising that progress is made in group formation—works on that plane at the helping of his kind. These facts are already half apprehended among students but by a slight elaboration I may make it clearer.

Relationship of the Ego to the Hierarchy.

The relationship of the Ego to some one Master is at this stage consciously realised, but is nevertheless, itself of evolutionary development. As we have been told, there are sixty thousand million units of consciousness or spirits in the evolving human hierarchy. These are found on causal levels, though the numbers are slightly less now, owing to the attainment of the fourth Initiation by individuals from time to time. These egos at different stages of development are all linked with their Monad, Spirit or Father in Heaven, in much the same way (only in finer matter) as the Ego is linked with the Personality.

All the Monads are, as you know, under the control, or rather form part, of the consciousness of one of the Planetary Spirits. On egoic levels, the egos are in a similar condition. An Adept of their ray supervises their general evolution, dealing with them *in groups*. These groups are formed under three conditions:

a—As to sub-ray of the egoic ray.

b—As to period of individualisation or of entrance into the human kingdom.

c—As to point of attainment.

The Adept of their ray handles the general supervision but under Him work the Masters each on His own ray, and with Their own individual groups, who are affiliated with Them through period, through karma and through point of vibration. Under the Masters work the disciples who have the consciousness of the Higher Self, and are therefore able to work on causal levels and aid in the development of those egos whose causal bodies are less developed than their own.

All is beautifully subject to law, and as the work of developing the egoic body is dependent upon the progress made in the threefold personality, the Ego is consequently aided on lower levels by two different disciples, one working on emotional levels and reporting to another disciple who works upon the mental vehicle. He in his turn reports to the disciple with causal consciousness, who reports again to the Master. All this is done with the co-operation of the indwelling consciousness in the causal body. This, as you see, entails five factors concerning themselves with the aiding of the Ego in his evolutionary development:

1—The Adept of his Ray.
2—The Master of his group.
3—A disciple with causal consciousness.
4—A disciple on the mental plane.
5—A helper on the emotional plane.

For a long period of lives the Ego remains practically unconscious of the Personality. The magnetic link exists, but that is all until the time comes when the personal life reaches a point where it has somewhat to add to the content of the causal body—a body at first small, colourless and insignificant. But the hour comes when the stones are first brought perfected from the quarry of the personal life, and the first colours are painted in by the man, the builder and the artist. Then the Ego begins to give attention, rarely at first, but with increasing frequency, until lives come around in which the Ego definitely works at the subjugation of the lower self, at the enlargement of the communicating channel, and at the transmission to the physical brain consciousness of the fact of its existence and the goal of its being. Once that is accomplished, and the inner fire is freer in its passage, lives are then given to the stabilising of that impression, and to the making of that inner consciousness a part of the conscious life. The flame radiates downward more and more until gradually the different vehicles come into line, and the man stands on the Probationary Path. He is ignorant yet of what lies ahead, and is conscious only of wild and earnest aspiration and of innate divine longings. He is eager to make good, longing to *know*, and dreaming always of someone or something higher than himself. All this is backed by the profound conviction that in service to humanity will the dreamed-of goal be reached, will the vision become reality, the longing fructify into satisfaction, and aspiration be merged in sight.

The Hierarchy begins to take action and his instruction is carried out as aforesaid. . . . Until now the Teachers have only watched and guided without definitely dealing with the man himself; all has been left to the Ego and the life divine to carry out the plan, the attention of the Masters being directed to the Ego on his own plane. The Ego bends every effort to quicken vibration, and to force the oft-rebelling lower vehicles to respond and measure up to the rapidly increasing force. It is largely a matter of increased fire or heat, and consequent intensification of vibratory capacity. The egoic fire waxes ever greater until the work is done, and the purificatory fire becomes the Light of Illumination. Ponder on this sentence. As above, so below; on each rung of the ladder the process is repeated; the

Monad, at the third Initiation, begins itself to be conscious of the Ego. The work, then, is more rapid owing to the rarity of the material and to the fact that resistance is a factor in the three worlds but not elsewhere.

Hence, pain ceases for a Master. That is, pain as we know it on earth, which is largely *pain in matter*. The pain that lies hid in comprehension, not resistance, is felt to the highest circles, yea, it reaches to the Logos Himself. But this is beside the point and well-nigh incomprehensible to you who are yet trammelled by matter.

Relationship of the Ego to its own development.

The Ego seeks to bring about the desired end in three ways:—

1—By definite work on abstract levels. It aspires to contact and enclose the permanent atom, its first direct approach to the Triad.

2—By definite work on colour and sound with the aim in view of stimulation and vivification, working thus in groups and under the guidance of a Master.

3—By frequent attempts to definitely control the lower self, a thing distasteful to the Ego, whose tendency is to rest content with consciousness and aspiration on its own plane. Forget not that the Ego itself has somewhat to wrestle with. The refusal to incarnate is not found only on spiritual levels, but is found also on that of the Higher Self. Certain developments also, incidental to the factors of time and space (as understood in the three worlds) are aimed at by the Ego, such as the increase of the causal periphery through the study of divine telepathy, systemic psychology and the knowledge of the laws of fire.

Relationship of the Ego to other egos.

Certain things need to be remembered:—

The factor of periodicity. Egos that are in incarnation, and egos that are out of incarnation are differentiated and capable of different work. Egos whose reflections are in incarnation are more limited than those who are not. It is almost as if the Higher Self were directed downwards, or willingly circumscribing itself to three-dimensioned existence, whereas the egos out of incarnation are not so limited but work in another direction or dimension. The difference lies in the focusing of attention, during physical plane life. The matter is hard for you to grasp, is it not so? I scarcely know how to express the difference more clearly. It is perhaps as if the incarnating egos were more positive, and the non-incarnating egos more negative.

The factor of activity. This is largely a matter of ray, and affects closely the relationship between egos. Those on similar rays coalesce and vibrate more readily to each other than those on different rays, and it is only as the second or wisdom aspect is developed that synthesis becomes possible.

On the third subplane of the mental plane egos are separated into groups—individual separation exists not, but group separation can be felt, incidental to ray and point in evolution.

On the second subplane the groups become merged and blend, and from their forty-nine groups are formed (by merging) forty-two. The process of synthesis might be tabulated as follows:

	1st subplane	35 groups, 7 x 5
Mental plane	2nd subplane	42 groups, 7 x 6
	3rd subplane	49 groups, 7 x 7

Buddhic plane $\Big\{$ 3rd subplane ..... 28 groups, 7 x 4
       1st subplane ..... 21 groups, 7 x 3

Atmic plane   Atomic subplane .. 14 groups, 7 x 2

Monadic plane .... 7 great groups

I have given a few hints here. It is so little, compared with what will later be known when those of you now studying expand the consciousness still further, but it is all I can as yet impart, and only this has been given with the intent of showing how much has to be considered, when meditation forms are duly set by a Master. He has to take into wise consideration the egoic ray, and the condition of the causal body in its relationship to the lower self and to the Hierarchy. The state of the body must be known, and its content; its relationship to other egos must be duly considered, for all is in group formation. Meditation must therefore be given which is in line with the *group* to which the Ego is assigned, for as each man meditates he contacts not only his own Ego but also his egoic group and through that group the Master to Whom he is consequently linked, though the efficacy of a meditation depends upon the work being done in an occult manner and under law. The group significance of meditation is little understood, but the above thoughts are commended to you for your wise study.

June 17, 1920

5—*Immediate Need of Period and Man's Availability.*

Today we will consider factor five in deciding methods of Meditation, and will deal with the need of the particular period and the suitability of the man to meet the need.

Let us first of all briefly recapitulate, for the value of reiteration is profound. We have taken up briefly the factor of the egoic ray, as it is considered by a teacher in assigning a meditation, and we have seen how each ray aimed at the same goal along a different route, and that each ray necessitated a different type of meditation. We have touched on the modification of the meditation through consideration of the personality ray. Then we took up the factor of time as shown in the causal body, its point of development, and the relationship of that body to its three lower expressions, finishing yesterday with a few brief hints anent the causal body on its own level and its scope of consciousness. All this will have indicated to you how wise must be the teacher who presumes to indicate meditation. One point I would here interpolate:— No meditation that is truly and occultly suitable can be assigned by a teacher who has not the capacity of causal consciousness and contact. When the teacher knows the note, the rate of vibration and the colour, then he can wisely assign, but not before. Before that time, generalisation only is possible, and a meditation given that may approximate the need and also be safe.

Another factor enters now,—a factor that varies somewhat according to the need of the period. All cycles are not as fundamentally important. The periods in a cycle that are of real moment are the termini, and those where overlapping and merging occur. They demonstrate on the physical plane in great revolutions, gigantic cataclysms, and fundamental upheavals in all three departments of the Hierarchy,—the department of the World Teacher, that of the Head of a root-race and that of the Ruler of civilisation or of force. At the points of merging in a cycle, cross-currents are found, and all the system seems to be in a chaotic condition. The middle part of a cycle, where the incoming vibration is stabilized and the old has passed away, manifests in a period of calm and apparent equilibrium.

At no time in the history of the race has this been better shown than in the present half century. The sixth Ray of Devotion passes away and the Ray of Ceremonial Law enters and with that entering comes a swinging into prominence of the outstanding features and faculties of the department of force and activity, the synthesis, forget not, of the four minor rays. Therefore you have the fighting for ideals and the devoted adherence to a cause, as demonstrated under the ray of the Master Jesus; therefore the clashing in every field of endeavor of the idealists (right or wrong) and their bitter warfare. What was the world war but the culmination of two opposing ideals, fighting it out on the physical plane?—it was an instance of the force of the sixth ray. Now will come, as the sixth ray passes out, a gradual cessation of the clashing, and the gradual domination of organisation, rule and order under the sway of the incoming force, that of the ray of the Master R—. Out of the present turbulence will arise the ordered and organised form of the new world. Gradually the new rhythm will impose itself on the disorganised communities of men, and instead of social chaos as now you will have social order and rule; instead of the religious differences and the differentiated sects of the many so-called religions, you will have religious expression itself regulated into form and all ordered by law; instead of economic and political strain and stress will be seen the harmonious working of the system under certain fundamental forms; all will be dominated by ceremonial with the inner results aimed at by the Hierarchy gradually taking shape. Forget not that in the apotheosis of law and order and their resultant forms and limitations lies, towards the close (I choose my words with deliberation), a fresh period of chaos, and the escape of the imprisoned life from even those limitations, bearing with it the imparted faculty and the essence of the development aimed at by the Logos of the seventh ray.

Such is the situation from time to time down through the ages. Each ray sweeps into power, bearing its own incarnating Spirits to whom the period marks a point of least resistance comparatively. They contact six other types of force in the worlds and six other groups of beings who must be impressed by that force and be carried forward in its sweep towards the universal goal. Such is also the specific situation in the period in which you live, a period wherein the seventh Logos of Ceremonial Law and Order seeks to straighten out the temporary chaos, and aims at the reduction within limits of the life escaping from the old and worn-out forms. The new forms are needed now and will be adequate. It is only after the middle period in a new cycle that limitation will again be felt and the attempt to escape be started anew.

Therefore the wise teacher at this time considers the situation and weighs the effect of the incoming ray on the spirits in incarnation. Here, therefore, you have a third ray and its bearing to be considered in the assigning of meditation. Complex you feel the task to be? Fortunately the Hall of Wisdom equips its graduates for the task.

At this particular period the aspect of the Form in meditation (whether meditation based principally on the egoic ray or on the personality ray) will be much developed. You can look to see very definite forms built up and assigned, both to individuals and to groups, resulting in an increase of white magic, and the consequent resultant, on the physical plane, of law and order. The coming period of reconstruction goes forward in line with the ray, and its ultimate success and achievement is more nearly possible than perhaps is looked for. The Great Lord comes in under the law and naught can stop His approach.

Just now the great need of the time is for those who understand the law and can work with it. Now is the opportunity, too, for the development of that principle and the training of people in the helping of the world.

The minor Rays of Harmony and Science respond quickly to this seventh influence; by that statement I mean that their monads are easily influenced in this direction. The monads of the sixth Ray of Devotion find conformity more difficult, until nearing the point of synthesis. The monads of the first and second rays find in this ray a field of expression. First ray monads have a direct link with this ray and seek to wield the law through power, whilst second ray monads, being the synthetic type, guide and rule through love.

I think I have today given you enough to engender thought on this fifth factor. This is all I seek to do. To the guiding light of the intuition is the rest left and what that inner guide reveals is of more value to the individual than aught exoterically imparted. Therefore, ponder and consider.

June 18, 1920

Some Words of Cheer.

......It is only as the disciple is willing to relinquish all in the service of the Great One, and to hold naught back, that liberation is achieved, and the body of desire becomes transmuted into the body of the higher intuition. It is the serving perfectly each day—with no thought or calculation about the future—that brings a man to the position of the perfect Server. And, may I suggest one thing? All care and anxiety is based primarily on selfish motive. You fear further pain, you shrink from further sad experience. It is not thus that the goal is reached; it is reached by the path of renunciation. Perhaps it may mean the renunciation of joy, or the renunciation of good reputation, or the renunciation of friends, and the renunciation of all that the heart clings to. I say *perhaps;* I say not, it is so. I but seek to point out to you that if that is the way you are to reach your goal, then for you it is the perfect way. Aught that brings you rapidly to Their Presence and to Their Lotus Feet, is by you to be desired and eagerly welcomed.

Cultivate daily, therefore, that supreme desire that seeks solely the commendation of the inner Guide and Teacher, and the egoic response to good action dispassionately performed.

Should bereavement come your way, smile through it all; it will end in a rich reward and the return of all that has been lost. Should scorn and despisings be your lot, smile still, for only the look of commendation that comes from the Master is the one to seek. Should lying tongues take action, fear not, but forge ahead. A lie is a thing of earth and can be left behind as a thing too vile to be touched. The single eye, the unalloyed desire, the consecrated purpose, and the ear that turns in deafness to all earth's noise—such is the aim for the disciple. I say no more. I but desire that you do not dissipate needless force in vain imaginings, feverish speculations and troubled expectations.

6—*The Groups, Inner and Outer, with which the Pupil is Affiliated.*

The point for consideration today is of practical interest. It deals with the factor of a man's groups. The relationship to a Master we have somewhat considered, and I will therefore proceed with the instruction on the group connection.

We showed yesterday the importance of meditation in connection with the group to which a man is allied on egoic levels. Today we deal with the group to which he may be called on earth. This group is not exactly a reflection of the group on egoic levels as might be anticipated, for only certain units of an egoic group will be in incarnation at any one time. We deal with the Law of Cause and Effect, as demonstrated in the groups national, religious or family.

Four groups connected with the pupils.

A man, when in incarnation, has four sets of people to consider as his group:—

1.   *The big national group* to which he belongs, the karma of which (through aggregation of numbers) is so strong that he cannot break away from it even if he will. Certain racial characteristics, certain temperamental tendencies are his because they are hidden in the racial physical body, and he must carry that constitution, and the tendencies inherent in that particular type of body, throughout his life on earth. That body provides the needed lesson, or (as evolution proceeds) it provides the best body for the type of work that has to be accomplished. An oriental type of body has one set of qualifications, and an occidental body has another set, and equally good, if I might so express it. I seek here to make this point clear, for the tendency of the westerner is to ape the oriental and to endeavor to force his vibrations to the same key as that of the oriental. At times, this causes concern to the inner Teachers, and occasionally leads to trouble in the vehicles.

There has been too much tendency to believe that to be an oriental holds the goal for all. Forget not that even the Great Ones Themselves are not all orientals, and the Masters in European bodies are of equal accomplishment to the better known Eastern Adepts. Ponder on this. It needs much wise consideration, hence my emphasis of the fact. When more is known along these lines, and when schools of meditation are founded and conducted on truly occult lines by graduated Teachers, forms of meditation will be planned, suited to nationality and to the temperamental differences existing among nations. Each nation has its virtues and each has its defects; it will therefore be the work of the superintending Teacher to apportion meditations that will intensify the virtues and remedy the defects. The field opened up by these ideas is so vast that I cannot deal with it here. Specialists will later take up the problem, and the time comes when the orient and the occident will each have their own schools, subject to the same basic rules and under the superintendence of the same inner Teachers, but wisely differing on certain points, and (though aiming at the same goal) following different routes. You will later see these schools founded in each nation; admission into them will not be easy of attainment, but each applicant for instruction will be subjected to a drastic entrance examination. You will find each school will differ somewhat, not in fundamentals but in methods of application, due to the wise discrimination of the Head of the School. This Head, being of the same nationality as the pupils, and having the faculties of the causal body fully developed, will apply the method to the immediate need.

Later I may further expand the future of the meditation schools for your edification, but I seek now principally to generalise.

2—The second group, which is of importance in the life of the pupil, is *his family group,* involving its special family heredity and characteristics. Every man, who has reached a point in evolution where occult meditation is desirable and possible, has entered some particular family from deliberate choice:—

a—To work off karma as rapidly as may be.

b—Because of the physical vehicle it provides.

You will easily see, therefore, that in the assigning of occult meditation to be carried out on the physical plane and in a physical vehicle, it will be the concern of the Teacher to know somewhat of the physical pedigree and the inherent characteristics of the pupil, both from the point of view of finding the line of least resistance and of demonstrating what must be overcome. (Some of you who meditate are apt to be so engrossed straining after intuitional consciousness that you overlook the very necessary physical vehicles.) The physical brain and the conformity of the head play a large part in the process and must not be overlooked in the future as they are at present. This is necessarily so, for the dearth of trained teachers in the physical bodies is so insuperable at present.

Therefore the family group is the second thing of moment that enters into consideration, and the matter is of more vital importance than perhaps you think.

In the coming schools of meditation there will be records kept as to the pupil's forbears, his family history, the progress of his youth and life and his medical history. This record will be minutely accurate, and much will be learnt this way. The life will be regulated and the scientific purification of the physical body will be one of the first things attempted. Incidentally (in speaking of these schools) I would like to urge that you picture not some isolated spot for their location. In the world, yet not of the world is the ideal, and only in the advanced stages or just prior to taking Initiation will the pupil be permitted to retire for periods of any length. It is the inner detachment that counts, and the ability to dissociate the self from the environment that matters, and not so much the physical plane isolation.

3—The third group that a man has to consider is the particular *band of servers* to which he may be affiliated. Any man who is ready for occult meditation must have demonstrated first for many lives his intelligent willingness to serve and to work among the sons of men. Unselfish service is the bed-rock of the life of the occultist, and danger lurks when it exists not, and occult meditation carries a menace. Hence, the man must be an active worker in some part of the field of the world, and on the inner planes he must likewise be playing his part. Certain things will then have to be considered by the Teacher:

      a—The group work a man is doing and how best he may be qualified to serve better in that group.

      b—The type of a man's work, and his relationship in that work to his associates—a very important occult factor—will be carefully weighed before a meditation is assigned, and certain types of meditation (perhaps desired by the man himself) may be withheld on account of their being unsuited to the work in hand, and because of their tendency to develop certain qualities which might handicap the server in his work. Those meditations which will increase ability to *serve* will ever be the aim. The greater aim includes, after all, the lesser.

4—The fourth group that has a place in the calculations of the Teacher *is that to which a man belongs on the inner plane,* the band of helpers to which he is assigned, or—if he is a disciple,—the group of pupils of which he forms a part. Their particular type of group work will be considered, the capacity of the pupil to progress with his fellows will be fostered, and his ability to fill his appointed post will be increased.

I have but hinted in these last few communications at the many things that arise for consideration in the assignment of a meditation. You have three rays to consider, the point in evolution of the causal body and its interrelation on its own plane with its group, with the Hierarchy, and with its reflection, the Personality. You have also the factor of karma, the need of the time and of the man himself, and his relationship with four different groups.

All this is possible and will some day be recognized, but the period of laying a foundation is not yet over, and for long will remain with you. The control of the mind is the present aim of meditation, and must always be the elementary step.

LETTER IV

THE USE OF THE SACRED WORD IN MEDITATION.

1—Fundamental postulates.
2—The creative effect of the Sacred Word.
3—The destructive effect of the Sacred Word.
4—Pronunciation and use of the Sacred Word.
5—Its effect on the centres and on each body.

LETTER IV

THE USE OF THE SACRED WORD IN MEDITATION.

June 19, 1920

The subject that we are to deal with today is of such profundity and of such vital moment that your shrinking from even considering it is exceedingly natural. No matter what we may say upon the matter, we can but touch the fringe of it, and the depths of what will be left unsaid may seem so great, that the data communicated may assume too small proportions.

Fundamental Postulates.

First, I seek to lay down certain basic postulates which, though realised as mental concepts, may yet be too deep for easy comprehension.

These postulates are five in number—five out of a number too vast for your apprehension. These postulates themselves are based on certain fundamental facts, and these facts (seven in number) are not as yet all comprehended. H.P.B. touched on three in his statement of the fundamentals of the Secret Doctrine. Four yet remain hid, though the fourth is emerging somewhat through the study of psychology and mental science. The other three fundamentals will emerge during the next three rounds. This round will see the apprehension of the fourth fundamental.

These postulates are as follows:

1—That all that exists is based on sound or on the Word.

2—That differentiation is the result of sound.

3—That on each plane the Word has a different effect.

4—That according to the note of the Word, or the vibration of the sound, will the work of building-in or casting-out be accomplished.

5—That the one threefold Word has seven keys, and these seven keys have their own subtones.

In the apprehension of these basic facts lies hid much light on the use of the Word in meditation.

In the great original sounding forth of the Sacred Word (the three original Breaths, with their seven sounds,—one Breath for each of the three solar systems) the note was different, and the sounds pitched to a different key.

In system one, the completion of the First Breath, the culmination, was the sounding forth, in note majestic, of the note FA,—the note which forms the basic note of this system, the note of manifested nature. This note *is,* and to it must be supplemented the second note for this the second system. It is not fully sounded or rounded out, nor to the end of the greater cycle will it be completed. The Logos sounds it now, and should He cease to breathe it forth, the whole system would disappear into complete obscuration. It would mark the end of manifestation.

In system two, the present system, the keynote may not be disclosed. It is one of the secrets of the sixth Initiation, and must not be revealed.

In system three the final third note will be added to the basic notes of the first and second systems, and then what will you have? You will have the major third of the Logoic Personality in its completeness, a correspondence to the major third of the microcosm,—one note for each plane. We have been told that the Solar Logos, on the cosmic planes, works at the problem of cosmic mind; that He functions in His physical solar system, is polarised in His cosmic astral, or emotional body, and is developing cosmic mind. So, on the planes of the solar system, is it as with the microcosm. In the realisation of this correspondence and its wise application lies illumination on the use of the Sacred Word in meditation.

System I........corresponds to the physical body.
System II......corresponds to the emotional body.
System III........corresponds to the mental body.

By the study of the Word or Sound in the formation of these three will help come on the use of that Word in the building of the intuitional vehicle, and the purification of the personality.

Now we will divide what we have to say under four heads, and take up each one of them separately:—

1—The creative effect of the Sacred Word.
2—The destructive effect of the Sacred Word.
3—Its pronunciation and use:—
    a—In individual meditation.
    b—In group and congregational work.
    c—For certain specific ends.
4—Its effect on the bodies and centres, and its efficacy in effecting egoic alignment.

June 20, 1920

The Dual Effect of the Sacred Word; constructive and destructive.

We can today continue with the subject we were considering yesterday. We divided the theme into four divisions and we will take the first two, the effect,—creative and destructive—of the Word. Just a few broad hints will be possible, to form a basis for the intelligent application of the law.

First, let us repeat the truism that the worlds are the effect of sound. First life, then matter; later the attraction of the matter to the life for purposes of its manifestation and expression, and the orderly arrangement of that matter into the necessary forms. Sound formed the allying factor, the propelling impulse, and the attractive medium. Sound, in an occult and deeply metaphysical sense, stands for that which we term "the relation between", and is the creating intermediary, the linking third factor in the process of manifestation. It is the akasha. On the higher planes it is the agent of the great Entity Who wields the cosmic law of gravitation in its relation to our solar system, whilst on the lower planes it demonstrates as the astral light, the great agent of reflection, that fixes and perpetuates on its vibratory bosom the past, the present and the future, or that which we call Time. In direct relation to the lower vehicle it manifests as electricity, prana and the magnetic fluid. A simplification of the idea may come to you perhaps in the recognition of sound as the agent of the law of attraction and repulsion.

The seven great Breaths.

In sounding forth the Sacred Word in its sevenfold completeness for this solar system, the Logos gathered through inspiration the matter needed for manifestation, and started the evolution of that matter at the first great Breath.

At the second great Breath came differentiation and the instilling of the second aspect logoic.

At the third great Breath the activity aspect was demonstrated, matter was impregnated with that faculty, and fivefold evolution became a possibility.

At the fourth great Breath certain of the Hierarchies responded, and the great Builders more clearly saw the plan. There is a definite connection between the fourth

Breath and the fourth Creative Hierarchy, that of the human Spirits. This fourth note of the Logos has a special significance for the human Spirit, and an unique effect in this earth and in this fourth cycle. The relativity of it is such that it is difficult for you in any way to realise that effect. It demonstrates as far as you can grasp it in the harmonic note of the fourth plane and ray. That note permeates the peoples of the world at this time and ever since the fourth root-race. It shows itself in the struggle of humanity to grasp the ideal of harmony and peace, and in the world-wide aspiration in that direction.

This fourth Breath is especially applicable to human evolution.

You have therefore:

Subtone one of the threefold Word gave the first vibratory note and started the movement of the spheres—solar or atomic. It embodies *Will*.

Subtone two of the threefold Word instilled the second aspect and called the cosmic ruler of the synthetic ray into manifestation. It marked duality or *reflex love*.

Subtone three of the threefold Word made our five-fold evolution possible. It is the basic note of the five lower planes. It marked *activity or adaptability*.

Subtone four of the threefold Word is the sound of the Human Hierarchy, and in its entirety might be called the "cry of Man."

Each of the sounds directly called into manifestation one ray, with all that enters in on a ray. Each sound demonstrates particularly on one plane, being the dominant note of that plane.

The fifth great Breath has an effect peculiar to itself, for in its reverberation it holds the key to all,—it is the *Breath of fire*. It created a similar vibration to that of the cosmic mental level, and is closely allied with the first Breath. It is the dominant note (in technical musical terminology) of the solar system, just as the third Breath corresponds to the major third. It is the note of the Logos. Each breath attracts to the Logos for purposes of manifestation, some entity on cosmic levels. The reflection of the method can be seen in the microcosm when the Ego sounds the egoic note in the three worlds and prepares to manifest or to come into incarnation. The note attracts around the permanent atoms or nuclei adequate matter for the purpose of manifestation, and that matter is itself informed by some vital entity. Similarly, the cosmic Lords of Fire, the great informing Entities of our solar system, respond when this fifth subtone is sounded forth. Again, the Lords of the Flame within the solar system itself responded when the microcosm sounded the fifth subtone of the monadic note, and involved themselves in human evolution.

The sixth great Breath drew to itself the Lords of the mysterious Pentacle, the volatile essences of the emotional plane, the desire faculty clothed in matter, the watery aspect of the logoic life.

At the sounding of the seventh subtone crystallisation occurred and absolute conformity to the law of approach. It resulted in the dense aspect of manifestation, the point of deepest experience. You will note its connection, therefore, with the Ray of Ceremonial Law, one of the great building rays,—a ray which adjusts matter, under set forms, to the desired shapes.

You may ask here: Why have I thus apparently disgressed? It seems to you wide of the mark and beside the question? Let me elucidate. The microcosm has but to repeat the work of the macrocosm. The Spirit or monad on his own plane sounds forth the note (his hierarchial note) and descends into incarnation. It is both the note of attraction and of out-breathing. The personality—the reflection of that monad at the densest point in evolution,—is linked to the monad by the attractive force of the Sacred Word sounded by its monad on its note and on its own subtone.

But the work of outbreathing is already accomplished. It is involution. The work of in-breathing or reabsorption into the source progresses. When the Personality finds for itself (after lives of stress and search) its spiritual note with the right key and subtone, what is the result? It accords with its monadic note, it vibrates to the same measure, it pulsates with the same colour, the line of least resistance is at last found, and the indwelling life is liberated and returns to its own plane. But this work of discovery is very slow and the man has to pick out the chord with infinite care and pains. First, he finds out the third of the Personality and sounds that forth, the result being an ordered harmonious life in the three worlds. Then he finds the dominant fifth of the Ego, the keynote of the chord, and sounds that in unison with the Personality note. The result is that a vacuum is formed (if I may so express it) and the liberated man with his informing soul,—the threefold spirit, plus mind and experience— the Three completed by the Quaternary and the Fifth, escapes upward to the Monad. It is the law of attraction demonstrating through sound. Like to like and kind to kind, driven thereto by unity of sound, of colour and of rhythm.

This leads to the second factor we are considering, the destructive factor. In emancipation comes the breaking of the chains, in liberation comes the abolition of the old forms, in the domination of matter is seen the liberation of spirit. So, in the sounding of the Sacred Word in its sevenfold sense, comes the escaping from the shattered forms; first in the out-breathing, the attraction of matter, then in the in-breathing, the gradual shattering of the material forms and the leaving of them behind.

Meditation and the Word.

I have pictured this for you on the systemic scale. Now let me apply it to meditation and see how it will work. Man, when meditating, aims at two things:—

- a—At the formation of thoughts, at the bringing down to the concrete levels of the mental plane, of abstract ideas and intuitions. This is what might be termed *meditation with seed.*
- b—At the aligning of the ego, and at the creation of that vacuum betwixt the physical brain and the Ego, which results in the divine outpouring, and the consequent shattering of the forms and subsequent liberation. This might be termed *meditation without seed.*

At a certain period in evolution the two blend, the seed is dropped and the vacuum is then created, not so much between the higher and the lower vehicles as between them and the intuitional plane or the plane of harmony.

Therefore, in the sounding of the Sacred Word in meditation man should (if rightly sounding it forth) be able to do both the creative work and the destructive work as does the Logos. It will be the reflection in the microcosm of the cosmic process. He will attract to his bodies matter of the finer kind and cast out that which is coarser. He will formulate thoughtforms that attract to themselves finer matter and repudiate that which is of a lower vibration. He should so sound the Word that alignment will be automatically made, and the necessary vacuum created, eventuating in a downflow from above. All these effects can transpire when the Word is correctly intoned, and each meditation should see the man more aligned, should disperse some of the matter of low vibration in one or other of his bodies, should open up the channel to a greater extent, and so provide a more adequate vehicle for the illumination from higher levels.

But—until correctness is possible—the effect produced by the use of the Word is very little, which is fortunate for the man who uses it. In the studying of the seven great Breaths and their effect on each plane, a man can find out much that should transpire on the different subplanes of each plane, especially in relation to his own development. In the studying of the basic note of the solar system (which was stabilised in System I), much can be found out about the use of the Word on the physical plane. A hint lies here for consideration. In the endeavour to find the note for this solar system, the note of love and wisdom, the student will make the necessary communication between the emotional or desire plane and the intuitional plane, and find out the secret of the emotional plane. In the study of the Word on mental levels and its effect in form building, the key to the erection of Solomon's Temple will be discovered, and the pupil will develop the faculties of the causal body, and eventually find liberation from the three worlds.

The student must remember, nevertheless, that he has first to find his personality note, and then the egoic, before he can touch the monadic chord. When he has done that he has, for himself, sounded his own threefold Word, and is now an intelligent creator animated by love. The goal is reached.

June 21, 1920

Some Practical Hints.

I wish to make clear this afternoon that it is not possible for me, nor wise and appropriate to give to you different keys in which the Sacred Word can be intoned; I can do no more than indicate general principles. Each human being, each unit of consciousness, is so unlike any other that the individual need can only be supplied when full causal consciousness exists on the part of the teacher, and when the pupil has himself reached a point where he is willing to know, to dare and to be silent. The dangers involved in the misuse of the Word are so great that we dare do no more than indicate basic ideas and fundamental principles, and then leave the aspirant to work out for himself the points necessary for his own development and to carry out the needed experiments until he finds *for himself* that which he needs. Only that which is the result of self-effort, of hard struggle and of bitter experience is of permanent and lasting value. Only as the disciple—through failure, through success, through hardly won victories, and the bitter hours that succeed defeat—adjusts himself to the inner condition, will he find the use of the Word scientifically and experimentally of value. His lack of will defends him largely from the misuse of the Word, whilst his endeavour to love guides him eventually to its correct intoning. Only that which we *know* for ourselves becomes inherent faculty. The statements of a teacher, no matter how profoundly wise he may be, are but mental concepts until experimentally part of a man's life. Hence, I can but point the way. I may give but general hints; the rest must be threshed out by the student of meditation for himself.

Pronunciation and Use in Individual Meditation.

I shall now be very practical. I speak for the man on the Probationary Path, who has therefore an intellectual grasp of what has to be accomplished. He realises approximately his place in evolution and the work to be done if he would some day pass through the portal of Initiation. In this way what I will say will teach the majority who study these letters........The man undertakes to meditate and seeks to conform to the necessary rules. Let me give a few preliminary hints:—

The aspirant seeks daily a quiet spot where he can be free from interference and interruption. If wise, he will always seek the same spot, for he will there build up a shell around it that will serve as a protection and make the desired higher contact more easy. The matter of that spot, the matter of what you might term the surrounding space, becomes then attuned to a certain vibration (the man's own highest vibration, reached in consecutive meditations) which makes it easier for him each time to start at his highest and so eliminate a long preliminary keying up.

The aspirant composes himself to a position in which he can be unconscious of his physical body. No hard and fast rules can be laid down as the physical vehicle itself has here to be considered,—it may be handicapped in some way, stiff or crippled. Ease of posture is to be aimed at, coupled with alertness and attention. Slothfulness and laxness lead a man nowhere. The position most suitable for the average is cross-legged upon the ground, sitting against something that affords support to the spine. In intensest meditation or when the aspirant is very proficient and the centres rapidly awakening (perhaps even the inner fire pulsating at the base of the spine) the back should be erect without support. The head should not be thrown back as tension is to be avoided, but it should be held level, or with the chin slightly dropped. When this is done, that tenseness that is the characteristic of so many will be gone and the lower vehicle will be relaxed. The eyes should be closed and the hands folded in the lap.

Then let the aspirant note if his breathing is regular, steady and uniform. Should this be so, let him then relax his entire person, holding the mind positive and the physical vehicle supple and responsive.

Then let him visualize his three bodies, and having decided whether his meditation shall be in the head or within the heart (I will later take up this point) let him withdraw his consciousness there and focus himself in one or other of the centres. In so doing let him deliberately realise that he is a Son of God, returning to the Father; that he is God Himself, seeking to find the God-consciousness which is His; that he is a creator, seeking to create; that he is the lower aspect of Deity seeking alignment with the higher. Then let him three times intone the Sacred Word, breathing it forth gently the first time and thereby affecting the mental vehicle; more loudly the second time, thereby stabilising the emotional vehicle; and in a still louder tone the final time, acting then upon the physical vehicle. The effect upon each body will be threefold. If correctly chanted with the centre of consciousness steadily held within whichever centre has been chosen, the effect will be as follows:

On Mental Levels:

   a-—The contacting of the head centre, causing it to vibrate. The stilling of the lower mind.

b—Linking up with the Ego to a more or less degree, but always to some extent through the permanent atom.

c—The driving out of coarse particles and the building in of finer.

On Emotional Levels:

a—The definite stabilisation of the emotional body through the permanent atom, and the contacting and setting in motion of the heart centre.

b—The driving out of coarse matter and the rendering of the emotional or desire body more colourless, so that it will be a true reflector of the higher.

c—It causes a sudden rush of feeling from the atomic levels of the emotional plane to the intuitional plane, via the atomic channel that exists between the two. It sweeps upward and clarifies the channel.

On the Physical Planes:

a—Here the effect is very similar, but the primary effect is on the etheric body; it stimulates the divine flow.

b—It passes beyond the periphery of the body and creates a shell that serves as a protection. It drives away discordant factors in the near environment.

June 22, 1920

The Logoic Chord and Analogy.

Now, let us proceed with the study of the use of the Sacred Word in its group application and in its employment for certain specific ends. We have very briefly studied the Word as used by the individual who begins to

meditate,—the effect of its use being very largely one of
purification, stabilisation and centralisation. This is all
that is possible until the student has reached a point
where he may be allowed to sound the note in one of the
subtones egoic. You will have in the egoic note just the
same sequence as in the note Logoic. What had you there?
You had a sevenfold chord of which the important points
at our stage of development are:

1—The basic note.
2—The major third.
3—The dominant or fifth.
4—The ultimate seventh.

A hint may here be given along the line of analogy.
There is a close connection between the fifth or dominant
and the fifth principle, Manas or Mind, and, for this solar
system (though not for the first or third), there is an
interesting response between the fifth plane of mind and
the dominant, and between the sixth plane of the emotions
and the major third. From some angles in this connection
the emotional vehicle forms a third vehicle for consciousness—counting the dense physical and the vehicle for
prana or electrical vitality as two units. More I cannot
say for the whole shifts and interpenetrates, but I have
indicated food for thought.

In the egoic note,—as before said—you have a similar
sequence, for it is the reflection on its own plane of the
Logoic. You will therefore have the basic note of the
physical, the third of the emotional, and the fifth of the
causal levels. When a man has mastered the key, and has
found his own subtone then he will sound the Sacred Word
with exactitude and thus reach the desired end; his alignment will be perfect, the bodies will be pure, the channel

free from obstruction, and the higher inspiration will be possible. This is the aim of all true meditation and can be reached by the right use of the Word. In the meantime, owing to the absence of a teacher and the defects of the pupil, all that is now possible is to sound the Word as well as may be, knowing that danger does not lurk where there is sincerity of purpose, and that certain results, such as protection, quieting and correction may be achieved.

Group Use of the Word.

In group formation the effect of the Word is intensified, provided the groups are correctly constituted, or rendered null and void and neutralised should the groups contain undesirable elements. Certain things, therefore, have to be ascertained before the Word may be used with adequacy by a group:—

a—It is desirable that people on the same ray or on a complementary ray form a group.

b—It is desirable that the Word be intoned on the same key, or in part harmonic. When this is done, the vibratory effect is far reaching and certain reactions will occur.

What results, therefore, when the Word is correctly sounded by a group of people rightly intermingled?

a—A strong current is set up that reaches the disciple or the Master responsible for the group and which enables him to put the group en rapport with the Brotherhood, permitting the channel to be cleared for the transmission of teaching.

b—A vacuum is created that corresponds somewhat to the vacuum that should exist between the Ego and the Personality, but this time between a group and Those on the inner side.

c—If all conditions are right, it likewise results in a linking with the egoic groups of the involved personalities, a stimulation of the causal bodies involved, and a linking of all three groups—the lower, the higher and the Brotherhood—in a triangle for the transmission of force.

d—It has a definite effect on the physical vehicles of the lower group; it intensifies the vibration of the emotional bodies, driving out countervibration and swinging all into line with the higher rhythm. This results in equilibrium; it stimulates the lower mind, yet at the same time opens the connection with the higher, which higher, entering in, stabilises the lower concrete mind.

e—It attracts the attention of certain of the devas or angels whose work lies with the bodies of men, and enables them to do that work with greater exactitude and make contacts that later will be of use.

f—It creates a protective shell around the group, which (though only temporary) leads to freedom from disturbance, enables the units of the group to work with greater ease and according to the law, and helps the inner Teachers to find the line of least resistance betwixt Themselves and those who seek Their instruction.

g—It aids in the work of evolution. Infinitestimal that aid may be, yet every effort that leads to the free play of the law, that acts in any way on matter for its greater refining, that stimulates vibration and facilitates the contact between the higher and the lower is an instrument in the hand of the Logos for the hastening of His plan.

I have touched here upon certain effects incident upon the chanting of the Word in unison. Later, as the rules of occult meditation are understood and experimentally applied, these effects will be studied. As the race becomes more clairvoyant, they will also be tabulated and checked. The geometrical forms created by the individual, and by the group, in sounding forth the Word will be recorded and noted. The elimination of individuals from different groups and their assignment to other groups more suitable will be effected by judicious consideration of the work done by them. Later, as individuals develop the higher consciousness, wardens of groups must be chosen—not only for their spiritual attainments and their intellectual capacity, but for their ability to see with the inner vision, and hence assist their members and group to rightful plans and to correct development.

Groups for Specific Purposes.

Groups will later be formed for specific purposes, which brings me to my third point, the use of the Word for certain calculated ends.

Let me enumerate for you some of the aims groups will have in view when they form themselves, and by the use of the Sacred Word, coupled to the true occult meditation, achieve certain results. The time for this is not yet, and need arises not for detailed description, yet if things progress as desired, even *you* may see it somewhat worked out in your lifetime.

1—Groups for the purpose of working on the emotional body, with the object of development, of subjugation, and clarification.

2—Groups for the purpose of mental development, of strengthening equilibrium, and the contacting of the higher mind.

3—Groups for the healing of the physical body.

4—Groups whose purpose is to effect alignment, and to clear the channel betwixt the higher and the lower.

5—Groups for the treatment of obsessions and mental diseases.

6—Groups whose work it will be to study reaction to the sounding of the Word, to record and tabulate the consequent geometrical forms, to note its effect on individuals in the groups, and to note the extraneous entities it draws by its attractive force. These must be rather advanced groups, capable of clairvoyant investigation.

7—Groups that definitely work at making contact with the devas, and collaborating with them under the law. During the seventh ray activity, this will be much facilitated.

8—Groups that are definitely and scientifically working on the laws of the rays, and studying colour and sound, their individual and group effects, and their interrelation. This is necessarily a select group and only those of high spiritual attainment and those nearing Initiation will be permitted to take part. Forget not that these groups on the physical plane are but the inevitable working out into manifestation of the inner groups of aspirants, pupils, disciples and initiates.

9—Groups that are definitely working under some one Master, and conforming to certain procedure laid down by Him. The members of these groups will therefore be chosen by the Master.

10—Groups working specifically under one of the three great departments and seeking—under expert guidance—to influence politically and religiously the world of men, and to speed the processes of evolution as directed from the department of the Lord of Civilisation. Some of these groups will work under the Church, others under Masonry, and others will work in connection with the Initiate heads of the great organizations. In considering this you need to remember that the whole world becomes ever more mental as time proceeds, —hence the ever-increased scope of this type of work.

11—Other groups will work entirely in what might be termed preparatory work for the future colony.

12—Problem groups, as they might be called, will be formed to deal with social, economic, political and religious problems as they arise, studying the effects of meditation, colour and sound.

13—Still other groups will deal with child culture, with the individual training of people, with the guidance of persons on the probationary path, and with the development of the higher faculties.

14—Later, when the Great Lord, the Christ, comes with His Masters, there will be a few very esoteric groups, gathered out of all the others, where the members (through graduation and karmic right) will be trained for discipleship and for the first Initiation. There will be seven such groups or centres formed for definite occult training...Only those whose vibratory capacity is adequate will find their way there.

I have given you enough to consider for today, and we will leave the consideration of point the fourth till tomorrow.

June 23, 1920

You are right in thinking that conditions today are not desirable. The whole world speeds towards a crisis—a crisis reconstructive, even though it seems to the onlooker to be destructive. On all sides, the tearing down of the old forms is progressing, nor is the work as yet fully accomplished. Enough has, nevertheless, been done to permit of the erection of the scaffolding for the new building. In serenity and steady adherence to the next duty will come the simplification of that which must be done.

Today we deal with the effect of the Word on the various centres, on each body, and its utility in aligning the bodies with the causal vehicle. This was our fourth point. The first two are closely allied, for the Sacred Word (when properly enunciated) acts on the various bodies through the medium of the centres, and their astral and mental counterparts. Some of the effects, such as the elimination of undesirable matter, and the building in of new, the protective effect of the Word and its work of stabilisation and purification, we have somewhat touched upon. We will now focus our attention largely upon the centres and the result upon them of the sounding of the Word.

The Seven Centres and the Sacred Word.

As is our custom, let us divide our thoughts under the following heads. Tabulation has its value; it systematises knowledge, thus tending to the orderly arrangement of the mental body; it facilitates recollection through the assistance of the eye.

1—Enumeration and discussion of the centres.
2—Growth and development of the centres.
3—The effect of meditation on the centres.
4—Their interrelation in the work of alignment.

First let me say that certain information that may seem to be the natural sequence and corollary of that which I have to impart will have to be withheld. The dangers involved through the injudicious development of the centres are too great for us to venture yet to give full and detailed instructions. We seek to develop Masters of Compassion, dispensers of the love of the universe. We seek not to develop Masters of Black Arts and specialists in ruthless self-expression at the expense of the un-initiated. Certain facts have been, and can be, imparted. They will lead to the development of the intuition, and inspire the seeker after light to more earnest endeavour. Others must be withheld for they would be weapons of great danger in the hands of the unscrupulous. If then it seems to you that I have but imparted only sufficient to arouse interest, know then that that is my aim. When your interest and the interest of all aspirants is suficiently aroused naught can then be withheld from you.

1—*Enumeration of the centres.*

The physical centres are, as you know:—
1—The base of the spine.
2—The solar plexus.
3—The spleen.
4—The heart.
5—The throat.
6—The pineal gland.
7—The pituitary body.

This enumeration is correct, but I seek to give you another division, based on earlier imparted facts, those anent the solar system. These seven centres may be enumerated as five if we eliminate the spleen and count the two head centres as one. The five centres thus specified are applicable to our fivefold evolution in this the second solar system.

In the first solar system the three lower centres were developed and with them the occultist has naught to do. They form the basis of the development of the lower quaternary before individualisation, but are now transcended and the divine fire must be focalised in other and higher centres.

The Spleen.

The spleen, the third centre, has a specific purpose. It has its correspondence in the third or activity aspect, and in the third or Activity (Adaptability) Ray, and is the basis of all the fundamental activities of the microcosm, and of the recurring adaptations of the microcosm to its environment, to its need and to the macrocosm. It controls the selective processes of the microcosm; it takes the vibratory force and energy of the macrocosm and transmutes it for the use of the microcosm. We might call it the organ of transmutation, and—as its functions are more completely understood,—it will be found that it provides a magnetic link between the conscious, thinking, three-fold man and his lower vehicles, regarding those lower vehicles as the Not-Self, and as themselves animated by informing entities. It is the life force contacting those entities that is the issue and aim.

In its emotional counterpart, it is the organ of emotional vitality, again in the same sense as providing a link; on the mental plane it serves somewhat the same purpose, only this time through this centre are the thoughtforms vitalised by means of the energising will. I will not, therefore, deal more fully with this centre beyond these general indications. Few people have the faculty of stimulating it through the use of the Word, nor is it desirable that they should. It develops normally if the aspirant himself —as a totality—progresses as desired:—if his physical body receives adequate application of the life forces of the sun, if his emotional body is moved by high desire, and open to the downflow of force from the causal and intuitional levels, and if his mental life is intense, vibrant, and animated by a powerful will. Then the spleen, with its inner counterparts, will progress and be in a healthy condition.

We will therefore thus dispose of it and give no further space to it in these letters.

The fundamental centres.

The three fundamental centres of vital importance from the standpoint of the average man, polarised in his emotional body and living the normal life of the man of the world, are:

1—The base of the spine.
2—The solar plexus.
3—The heart centre.

The three major centres for the man nearing the Probationary Path, and for the man who is aiming at a life of altruism, having examined the attractions of the three worlds, are:

1—The base of the spine.
2—The heart.
3—The throat.

His solar plexus is left then to normal functioning, having served its purpose as a centre for the emotional focussing. The activity of the fire becomes more centered in the throat.

The three major centres for the man on the Path itself in its twofold divisions are:—

1—The heart.
2—The throat.
3—The head.

The divine activity has developed the solar plexus centre, is controlling all the centres below the solar plexus, and is passing upward in ordered progression until it is focussed and vivifying the head centres.

Earlier we divided the life of the man into five main periods, tracing his development in each. We might (if we are careful to generalise widely) apply the same to the five centres.

Period I—wherein the base of the spine is the most active in the purely rotary sense and not in a fourth-dimensional. The inner fire is focussed on the vivification of the organs of generation and on the functional physical life of the personality.

Period II—wherein the solar plexus is the goal of the attention of the fire and when the emotional counterpart vibrates synchronously. Two centres are thus vibrating, even though the measure be slow; the others are alive; pulsation can be seen, but there is no circular movement.

Period III—The divine fire now mounts to the heart centre and the three rotate in ordered measured unison. I would point out that the vivification of any one centre causes an accession of force in all, and I would further point out that in the head are seven centres (three major and four minor) and that these centres directly correspond to one or other centre in the body. They are the synthesis, and, on the stimulation of their corresponding centre, receive themselves a corresponding acquisition of rotary power.

Period IV—marks the definite stimulation of the throat centre. All the creative activity of the three-fold man—physical, emotional and mental,—is turned upward in service, and his life begins occultly to *sound*. He is *occultly productive*. He manifests forth and his sound goes out before him. This is an occult statement of fact definitely apparent to those who have the inner vision. Coordination between the centres becomes apparent; rotation is intensified, and the centres themselves change in appearance, becoming unfolded, and the rotary movement becomes fourth-dimensional, turning inward upon itself. The centres are then radiating nuclei of light, and the corresponding four lower head centres are equally alive.

Period V—marks the application of the fire to the head centres and their complete awakening.

Before initiation, all the centres will be rotating in fourth dimensional order, but after initiation they become flaming wheels, and—seen clairvoyantly—are of rare beauty. The fire of Kundalini is then awakened and is progressing in the necessary spirals. At the second initiation the emotional centres are similarly awakened, and at the third initiation those on the mental plane are touched. The initiate can then stand in the Presence of the Great King, the One Initiator.

I seek to point out that the student must ever remember that here generalisations only are given. The complexity in the development of the microcosm is as great as in the macrocosm. The awakening of the centres and their particular order is dependent on several factors, such as:

a—The Ray of the Spirit or Monad.
b—The Ray of the Ego, Higher Self, or Son, or the sub-ray.

c—Race and nationality.
d—The special type of work to be done.
e—The application of the student.

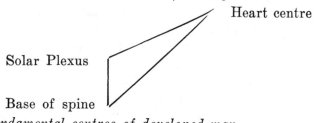

Fundamental centres of average man.

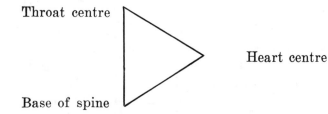

Fundamental centres of developed man.

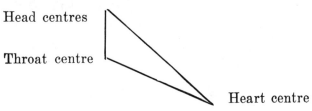

Fundamental centres of man on Path.

Hence you can see for yourself that it is useless to lay down rules for the development of the centres and to formulate methods whereby the fire can be circulated until such time as trained teachers with expert knowledge and clairvoyant faculty are in charge of the work on the physical plane. It is not desirable for aspirants to focus their thought on any one centre. They run the risk of over-stimulation, or of attrition. It is not wished that effort be made to turn the fire towards any particular point; in ignorant manipulation lies insanity and fell disease. If the aspirant but seeks spiritual development, if he but aims at sincerity of purpose and at compassionate altruism, if he, with serene application, concentrates on the subjugation of the emotional body and the enlargement of the mental, and cultivates the habit of abstract thinking, the desired results upon the centres will be produced from necessity, and danger will be eliminated.

When these triangles are paths of threefold fire, emanating from the base of the spine, when the interlacing is complete and the fire progresses along the path from centre to centre in the correct manner, and when this is accomplished in the order required by the man's primary ray, then the work is completed. The fivefold man has attained perfection for this present greater cycle and the goal is reached.

(Note that this order has to be attained in the head centres likewise.)

Tomorrow we will continue the study of the centres more specifically and somewhat describe them, pointing to the effect upon the life through the awakening of these wheels.

June 25, 1920.

2—*The growth and development of the centres.*

We will now enumerate the centres again, this time considering their psychic correspondences and will note the colours and the number of the petals.

1—*The base of the spine.* Four petals. These petals are in the shape of a cross, and radiate with orange fire.

2—*The solar plexus.* Ten petals. The colour rosy, with an admixture of green.

3—*The heart centre.* Twelve petals. Colour glowing golden.

4—*The throat centre.* Sixteen petals. Colour silvery blue, the blue predominating.

5—*The head centres.* These are in a twofold division:—

a—Between the eyebrows. Ninety-six petals. Colour, one-half of the lotus is rose and yellow, and the other half is blue and purple.

b—The top of the head. There are twelve major petals of white and gold, and 960 secondary petals are arranged around the central twelve. This makes a total of 1068 petals in the two head centres, or 356 triplicities. All these figures have an occult significance.

This description is taken from "The Inner Life." This description applies to the etheric centres, which are themselves the working out into physical plane manifestation of corresponding vortices on the emotional plane, with emotional vitality playing through. They have their mental counterparts, and in their awakening as aforesaid, and in their growth and development, comes the final vivification, and the resultant liberation.

The connection between the centres, the causal body and meditation lies hid in the following hint: it is through the rapid whirling and interaction of these centres and their increased force through meditation (the ordered occult meditation) that the shattering of the causal body is effected. When the inner fire is circulating through each centre and when kundalini is spiralling accurately and geometrically from vortex to vortex, the intensification interacts in three directions.

a—It focuses the light or the consciousness of the Higher Self into the three lower vehicles, drawing it downward into fuller expression and widening its contact on all the three planes in the three worlds.

b—It draws down from the threefold Spirit more and more of the fire of the Spirit, doing for the causal body what the Ego is doing for the three lower vehicles.

c—It forces the unification of the higher and lower, and it attracts the spiritual life itself. When this is done, when each successive life sees an increase of vitality in the centres, and when kundalini in its seven-fold capacity touches each centre, then even the causal body proves inadequate for the influx of life from above. If I might so express it, the two fires meet, and eventually the egoic body disappears; the fire burns up entirely the Temple of Solomon; the permanent atoms are destroyed, and all is reabsorbed into the Triad. The essence of the Personality, the faculties developed, the knowledge gained, and the remembrance of all that has transpired becomes part of the equipment of the Spirit and eventually finds its way to the Spirit or Monad on its own plane.

Now let me enumerate for you the things as to which it will not be possible as yet to furnish more information; the risks involved would be too great.

1—The method of arousing the Sacred Fire.
2—The order of its progression.
3—The geometrical forms it makes as it mounts.
4—The order of the development of the centres, according to the ray of the Spirit. The complexity is too great.

You will therefore observe that the subject really becomes more abstruse, the longer it is studied. It is complicated by ray development, by the man's own place upon the ladder of evolution, by the uneven awakening of the different centres due to the type of a man's lives; it is rendered more complex by the threefold nature of the centres themselves,—etheric, emotional and mental—by the fact that some people have one or other emotional centre completely awakened and demonstrating etherically whilst the mental counterparts may be quiescent; others may have the mental centres awake and the emotional not so vivified and be etherically quiet. Therefore, it will be obvious how great is the need for conscious clairvoyant teachers, who can judiciously work with the pupils, stimulating through scientific knowledge and methods the dormant or sluggish centres, and aligning them so that the current can freely flow back and forth between the external vortices and the inner centre. Later the teacher can train the pupil in the safe awakening of the inner fire, in its scientific culture and transmission, and instruct him in the order required for its convolutions along the path of the triangles until it reaches the head centres. When kundalini has traversed these geometrical lines the man is perfected, the personality has served its purpose, and the goal is reached. Hence the fact that all the centres have petals whose numbers are multiples of four, for four is the number of the lower self, of the quaternary. The total number of petals in the centres, if we eliminate the spleen which has a purpose all its own, and the three lower organs of creation, is one thousand, one hundred and ten, the total number signifying the perfection of the microcosm,—ten the number of perfected personality, one hundred the number of causal perfection, and one thousand the number of spiritual achievement. When every petal vibrates in all the dimensions, then the goal for this manvantara is reached. The lower lotus is full blown, and reflects the greater with precision.

June 26, 1920.

The effect of occult meditation on the centres.

We shall study today the effect of occult meditation upon the centres and their consequent vivification, positing a meditation prefaced always by the use of the Sacred Word, uttered according to rule.

We speak also of a meditation followed under the guidance of a teacher. The man therefore will meditate correctly or approximately so; thus what we are to consider today is the factor of *time*, in its relationship to the centres, for the work is slow and necessarily gradual. Here I would pause to emphasize to you the need of ever remembering that in all work that is truly occult expected effects are very slowly achieved. Should a man seem in any one incarnation to make spectacular progress it is due to the fact that he is but demonstrating what has already been earlier acquired (the manifesting forth of innate faculty, acquired in previous incarnations) and is preparing for a fresh period of slow, careful and painstaking endeavor. He recapitulates in the present life the processes surmounted in the past, and thus lays the foundation for renewed effort. This slow and laborious effort, which is the consistent method of all that evolves, is after all but an illusion of *time* and is due to the fact that consciousness is at present for the majority polarised in the lower vehicles and not in the causal. The states of consciousness succeed each other apparently slowly, and in their slow progression lies the chance for the Ego to assimilate the fruit of these stages,

It takes a long time to establish a stable vibration, and it takes as long to shatter it, and to impose another and still higher rhythm. Growth is one long period of building in order to destroy, of constructing in order to disorganise later, of developing certain rhythmic processes in order to later disrupt them, and to force the old rhythm to give place to the new. What the Personality spends many thousands of lives in establishing is not going to be lightly altered when the Ego—working in the lower consciousness—seeks to effect a change. The shifting of polarisation from emotional to mental, and thence to the causal and later to the three-fold Spirit inevitably entails a period of great difficulty, of violent conflict both internally and with the environment, intense suffering and apparent darkness and disruption—all these things characterise the life of the aspirant or the disciple. What causes this and why is this so? The following reasons may make it apparent why the path is so hard to tread and the process of mounting the ladder (as one nears the higher rungs) becomes ever more complicated and difficult.

1—Each body has to be dealt with and disciplined separately and thus purified.

2—Each body has to be readjusted and aligned.

3—Each body has to be subjected to repolarisation.

4—Each body is practically reconstructed.

5—Each subplane above the fourth (for on the fourth the life of the aspirant starts) has to be dominated.

6—Each centre has to be gradually, carefully and scientifically awakened, its revolutions have to be intensified, its radiations electrified (if I may borrow that term and apply it to the centres) and its force must demonstrate through the higher dimension.

7—Each etheric centre has to be magnetically linked, in full alignment, with the corresponding centres in the emotional and mental bodies, so that the flow of force is unimpeded.

8—Each centre has then to be awakened afresh by the Sacred Fire till the radiations, the velocity and the colours are keyed to the egoic note. This is part of the work of Initiation.

As each change is gradually made, it responds to the same law that governs all cyclic growth in the macrocosm:

1—First comes the clashing of the old with the new rhythm.

2—This is followed by a period of gradual dominance of the new, elimination of the old, and the stabilisation of the new vibration.

3—Then finally comes the passing on and out, and again a repetition of the process.

It is this work that is done on the bodies and on the centres by the work of meditation and the use of the Sacred Word. This Word aids in the adjustment of the matter, its vitalisation by fire, and enables the aspirant to work in line with the law. This unfoldment of the centres is a gradual process, paralleling the work done on the bodies, the refining of the vehicles and the slow development of causal consciousness.

Concluding remarks.

In concluding this division upon the use of the Sacred Word in meditation, I would like to indicate certain things, though more than a hint is not possible. This matter has been difficult for you to comprehend, and I fully realise it. The difficulty lies in the fact that so little can be safely said, that the real use of the Word is one of the secrets of initiation and may not therefore be divulged, and that what little can be indicated is of small value to the student apart from the wise attempt to experiment, which experiment must be carried on under the guidance of one who *knows*. Still, I will indicate certain things which, wisely pondered upon, may lead to illumination.

When meditating in the heart centre, picture it as a golden lotus *closed*. When the Sacred Word is enunciated, picture it as a lotus slowly expanding until the inner centre or vortex is seen as a radiating whirlpool of electric light, more blue than golden. Build there the picture of the Master, in etheric, emotional and mental matter. This entails the withdrawing of the consciousness ever more and more inwards. When the picture is fully built then gently sound the Word again, and with an effort of the will withdraw still further inwards and link up with the twelve petalled head centre, the centre of causal consciousness. Do all this very slowly and gradually, maintaining an attitude of perfect peace and calm. There is a direct relationship between the two twelve petalled centres and occult meditation, and the action of the kundalini fire will later reveal its significance. This visualization leads to synthesis, to causal development and expansion, and eventually conducts a man into the presence of the Master.

The solar plexus is the seat of the emotions and should not be centred upon in meditation. It is a basis for physical healing and will later be more completely understood. It is the centre of activity—an activity which must later be intuitional. The throat centre works radiantly when the polarisation is shifting from the physical atom to the mental permanent atom as dealt with earlier.

The mental permanent atom becomes the centre of pure reason or of abstract thought. Then comes a time in the development of consciousness when the emotional force which governs so many is transcended and superseded by the force of the higher intellect. It often marks a period when a man is swayed purely by reason and his emotions do not control him. This may demonstrate in the personal life on the physical plane as intellectual hardness. Later, the emotional permanent atom gives place to the intuitional, and pure intuition and perfect comprehension through love is the motive power, with the faculty of reason added. Then the solar plexus is distinguished by the preponderance of the green of activity, for the emotional body is actively the agent of the higher, and engenders but little of the rose of human desire.

In the whirling of the force through the vortex (which whirling forms the petals of the lotus) it will be observed that certain petals predominantly stand out, and each centre demonstrates one particular type of cross, with the exception of the two head centres which are the synthesis of the lower crosses. The four-armed cross of the third Logos is found at the base of the spine and the cross of the fourth human Hierarchy in the heart.

When the Sacred Word is intoned by the average aspirant, it carries force through all the inner centres to the etheric, and causes a definite stimulation of the petals in each centre. If the lotus is only partially unfolded, then only some of the petals receive the stimulation. This stimulation creates a vibration (especially in the centre in which a man meditates—the head or the heart) which causes reflex action in the spine and down to the base. This is not in itself sufficient to arouse the fire; that can only be done in due form, in the right key and subject to certain rules.

When meditation is done in the heart and under occult laws, with the correct intoning of the Word, the force comes through the emotional centres from the intuitional levels. When it is done in the head, the force comes through the mental centres from the abstract manasic levels, and later from the atmic. The one gives spiritual intuition, and the other causal consciousness.

The advanced man is the man who is linking up the two major centres,—the head and the heart,—into one synthetic instrument, and whose throat centre vibrates to the same measure. Then you have will and love blended in harmonious service, and the lower physical activity is transmuted into idealism and altruism. When this stage is reached, the man is ready for the awakening of the inner fire. His bodies are refined enough to withstand the pressure and the onrush; they contain nothing dangerous to its progress; the centres are keyed high enough to receive the acquisition of fresh stimulation. When this has been done, the hour of initiation comes when the would-be server of humanity will stand before his Lord, with purified desire, consecrated intellect, and a physical body that is his servant and not his master.

Today we will bring this letter to a close. Tomorrow, we will take up the dangers that confront the man who meditates. I shall seek to point out what he must guard against and wherein he must move with caution.

LETTER V

DANGERS TO BE AVOIDED IN MEDITATION.

1—Dangers inherent in the Personality.
2—Dangers arising from Karma.
3—Dangers arising from subtle forces.

LETTER V

July 22, 1920.

DANGERS TO BE AVOIDED IN MEDITATION.

The Withholding of Information.

We have reached a point now where the foundations of knowledge have been laid,—that knowledge which instills into the wise student the desire to submit to the necessary rules, to conform to the prescribed requirements, and to make the comprehended mental concepts practical experiences in daily life. This desire is wise and right, and the object of all that has been imparted, but at this juncture it may be wise to sound a warning note, to point out certain dangerous possibilities, and to put the student on his guard against an enthusiasm that may lead him along paths that will hinder development, and that may build up vibrations that will ultimately have to be offset. This entails delay and a recapitulation in work that (if realised in time) might be obviated.

Certain statements and instructions cannot be made or given in writing to students for three reasons:—

1—Some instructions are always given orally, as they appeal to the intuition and are not for the pondering and logical reasoning of lower mind; they also contain elements of danger if submitted to the unready.

2—Some instructions pertain to the secrets of the Path, and are mainly applicable to the groups to which the student is attached; they can only be given in joint instruction when out of the physical body. They pertain to the group causal body, to certain ray secrets, and to the invoking of the assistance of the higher devas to bring about desired results. The dangers attached thereto are too great to permit of their being communicated in an exoteric publication. The occult effects of the spoken word and of the written word are diverse and interesting. Until such time as you have among you a wise Teacher in physical person, and until it is possible for Him to gather around Him His students, thus affording them the protection of His aura and its stimulating vibration, and until such time as world conditions permit of a certain period of relaxation from the present strain and suspense, it will not be possible to impart forms, invocations and mantrams of a specific character; it will not be possible to arouse the centres ahead of the necessary evolutionary rate, except in a few individual cases where certain pupils (perhaps unconsciously to themselves) are being subjected to definite processes, which result in a greatly increased rate of vibration. This is only being done to a few in each country, and is directly under the eye of a Master, focusing through H.P.B.

3—Information as to the invoking of devas in meditation cannot yet be safely given to individuals, though a beginning is being made with groups such as in the rituals of the Masons and of the Church. Formulas that put the lesser devas under the control of man will not yet be imparted. Human beings are not yet to be trusted with that power, for the majority are but animated by selfish desire and would misuse it for their own ends. It is deemed by the wise Teachers of the race,—as I think I have before said—that the dangers of too little knowledge are much less than the dangers of too much, and that the race can be more seriously hindered by the misapplication of powers gained by incipient occultists than it can by a lack of knowledge that engenders not karmic results. The powers gained in meditation, the

capacities achieved by the adjustment of the bodies
through meditation, the faculties developed in each vehicle by definite formulas in meditation, the manipulation of matter that is one of the functions of the occultist
(the result of well-adjusted vehicles that respond perfectly to plane conditions) and the attainment of causal
consciousness—a consciousness that carries with it the
ability to include within itself all the lesser—are of too
serious a character to be lightly disposed of, and in the
training of man along these lines only those are encour-
aged by the teacher who can be trusted. Trusted in what
sense? Trusted to think in group terms and not in terms
of self, trusted to use the knowledge gained anent the
bodies and the karma of environing associates solely for
their wise assistance and not for selfish purposes, and
trusted to use occult powers for the furtherance of evolution and for the development on all planes of the schemes
of evolution as planned by the three Great Lords.

Let me illustrate:—

One of the things accomplished in meditation when
pursued with regularity and under correct instruction is
the transference of the consciousness of the lower self
into the higher. This carries with it the capacity to see
on causal levels, intuitively to recognize *facts* in the lives
of others, to foresee events and occurrences and to *know*
the relative value of a personality. This can only be permitted when the student can be silent, selfless and stable.
Who as yet answers to all these requirements?

I am endeavoring to give you a general idea of the
dangers incident to the too early development of the
powers achieved in meditation. I seek to sound a note—
not of discouragement—but of insistence upon physical
purity, on emotional stability and on mental equilibrium
before the student passes on to greater knowledge. Only

as the channel opens to the intuition and closes to the animal nature can a man wisely proceed with his work. Only as the heart enlarges its capacity to suffer with all that breathes, to love all that is contacted, and to understand and sympathise with the least desirable of God's creatures, can the work go forward as desired. Only when the development is equable, only when the intellect runs not too far ahead of the heart, and the mental vibration shuts not out the higher one of the Spirit can the student be trusted to acquire powers that, wrongly used, may result in disaster to his environment as well as to himself. Only as he formulates no thoughts save such as he *purposes* to make for the helping of the world can he be trusted wisely to manipulate thought matter. Only as he has no desire save to find out the plans of the Master, and then to assist definitely in making those plans facts in manifestation, can he be trusted with the formulas that will bring the devas of lesser degree under his control. The dangers are so great and the perils that beset the unwary student so many that before I proceed further I have sought to urge caution.

Let us now specify and enumerate certain dangers that must be guarded against by the man who progresses in meditation. Some of them are due to one cause and some to another, and we shall have to specify with accuracy.

1—*Dangers inherent in the Personality of the pupil.* They can, as you foresee, be grouped under the three heads:—physical dangers, emotional dangers, and mental dangers.

2—*Dangers arising from the karma of the pupil*, and from his environment. These also may be enumerated under three divisions:

a—The karma of his present life, his own individual "ring-pass-not," as represented by his present life.

b—His national heredity and instincts as, for instance, whether he possesses an occidental or an oriental type of body.

c—His group affiliations, whether exoteric or esoteric.

3—*Dangers arising from the subtle forces* that you ignorantly call evil; such dangers consist in attack on the pupil by extraneous entities on some one plane. These entities may simply be discarnate human beings; they may be the denizens of the other planes who are non-human; later on, when the student is of sufficient importance to attract notice, the attack may come from those who deal purely with matter to the hindrance of spiritual growth,—the black magicians, the dark brothers, and other forces that appear destructive. This appearance is only such when viewed from the angle of time and in our three worlds, and is but incidental to the fact that our Logos Himself is also evolving, and (from the standpoint of the infinitely greater Ones Who assist Him in His development) it is dependent upon His transitory imperfections. The imperfections of nature—as we term them—are the imperfections of the Logos, and will eventually be transcended.

I have therefore outlined for you this morning the material I shall seek to impart during the coming days.

July 24, 1920.

The dangers that beset the student of meditation are dependent upon many factors, and it will not be possible to do more than briefly indicate certain menacing conditions, to warn against certain disastrous possibilities, and to caution the pupil against results that are to be reached by undue strain, by over-excess of zeal, and by a one-pointedness that may lead to an unbalanced development. One-pointedness is a virtue, but it should be the one-pointedness of purpose and of aim, and not that which develops one sole line of method to the exclusion of all others.

The dangers of meditation are largely the dangers of our virtues, and therein lies much of the difficulty. They are largely the dangers of a fine mental concept that runs ahead of the capacity of the lower vehicles, especially of the dense physical. Aspiration, concentration and determination are necessary virtues, but if used without discrimination and without a sense of *time* in evolution they may lead to a shattering of the physical vehicle that will delay all progress for some one particular life. Have I made my point clear? I seek but to bring out the absolute necessity for the occult student to have a virile common sense for one of his basic qualities, coupled with a happy sense of proportion that leads to due caution and an approximation of the necessary method to the immediate need. To the man therefore who undertakes wholeheartedly the process of occult meditation I would say with all conciseness:—

a—Know thyself.

b—Proceed slowly and with caution.

c—Study effects.

d—Cultivate the realisation that eternity is long and that that which is slowly built up endures forever.

e—Aim at regularity.

f—Realise always that the true spiritual effects are to be seen in the exoteric life of service.

g—Remember likewise that psychic phenomena are no indication of a successful following of meditation. The world will see the effects and be a better judge than the student himself. Above all, the Master will know, for the results on causal levels will be apparent to Him long before the man himself is conscious of any progress.

Let us now take up these points in detail.

Dangers inherent in the Personality.

Let us, therefore, consider first those dangers most closely connected with the man's own personal life, and which are dependent upon his three bodies, their separate condition and their interrelation. This subject is so vast that it will not be possible to do more than indicate certain results due to certain conditions; each man presents a different problem, and each body causes a different reaction, and each totality in his threefold nature is affected by its alignment or by its lack of alignment. Let us take each body separately at first and then in their threefold totality. In this way some specific facts may be imparted.

I begin with the mental body as it is for the student of meditation the one that is the centre of his effort and the one that controls the two lower bodies. The true student seeks to draw his consciousness away from his physical body, and away from the emotional body into the realms of thought, or into the lower mind body. Having achieved that much, he seeks then to transcend that lower mind and to become polarised in the causal body, using the antahkarana, as the channel of communication between the higher and the lower, the physical brain being then but the quiescent receiver of that which is transmitted from the Ego or Higher Self, and later from the threefold Spirit, the Triad. The work to be done necessitates a working from the periphery inwards, and a consequent centralisation. Having achieved that centralisation and focussed in that stable centre—with the solar plexus and the heart quiet—a point within the head, one of the three major head centres, becomes the centre of consciousness, the ray of a man's ego deciding which that centre will be. This is the method of the majority. Then that point having been reached, a man will follow the meditation of his ray as indicated to you in general terms earlier in these letters. In each case, the mental body becomes the centre of consciousness and then later—through practice—it becomes the point of departure for the transference of the polarisation into a higher body, first the causal and later into the Triad.

The dangers to the mental body are very real and must be guarded against. They are paramountly two, and might be termed *the dangers of inhibition* and those due to the *atrophying of the body*.

a—Let us take first the dangers due to inhibition. Some people, by their sheer strength of will, reach a point in meditation where they directly inhibit the processes of the lower mind. If you picture the mental body as an ovoid, surrounding the physical body and extending much beyond it, and if you realise that through that ovoid are constantly circulating thoughtforms of various kinds (the content of the man's mind and the thoughts of his environing associates) so that the mental egg is coloured by predominant attractions and diversified by many geometrical forms, all in a state of flux or circulation, you may get some idea of what I mean. When a man proceeds to quiet that mental body by inhibiting or suppressing all movement, he will arrest these thoughtforms within the mental ovoid, he will stop circulation and may bring about results of a serious nature. This inhibition has a direct effect upon the physical brain, and is the cause of much of the fatigue complained of after a period of meditation. If persisted in, it may lead to disaster. All beginners do it more or less, and until they learn to guard against it they will stultify their progress and retard development. The results may indeed be more serious.

What are the right methods of thought elimination? How can placidity of mind be achieved without the use of the will in inhibition? The following suggestions may be found useful and helpful:—

The student having withdrawn his consciousness on to the mental plane at some point within the brain, let him sound forth the Sacred Word gently three times. Let him picture the breath sent forth as a clarifying, expurgating force that in its progress onward sweeps away the thoughtforms circulating within the mental ovoid. Let him then at the close realise that the mental body is free and clear of thoughtforms.

Let him then raise his vibration as high as may be, and aim next at lifting it clear of the mental body into the causal, and so bring in the direct action of the Ego upon the lower three vehicles. As long as he can keep his consciousness high and as long as he holds a vibration that is that of the Ego on its own plane, the mental body will be held in a state of equilibrium. It will hold no lower vibration analagous to the thoughtforms circulating in its environment. The force of the Ego will circulate throughout the mental ovoid, permitting no extraneous geometrical units to find entrance, and the dangers of inhibition will be offset. Even more will be done,—the mental matter will in process of time become so attuned to the higher vibration that in due course that vibration will become stable and will automatically throw off all that is lower and undesirable.

b—What do I mean by the dangers of atrophy?

Simply this: Some natures become so polarised on the mental plane that they run the risk of breaking connection with the two lower vehicles. These lower bodies exist for purposes of contact, for the apprehension of knowledge on the lower planes and for reasons of experience in order that the content of the causal body may be increased. Therefore it will be apparent to you that if the indwelling consciousness comes no lower than the mental plane and neglects the body of emotions and the dense physical, two things will result. The lower vehicles will be neglected and useless and fail in their purposes, atrophying and dying from the point of view of the Ego, whilst the causal body itself will not be built as desired and so time will be lost. The mental body will be rendered useless likewise, and will become a thing of selfish content, of no use in the world and of little value. A dreamer whose dreams never materialise, a builder who stores up material which he never employs, a visionary whose visions are of no use to gods or men, is a clog upon the system universal. He is in great danger of atrophying.

Meditation should have the effect of bringing all three bodies more completely under the control of the Ego, and lead to a co-ordination and an alignment, to a rounding-out and a symmetrical development that will make a man of real use to the Great Ones. When a man realises that mayhap he is too much centralised on the mental plane he should definitely aim at making all his mental experiences, aspirations and endeavours matters of *fact* on the physical plane, bringing the two lower vehicles under control of the mental and making them the instruments of his mental creations and activities.

I have here indicated two of the dangers most frequently met with, and I advise all students of occultism to remember that all the three bodies are of equal importance in carrying out the work to be done, both from the egoic standpoint and from the standpoint of service to the race. Let them aim at a wise co-ordination in expression, that will enable the God within to manifest for the aiding of the world.

July 25, 1920.

The emotional body is at this time the most important body in the Personality for several reasons. It is a complete unit, unlike the physical and mental bodies; it is the centre of polarisation for the majority of the human family; it is the most difficult body to control, and is practically the very last body to be completely subjugated. The reason for this is that the vibration of desire has dominated, not only the human kingdom but also the animal and vegetable kingdoms in a lesser sense, so that the evolving inner man has to work against inclinations set up in three kingdoms. Before the spirit can function through forms of the fifth or spiritual kingdom, this desire vibration has to be eliminated, and selfish inclination transmuted into spiritual aspiration. The emotional body forms practically a unit with the physical body, for the average man functions almost entirely at the instigation of the emotional,—his lowest vehicle automatically obeying the behests of a higher. It is also the body that connects most directly, as has been oft-times said, with the intuitional levels, and one path of attainment lies that way. In meditation the emotional body should be controlled from the mental plane, and when the polarisation has been transferred into the mental body through forms of meditation and intensity of purpose and of will, then the emotional becomes quiescent and receptive.

This negative attitude in itself, if carried too far, opens the door to serious dangers, which I will later enlarge upon when we take up the subject of obsessions, divine sometimes, but more oft the reverse. A negative condition is not desired in either of the bodies, and it is just this very negativeness that beginners in meditation so oft achieve, and so run into danger. The aim should be to make the emotional ovoid positive to all that is lower and to its environment and only receptive to the Spirit via the causal. This can only be brought about by the development of *the faculty of conscious control*— that control which even in the moments of highest vibration and contact is alert to watch and guard the lower vehicles. "Watch and pray," the Great Lord said when last on earth, and He spoke in occult terms, that have not as yet received due attention or interpretation.

What must therefore be watched?

1—The attitude of the emotional ovoid and its positive-negative control.

2—The stability of the emotional matter and its conscious receptivity.

3—Its alignment with the mental and with the causal bodies. If this alignment is imperfect (as it so frequently is) it causes inaccuracy in reception from the higher planes, distortion of the truths sent down via the Ego, and a very dangerous transference of force to undesirable centres. This lack of alignment is the cause of the frequent straying from sexual purity of many apparently spiritually inclined persons. They *can* touch the intuitional levels somewhat, the Ego *can* partially transmit power from on high, but as the alignment is imperfect the force from those higher levels is deflected, the wrong centres are over-stimulated, and disaster results.

4—Another danger to be guarded against is that of

obsession, but in pure thoughts, spiritual aims, and unselfish brotherly conduct, lie the fundamentals of protection. If to these essentials is added common sense in
meditation and a wise application of occult rules, with
due consideration of ray and karma, these dangers will
disappear.

July 28, 1920.

Some thoughts on FIRE.

Just prior to beginning the consideration of the matter on hand, I would like to point out to you a certain
rather interesting fact. Most of the psychological phenomena of the earth are—as you will realise, if you think
clearly,—under the control of the Deva Lord Agni, the
great primary Lord of Fire, the Ruler of the mental
plane. Cosmic fire forms the background of our evolution; the fire of the mental plane, its inner control and
dominance and its purifying asset coupled to its refining
effects, is the aim of the evolution of our three-fold life.
When the inner fire of the mental plane and the fire latent
in the lower vehicles merge with the sacred fire of the
Triad, the work is completed, and the man stands adept.
The at-one-ment has been made and the work of aeons
is completed. All this is brought about through the co-
operation of the Lord Agni, and the high devas of the
mental plane working with the Ruler of that plane, and
with the Raja-Lord of the second plane.

Macrocosmic evolution proceeds in like manner to the
microcosmic. The internal fires of the terrestrial globe,
deep in the heart of our earth sphere, will merge with
the sacred fire of the sun at the end of the greater cycle,
and the solar system will then have reached its apotheosis. Little by little as the aeons slip away and the lesser
cycles run their course, fire will permeate the ethers and
will be daily more recognisable and controlled till even-

tually cosmic and terrestrial fire will be at-one (the bodies of all material forms adapting themselves to the changing conditions) and the correspondence will be demonstrated. When this is realised the phenomena of the earth—such as, for instance, seismic disturbance—can be studied with greater interest. Later, when more is comprehended, the effects of such disturbances will be understood and likewise their reactions on the sons of men. During the summer months—as that great cycle comes around in different quarters of the earth—the fire devas, the fire elementals and those obscure entities the "agnichaitans" of the internal furnaces, come into greater activity, relapsing as the sun moves further away, into a less active condition. You have here a correspondence between the fiery aspects of the earth economy in their relationship to the sun similar to the watery aspects and their connection with the moon. I give you quite an occult hint here. I would like also to give you here a very brief though occult fragment that . . . may now be made public. If pondered on, it carries the student to a high plane and stimulates vibration.

"The secret of the Fire lies hid in the second letter of the Sacred Word. The mystery of life is concealed within the heart. When that lower point vibrates, when the Sacred Triangle glows, when the point, the middle centre, and the apex likewise burn, then the two triangles—the greater and the lesser—merge into one flame which burneth up the whole."

It is our task now to deal briefly with the dangers that attend the practice of meditation as they manifest in the physical body. These dangers—like so much else in the Logoic scheme—assume a three-fold nature, attacking three departments of the physical body. They show themselves:—

a—In the brain.

b—In the nervous system.

c—In the sex organs.

It is needless to point out now the reason why I dealt first with the dangers of the mental and emotional bodies. It was necessary so to do, for many of the perils besetting the dense vehicle find their commencement on the subtler planes, and are only the outer manifestations of inner evils.

Each human being enters into life equipped with a physical and etheric body of certain constituents, those constituents being the product of a previous incarnation; they are virtually the body, reproduced exactly, that the man finally left behind him when death severed him from physical plane existence. The task ahead of everybody is to take that body, realise its defects and requirements, and then deliberately set in and build a new body that may prove more adequate to the need of the inner spirit. This is a task of large dimensions and involves time, stern discipline, self-denial and judgment.

The man who undertakes the practice of occult meditation literally "plays with fire." I wish you to emphasise this statement for it embodies a truth little realised. "Playing with fire" is an old truth that has lost its significance through flippant repetition, yet it is absolutely and entirely correct, and is not a symbolic teaching but a plain statement of fact. Fire forms the basis of all—the Self is fire, the intellect is a phase of fire, and latent in the microcosmic physical vehicles lies hid a veritable fire that can either be a destructive force, burning the tissue of the body and stimulating centres of an undesirable character, or be a vivifying factor, acting as a stimulating and awakening agent. When directed along certain prepared channels, this fire may act as a purifier and the great connector between the lower and the Higher Self.

In meditation the student seeks to contact the divine flame that is his Higher Self, and to put himself likewise en rapport with the fire of the mental plane. When meditation is forced, or is pursued too violently, before the alignment between the higher and lower bodies via the emotional is completed, this fire may act on the fire latent at the base of the spine (that fire called kundalini) and may cause it to circulate too early. This will produce disruption and destruction instead of vivification and stimulation of the higher centres. There is a proper geometrical spiralling which this fire should follow, dependent upon the ray of the student and the key of the vibration of his higher centres. This fire should only be permitted to circulate under the direct instruction of the Master and consciously distributed by the student himself, following the specific oral instructions of the teacher. Sometimes the fire may be aroused and spiral with correctness without the student knowing what is occurring on the physical plane; but on the inner planes he knows and has but failed to bring the knowledge through to the physical plane consciousness.

Let us take up for a moment the three dangers that principally beset the physical vehicles. I would like to point out that I deal with the trouble in its extreme, and that there are many intermediate stages of risk and trouble that attack the unwary student.

Dangers to the physical brain.

The brain suffers principally in two ways:—
From congestion, causing a suffusion of the blood

vessels and a consequent strain upon the delicate brain tissue. This may result in permanent injury, and may even cause imbecility. It shows in the initial stages as numbness and fatigue, and if the student persists in meditation when these conditions are sensed the result will be serious. At all times a student should guard against continuing his meditation when any fatigue is felt, and should stop at the first indications of trouble. All these dangers can be guarded against by the use of common-sense, and by remembering that the body must ever be trained gradually and be built slowly. In the scheme of the Great Ones, hurry has no place.

From insanity. This evil has often been seen in earnest students who persist in unwise pressure or seek unguardedly to arouse the sacred fire through breathing exercises and similar practices; they pay the price of their rashness through the loss of their reason. The fire does not proceed in due geometrical form, the necessary triangles are not made, and the electrical fluid rushes with ever increasing speed and heat upwards, and literally burns away all or part of the brain tissue, thus bringing about insanity and sometimes death.

When these things are more widely comprehended and openly acknowledged, doctors and brain specialists will study with greater care and accuracy the electrical condition of the spinal column, and correlate its condition with that of the brain. Good results will thus be achieved.

Dangers to the nervous system.

The troubles connected with the nervous system are more frequent than those attacking the brain, such as insanity and disruption of the brain tissue. Almost all who undertake meditation are conscious of an effect in the nervous system; sometimes it takes the form of sleeplessness, of excitability, of a strained energy and restlessness that permit of no relaxation; of an irritability that has been foreign perhaps to the disposition until meditation was pursued; of a nervous reaction—such as a twitching of the limbs, the fingers or the eyes—of depression or a lowering of the vitality, and of many individual modes of showing tension and nervousness, differing according to nature and temperament. This display of nervousness may be either severe or slight, but I seek earnestly to point out it is quite needless, provided the student adheres to *the rules of common-sense*, that he studies wisely his own temperament, and that he does not blindly proceed with forms and methods but insists on knowing the raison d'etre of instituted action. If occult students disciplined the life more wisely, if they studied the food problem more carefully, if they took the needed hours of sleep with more determination, and if they worked with cautious slowness and not so much from impulse (no matter how high the aspiration) greater results would be seen and the Great Ones would have more efficient helpers in the work of serving the world.

It is not my purpose in these letters to take up specifically the diseases of the brain and of the nervous system. I only desire to give general indications and warnings and (for your encouragement) to point out that later when the wise Teachers move among men and openly teach in specific schools, many forms of brain trouble and of nervous complaints will be cured through meditation wisely adjusted to the individual need. Proper meditations will be set to stimulate quiescent centres, to turn the inner fire to proper channels, to distribute the divine heat in equable arrangement, to build in tissue and to heal. The time for this is not yet, though it lies not so far ahead as you might imagine.

Dangers to the sex organs.

The danger of the over-stimulation of these organs is well recognised theoretically, and I do not purpose to enlarge on it greatly today. I but seek to point out that this danger is very real. The reason is that in the over-stimulation of these centres the inner fire is but following the line of least resistance, owing to the polarisation of the race as a whole. The work, therefore, that the student has to do is twofold:—

a—He has to withdraw his consciousness from those centres; this is no easy task for it means working against the results of age-long development.

b—He has to direct the attention of the creative impulse to the mental plane. In so doing, if successful, he will turn the activity of the divine fire to the throat centre and its corresponding head centre, instead of to the lower organs of generation. Therefore, it will be apparent to you why—unless a man is very advanced—it is not wise to spend much time in meditation during the earlier years. There was wisdom in the old Brahmanical rule that a man must give his early years to household endeavour, and only when he had fulfilled his function as a man could he go on to the life of the devotee. This was the rule for the average. With advanced egos, pupils and disciples, it is not so, and each must then work out his own individual problem.

July 29, 1920.

Dangers arising from the Karma of the student.

These as you know may be grouped under three heads, as follows:

1—Those incidental to the karma of his present life.
2—Those based on his national heredity and his type of body.
3—Those attendant on his group affiliations, whether on the physical plane and so exoteric, or on the subtle planes and so esoteric.

Just what do you mean by the "karma of the student?" We use words lightly, and I presume that the thoughtless reply would be that the student's karma is the inevitable happenings of the present or the future that he cannot evade. This is somewhat right, but is only one aspect of the whole. Let us look at the matter first in a large manner, for oft in the just apprehension of big outlines comes comprehension of the small.

When our Logos founded the solar system He drew within the circle of manifestation matter sufficient for His project, and material adequate for the object He had in view. He had not all possible objects in view for this one solar system: He had some specific aim that necessitated some specific vibration and required therefore certain differentiated material. This circle that we term the systemic or solar "ring-pass-not" bounds all that transpires within our system, and contains within its bounds our dual manifestation. All within that ring vibrates to a certain key-measure, and conforms to certain rules with the aim in view of the achievement of a particular goal, and the attainment of a certain end, known in its entirety only to the Logos Himself. All within that circle is subject to specific rules and governed by a certain key measure, and might be regarded as being subject to the karma of that sevenfold periodic existence, and actuated by causes dating back prior to the ringing of that circle, thus linking our system to its forerunner and affiliating it with that which will come after. Not an isolated unit are we, but part of a greater whole, governed in our totality by cosmic law and working out (as a whole) certain definite aims.

Microcosmic purpose.

So it is with the Microcosm. The Ego on his own plane and on a tiny scale, repeats the action of the Logos. For certain ends he builds a certain form; he gathers certain material, and aims at a definite consummation that shall be the result of that gathered material vibrating to a certain measure, governed in one specific life by certain rules and aiming at some one particular object,— *not all possible objects.*

Each Personality is to the Ego what the solar system is to the Logos. It is his field of manifestation and the method whereby he attains a demonstrable object. That aim may be the acquirement of virtue by paying the price of vice; it may be the attainment of business acumen by the struggle to provide the necessities of life; it may be the development of sensitiveness by the revealing cruelties of nature; it may be the building in of unselfish devotion by the appeal of needy dependents; or it may be the transmutation of desire by the method of meditation on the path. It is for each soul to find out. What I want to impress upon you is the fact that there is a certain danger incident to this very factor. If, for instance, in the acquirement of the mental capacity to meditate, the student misses the very thing he came into the physical body to acquire, the result is not so much a gain as an unequal development and a temporary loss of time.

Let us be specific and illustrate:—An Ego has formed his three-fold body of manifestation and set his ring-pass-not with the purpose in view of building into his causal body the faculty of "mental apprehension of the basic facts of life." The object of that one incarnation is to develop the mental capacity of the student; to teach him concrete facts and science and thus to enlarge the content of his mental body, with a view to future work. He may be over-developed on the heart side, too much of the devotee; he may have spent many lives in dreaming dreams and in seeing visions and in mystic meditation. To be practical, full of common sense, to know the curriculum of the Hall of Learning and to apply practically the knowledge learnt on the physical plane is his great need. Yet, even though his ring-pass-not seems to proscribe and limit his inherent tendencies, and even though the stage is set so that it would seem he *must* learn the lessons of practical living in the world, he learns not, but follows what is to him the line of least resistance. He dreams his dreams, and stays aloof from world affairs; he does not fulfil the desire of the Ego, but misses opportunity; he suffers much, and in the next life is necessitated a similar staging and a stronger urge, and a closer ring-pass-not until he complies with the will of his Ego.

For such an one, meditation helps not, but mainly hinders. As before I have said, meditation (to be wisely undertaken) is for those who have reached a point in evolution where the rounding out of the causal body is somewhat matured and where the student is in one of the final grades in the Hall of Learning. You need to remember that I refer not here to the mystic meditation but to the scientifically occult meditation. The dangers are, therefore, practically those of wasted time, of an intensification of a vibration out of all proportion to the key of the other vibrations, and of an unequal rounding out and a lop-sided building that will necessitate reconstruction in other lives.

July 30, 1920.

Dangers based on national heredity and type of body.

. . . As you may well imagine it is not my purpose to enlarge upon the dangers incidental to a defective body, save in general terms to lay down the ruling that where there is definite disease, congenital trouble or mental weakness of any kind, meditation is not the part of discretion, but may serve but to intensify the trouble. I wish specifically to point out for the guidance of future students and as a prophetic statement, that in days to come when the science of meditation is more comprehended, two factors will be wisely weighed and considered before assigning a meditation. These factors are:—

    a—The man's subrace characteristics.

    b—His type of body, whether it is oriental or occidental.

In this way, certain disasters will be avoided and certain troubles obviated that are now found in a more or less degree in every occult group.

It is generally recognised that each race has for its predominant feature some one outstanding quality of the emotional body. This is the general rule. In contrasting the Italian and the Teutonic racial differences, those differences are summed up in our minds in terms of the emotional body. We think of the Italian as fiery, romantic, unstable and brilliant; we think of the Teuton as phlegmatic, matter-of-fact, sentimental and stolidly, logically clever. It will, therefore, be apparent to you that these different temperaments carry with them their own dangers, and that in the unwise pursuit of unsuitable meditations, virtues could be emphasised till they approximated vices, temperamental weaknesses could be intensified till they became menaces, and consequently lack of balance would result instead of that attainment of equilibrium and that fine rounding out of the causal body which is one of the aims in view. When, therefore, the wise Teacher moves among men and Himself apportions meditation, these racial differences will be weighed and their inherent defects will be offset and not intensified. Over-development and disproportionate attainment will be obviated by the equalising effects of occult meditation.

Meditation as followed now and as followed in Atlantean days differs fundamentally. In the fourth root race an effort was made to facilitate attainment via the atomic subplane, from the emotional plane to the intuitional, to the practical exclusion of the mental. It followed the line of the emotions and had a definite effect on the emotional body. It worked upwards from the emotional instead of, as now, working on mental levels and from those levels making the effort to control the two lower. In the Aryan root-race, the attempt is being made to bridge the gap between the higher and the lower and, by centering the consciousness in the lower mind and later in the causal, to tap the higher until the downflow from that higher will be continuous. With most of the advanced students at present all that is felt is occasional flashes of illumination, but later will be felt a steady irradiation. Both methods carry their own dangers. In Atlantean days, meditation tended to over-stimulation of the emotions and although men touched great heights, yet they also touched great depths. Sex magic was unbelievably rampant. The solar plexus was apt to be over vivified, the triangles were not correctly followed, and the lower centres were caught in the reaction of the fire with dire results.

The dangers now are different. The development of

mind carries with it the dangers of selfishness, of pride, of blind forgetfulness of the higher that it is the aim of the present method to offset. If the adepts of the dark path attained great powers in Atlantean days they are still more dangerous now. Their control is much more widespread. Hence the emphasis laid on service, and on the steadying of the mind as an essential in the man who seeks to progress and to become a member of the Brotherhood of Light.

The matter I now seek to give some instruction upon is one of very real importance to all earnest students at this time. The orient is to the evolving race of men what the heart is to the human body; it is the source of light, of life, of heat, and of vitality. The occident is to the race what the brain or mental activity is to the body,—the directing organising factor, the instrument of the lower mind, the accumulator of facts. The difference in the entire ''make-up'' (as you term it) of the oriental and of the European or American is so great and so well recognised that it is mayhap needless for me to dwell upon it.

The oriental is philosophical, naturally dreamy, trained through centuries to think in abstract terms, fond of obstruse dialectics, temperamentally lethargic, and climatically slow. Ages of metaphysical thinking, of vegetarian living, of climatic inertia and of a rigid adherence to forms and to the strictest rules of living have produced a product the exact opposite of his occidental brother.

The occidental is practical, businesslike, dynamic, quick in action, a slave to organization (which is after all but another form of ceremonial), actuated by a very concrete mind, acquisitive, critical, and at his best when affairs move quickly and rapid mental decision is required. He detests abstract thought yet appreciates it when apprehended, and when he can make those thoughts *facts* on the physical plane. He uses his head more than his heart centre, and his throat centre is apt to be vitalised. The oriental uses his heart centre more than the head and necessarily the corresponding head centres. The centre at the top of the spine at the base of the skull functions more actively than the throat.

The oriental progresses by the withdrawing of the centre of consciousness to the head through strenuous meditation. That is the centre that he needs to master, he learns by the wise use of mantrams, by retiring into seclusion, by isolation and by the careful following of specific forms for many hours each day for many days.

The occidental has in view the withdrawal of his consciousness to the heart at first, for already he works so much with the head centres. He works more by the use of collective forms and not individual mantrams; he does not work so much in isolation as his oriental brother, but has to find his centre of consciousness even in the noise and whirl of business life and in the throngs of great cities. He employs collective forms for the attainment of his ends, and the awakening of the heart centre shows itself in service. Hence the emphasis laid in the occident on the heart meditation and the subsequent life of service.

You will see, therefore, that when the real occult work is begun, the method may differ—and will necessarily differ—in the east and in the west, but the goal will be the same. It must be borne in mind, for instance, that a meditation that would aid the development of an oriental, might bring danger and disaster to his western brother. The reverse would also be the case. But always the goal will be the same. Forms may be individual or collective, mantrams may be chanted by units or by groups, different centres may be the object of specialised attention, yet the results will be identical. Danger arises when the occidental bases his endeavour on rules that suffice for the oriental, as has at times been so wisely pointed out. In the wisdom of the Great Ones this danger is being offset. Different methods for different races, diverse forms for those of various nationalities, but the same wise guides on the inner planes, the same great Hall of Wisdom, the same Gate of Initiation, admitting all into the inner sanctuary. . . .

In concluding this subject, I seek to give a hint:— The Seventh Ray of Ceremonial Law or Order (the ray now coming into power) provides for the occidental what has long been the privilege of the oriental. Great is the day of opportunity, and in the sweeping onward of this seventh force comes the needed impetus that may—if rightly grasped—drive to the Feet of the Lord of the World the dweller in the occident.

August 2, 1920.

Dangers attendant on group affiliations.

Very briefly would I seek this morning to take up the question of the dangers involved in meditation that are incidental to a man's group affiliations, whether exoteric or esoteric. There is not much that can be said on this particular matter, save broad indications. Each of these various subjects that I have touched upon might warrant the writing of a weighty treatise, and I shall not, therefore, attempt to cover what might be said but only point out certain aspects of the matter that will (if pondered on with care) open up to the earnest seeker after truth many avenues of knowledge. All occult training has this in view,—to give to the pupil some seed thought which (when brooded over in the silence of his own heart) will produce much fruit of real value, and which the pupil can then conscientiously consider his own. What we produce through wrestling and strenuous endeavour remains forever our own, and vanishes not into forgetfulness as do the thoughts that enter through the eye from the printed page, or through the ear from the lips of any teacher no matter how revered.

One thing that is oft overlooked by the pupil when he enters upon the path of probation and starts meditation is that the goal ahead for him is not primarily the completing of his own development, but his equipping for service to humanity. His own growth and development are necessarily incidental but are not the goal. His immediate environment and his close associates on the physical plane are his objectives in service, and if in the endeavour to attain certain qualifications and capacities he overlooks the groups to which he is affiliated and neglects to serve wisely and to spend himself loyally on their behalf he runs the danger of crystallisation, falls under the spell of sinful pride, and mayhap even takes the first step toward the left-hand path. Unless inner growth finds expression in group service the man treads a dangerous road.

Three types of affiliated groups.

Perhaps I could here give some indications of the groups on the various planes to which a man is assigned. These groups are many and diverse and at different periods of a man's life may change and differ, as he works out from under the obligating karma that governs the affiliations. Let us remember too that as a man enlarges his capacity to serve he at the same time increases the size and number of the groups he contacts till he reaches a point in some later incarnation when the world itself is his sphere of service and the multitude those whom he assists. He has to serve in a threefold manner before he is permitted to change his line of action and pass on to other work,—planetary, systemic or cosmic.

a—He serves first *through activity*, through the use of his intelligence, using the high faculties of mind and the product of his genius to aid the sons of men. He builds slowly great powers of intellect and in the building overcomes the snare of pride. He takes, then, that active intelligence of his and lays it at the feet of collective humanity, giving of his best for the helping of the race.

b—He serves *through love*, becoming, as time elapses, one of the saviours of men, spending his life and giving of his all through perfect love of his brothers. A life then comes when the utmost sacrifice is made and in love he dies that others may live.

c—He serves then *through power*. Proved in the furnace to have no thought save the good of all around, he is trusted with the power that follows from active love intelligently applied. He works with the law, and bends all his will to make the power of the law felt in the three-fold realms of death.

In all these three branches of service you will notice that the faculty of working with groups is one of paramount importance. These groups are diverse, as before I have said, and vary on different planes. Let us briefly enumerate them:—

1—*On the physical plane.* The following groups will be found:—

a—His family group to which he is usually affiliated for two reasons, one to work out karma and repay his debts; the second, to receive a certain type of physical vehicle that the Ego needs for adequate expression.

b—His associates and friends; the people his environment throws him with, his business associates, his church affiliations, his acquaintances and casual friends, and the people he touches for a brief period and then sees no more. His work with them is twofold again; first to repay an obligation should such a debt have been incurred; and secondly to test out his powers to influence for good those around him, to recognise responsibility and to direct or help. In doing thus, the Guides of the race find out the actions and reactions of a man, his capacity for service, and his response to any surrounding need.

c—His associated band of servers, the group under some Great One that is definitely united for work of an occult and spiritual nature. It may be either a band of church workers among the orthodox (beginners are tried out here); it may be in social work such as in the labor movements or in the political arena; or it may be in the more definitely pioneer movements of the world, such as the Theosophical Society, the Christian Science movement, the New Thought workers and the Spiritualists. I would add to this, one branch of endeavour that may surprise you,—I mean the movement of the Soviet in Russia and all the aggressive radical bodies that sincerely serve under their leaders (even when misguided and unbalanced) for the betterment of the condition of the masses.

Thus on the physical plane you have three groups to which a man belongs. He owes a duty to them and he must play his part. Now wherein could danger enter through meditation? Simply in this: that as long as a man's karma holds him to some particular group the thing that he must aim at is to play his part perfectly, so that he may work out from under karmic obligation and advance toward ultimate liberation; besides this he must carry on his group with him to greater heights and usefulness. Therefore, if through meditation of an unsuitable nature he neglects his proper obligation he delays the purpose of his life, and in another incarnation he will have to play it out. If he builds into that group's causal body (the composite product of the several lines) aught that has not its place properly there, he aids not but hinders, and again that involves danger. Let me illustrate, for clarity is desired:—A student is affiliated with a group that has an over-preponderance of devotees, and he has come in for the express purpose of balancing that quality with another factor, that of wise discrimination and mental balance. If he permits himself to be overcome by the group thoughtform and becomes himself a devotee, following a devotional meditation and unwisely omitting to balance that group's causal body, he runs into a danger that hurts not only himself but the group to which he belongs.

2—*On the emotional plane:* Here he belongs to several groups such as:—

a—His emotional plane family group, which is more thoroughly his own group than the family into which he happens to be born on the physical plane. You will see this demonstrated many times in life when members of an emotional plane family contact each other on the physical plane. Instant recognition ensues.

b—The class within the Hall of Learning to which he is assigned and in which he receives much instruction.

c—The band of Invisible Helpers with whom he may be working and the band of Servers.

All these groups involve obligation and work and all must be allowed for in studying the wise use of meditation. Meditation should increase a man's capacity to discharge his karmic debts, giving clear vision, wise judgment and a comprehension of the work of the immediate moment. Anything that militates against this is dangerous.

3—*On the mental plane:* The groups to be found there may be enumerated as follows:

a—The groups of pupils of some one Master to Whom he may be attached, and with Whom he may be working. This is usually only the case when the man is rapidly working out his karma and is nearing the entrance to the Path. His meditation, therefore, should be directly under the guidance of his Master, and any formula followed that is not adjusted to a man's need carries with it elements of danger, for the vibrations set up on the mental plane and the forces engendered there are so much more potent than on the lower levels.

b—The egoic group to which he belongs. This is most important for it involves the consideration of the man's ray in the apportioning of meditation. This matter has already been somewhat touched upon.

As you will see, I have not specified certain dangers attacking any particular body. It is not possible to cover the subject thus. In later days, when occult meditation is more comprehended and the matter scientifically studied, students will prepare the necessary data and treatises covering the entire subject as far as then may be. I sound, however, a note of warning, I indicate the way,—the teachers on the inner side seldom do more. We aim at developing thinkers and men of clear vision, capable of logical reasoning. To do this we teach men to develop themselves, to do their own thinking, reason out their own problems, and build their own characters. Such is the Path. . . .

August 3, 1920.

Dangers arising from subtle forces.

. . . We have for our topic this morning the final section of our letter on the dangers incidental to meditation. We have dealt somewhat with individual dangers inherent in the three bodies; we have touched upon the risks that may be run when the karma of the student and his group affiliations are overlooked. Today the subject involves real difficulty. We have to deal with the dangers that may arise from forces and persons, from entities and groups working on the subtler planes. The difficulty arises in three ways:—

1—The ignorance of the average student as to the nature of those forces and as to the personnel of the groups on the subtler planes.

2—The risk of revealing more than would be wise in an exoteric publication.

3—An occult risk that is little comprehended by the uninitiated. It lies in the fact that in the concentration of thought that necessarily arises in discussing these problems, thought-waves are set in motion, currents are contacted and thoughtforms circulated that attract the attention of those under discussion. This may lead at times to undesirable results. Therefore, I shall with brevity touch upon the subject. Upon the inner planes the needed light and protection are afforded.

Three groups of entities:—

These groups of entities can be differentiated in a threefold manner:—

1—Groups of discarnate beings on either the emotional or the mental planes.

2—Devas, either singly or in groups.

3—The dark Brotherhood.

Let us take each division and deal with it carefully, first laying the foundation of knowledge by pointing out that the dangers arise from a threefold condition of the bodies of the student which may be the result sometimes of meditation. These conditions are:—

A negative condition that makes the entire three bodies of the personality receptive and quiescent, and open therefore to the attack of the watching denizens of other planes.

A condition of ignorance or foolhardiness that, in attempting to use certain forms and mantrams without the permission of the Teacher, involves the student with certain groups of devas, bringing him into contact with the devas of the emotional or mental planes and making him therefore (through his ignorance) the butt of their attack and the plaything of their destructive instincts.

A condition which is the reverse of the above, which makes a man positive and a channel, therefore, for force or power. When this is the case, the man proceeds, under occult rule or law and with the aid of his Teacher, to wield the electrical fluid of the inner planes. He becomes then a centre of the attention of those who strive against the Brothers of Light.

The first two conditions are all the result of meditation unwisely and ignorantly practised, the last state of affairs is frequently the reward of success. In the first two, the remedy lies within the student himself and in the wise correction of the type of meditation and its more careful following; in the third case the remedy must be sought in various ways which I will later indicate.

Dangers of obsession.

Dangers from discarnate entities are frankly those of obsession, either of a temporary nature and lasting for a few moments or more enduring and lasting for a longer period. It may even be permanent and lasting through a lifetime. I have earlier written to you a letter upon this subject which you might here incorporate. We never duplicate effort if it can be avoided. I seek primarily to emphasise the point that this entrance which we call obsession is effected largely through the negative attitude assumed through the unwise following of an unsuitable meditation. In his anxiety to be the recipient of light from above, in his determination to force himself to a place where he can contact the teachers or even the Master, and in his endeavour to eliminate all thought and lower vibrations, the student makes the mistake of rendering his entire lower personality receptive. Instead of making it firmly positive to environing factors and to all lower contacts, and instead of only allowing the "apex of the mind" (if I may use so unusual a term) to be receptive and open to transmission from the causal or the abstract levels and even from the intuitional, the student permits reception from all sides. Only a point within the brain should be receptive, all the rest of the consciousness should be so polarised that outer interference will not be possible. This refers to the emotional and to the mental bodies, though with the majority these days it refers solely to the emotional. At this particular period of the world's history the emotional plane is so densely populated and the response of the physical to the emotional is now becoming so exquisitely attuned, that the danger of obsession is greater than ever heretofore. But for your cheering—the reverse holds good also, and response to the divine and rapid reaction to the higher inspiration has never been so great. Divine inspiration or that "divine obsession" which is the privilege of all advanced souls, will be understood in the coming years as never before, and will be definitely one of the methods used by the coming Lord and His Great Ones for the helping of the world.

The thing to be remembered is that in the case of wrong obsession the man is at the mercy of the obsessing entity, and is unconsciously or unwillingly a partner in the transaction. In divine obsession the man *consciously* and willingly co-operates with the One Who seeks to inspire, or to occupy or employ his lower vehicles. The motive is ever the greater helping of the race. The obsession is then not the result of a negative condition but of a positive collaboration and proceeds under law and for a specific period. . . . As more and more of the race develop continuity of consciousness between the physical and the emotional and later the mental, this act of transference of the vehicles will be more frequent and more understood.

October 9, 1919.

Causes of Obsession.

One of the activities ahead of the occult student is the study and the scientific observation of this matter. We have been told in various occult books that obsession and insanity are very closely allied. Insanity may exist in all three bodies, the least harmful being that of the physical body, whilst the most enduring and the hardest to cure is that of the mental body. Insanity in the mental body is the heavy fate that descends upon those who for many incarnations have followed the path of selfish cruelty, using the intelligence as a means to serve selfish ends and using it wilfully, knowing it to be wrong. But insanity of this type is a means whereby the Ego sometimes arrests the progress of a man towards the left-hand path. In this sense it is a disguised blessing. Let us deal first with the causes of obsession, leaving the subject of in-

sanity for another day. These causes are four in number
and each responds to a different treatment:—

One cause is a definite weakness of the etheric
double, in the separating web, which like a piece of relaxed elastic permits entry of an extraneous entity from
the emotional plane. The door of entrance which is
formed by this web is not closed tight, and entrance can
be effected from without. This is a physical plane cause,
and is the result of the maladjustment of physical plane
matter. It is the result of karma, and is prenatal, existing
from the earliest moment. Usually the sufferer is physically weak, intellectually feeble, but possessed of a powerful emotional body which suffers and fights and struggles to prevent entrance. The attacks are intermittent,
and more frequently attack women than men.

Another cause is due to emotional reasons. A lack
of co-ordination exists between the emotional and the
physical and when the man functions in the emotional
body (as at night) the moment of re-entry is attended
with difficulty, and opportunity exists for other beings to
enter the physical vehicle, and prevent its occupation by
the real Ego. This is the most common form of obsession, and affects those with powerful physical bodies and
strong astral vibrations, but with weak mental bodies.
It leads, in the ensuing struggle, to the violent scenes of
screaming lunatics and to the paroxysms of the epileptic.
Men are more subject to this than women, as women are
usually more definitely polarised in the emotional body.

A rarer kind of obsession is the mental. In coming
days as the mental body develops, one may expect perhaps to see more of it. Mental obsession involves the
displacement taking place on the mental levels—hence its
rarity. The physical body and the emotional body remain
as a unit, but the Thinker is left in his mental body,

whilst the obsessing entity (clothed in mental matter) enters the two lower vehicles. In the case of emotional obsession the Thinker is left with his emotional body and his mental body but with no physical. In this latter case he is left with neither emotional nor physical. The cause lies in the fact of the over-development of the mental, and of the relative weakness of the emotional and physical bodies. The Thinker is too powerful for his other bodies and disdains their use; he is too interested in work on mental levels, and thus gives opportunity to obsessing entities to assume control. This, as I said before, is rare and is the result of lop-sided development. It attacks women and men equally; it principally shows itself in childhood and is difficult to cure.

A still rarer cause of obsession is definitely the work of the dark Brothers. It takes the form of snapping the magnetic link that attaches the Ego to the lower physical body, leaving him in his emotional and mental bodies. This would normally result in the death of the physical body, but in cases such as these the dark Brother, who is to use the physical body, enters it and makes connection with his own cord. These cases are not common. They involve only two classes of people:—

Those who are highly evolved and on the Path, but who through some wilful shortcoming fail for some one incarnation and so lay themselves open to the evil force. Sin (as you call it) in the Personality of a disciple leads to a weakness in some one spot, and this is taken advantage of. This type of obsession shows itself in the transformation that is sometimes seen when a great soul suddenly plunges on an apparent downward path, when he changes the whole trend of his existence and besmirches a fair character with mud. It carries with it its own punishment, for on the inner planes the disciple looks on, and in agony of mind sees his lower vehicle dishonouring the fair name of its real owner and causing evil to be said of a loved cause.

The little evolved, weakly organised, and so unable to resist.

The Kinds of Obsessing Entities.

These are too numerous to mention in detail but I might enumerate a few.

1—Discarnate entities of a low order awaiting incarnation, and who see, in cases one and two, their wanted opportunity.

2—Suicides, anxious to undo the deed and to again get into contact with earth.

3—Earth-bound spirits, good and bad, who from anxiety over loved ones, over their business affairs, or eager to do some wrong or to undo some evil act, rush in and take possession of cases one and two.

4—Dark Brothers as aforesaid, who avail themselves principally of the third and fourth cases already cited. They require highly developed bodies, having no use for weak or unrefined bodies. In case three the weakness is entirely relative, due to over-accentuation of the mental vehicle.

5—Elementals and subhuman entities of a malicious nature who rush in on the slightest opportunity and where kindred vibration may be felt.

6—Some of the lower devas, harmless but mischievous who, from sheer freakishness and fun, enter another body in much the same way that a child loves to dress up.

7—Occasional visitors from other planets who enter certain highly evolved bodies for purposes of their own. This is very, very rare. . . .

Let me now give you some of the methods that eventually will be the first attempts at cure.

In the first type of cases, those due to physical plane weakness, the stress of the cure will be laid first on building up a strong physical body in both its departments, though especially the etheric body. This will be done in future years with the direct aid of the devas of the shadows (the violet devas or devas of the ethers). The strengthening of the etheric web will be aided by means of the violet light, with its corresponding sound, administered in quiet sanitariums. Coincident with this treatment will be the attempt to strengthen the mental body. With the strengthening of the physical body will come longer and longer periods of freedom from attack. Eventually the attacks will cease altogether.

When the cause is lack of co-ordination between the physical and the emotional vehicles the first methods of cure will be definite exorcism by the aid of mantrams and ceremonial (such as religious ritual). Qualified persons will use these mantrams at night when the obsessing entity may be supposed to be absent during the hours of sleep. These mantrams will call the real owner back, will build a protective wall after his re-entry and will seek to force the obsessing one to stay absent. When the real owner has returned, the work then will be to keep him there. Educative work during the day and protective measures at night for longer or shorter periods will gradually eliminate the evil occupant, or unwanted tenant, and in the course of time the sufferer will continue to procure immunity. More anent this can later be given.

Where mental obsession is involved the matter is more difficult. Most of the first cures achieved in the future will centre around the first two groups. Mental obsession must await greater knowledge, though experimentation from the very first should be undertaken. The work will have to be done mostly from the mental plane by those who can function there freely and so contact the Thinker in his mental body. The co-operation of the Thinker must then be procured and a definite attack conjointly made on the obsessed physical and emotional bodies. During the night much of the work in the first two cases of cures will be done, but in the latter case the Thinker has to win back his physical and his emotional bodies as well, hence the exceeding difficulty. Death often eventuates in these cases.

In the severing of the magnetic cord naught can be done as yet.

Dangers from the deva evolution.

This second point is more complex. You will remember how it has been said earlier in these letters that contact with the devas can be brought about through specific forms and mantrams and that in this contact lies peril for the unwary. This danger is curiously real now, owing to the following reasons:

a—The coming in of the violet ray, the seventh or Ceremonial Ray, has rendered this contact more easy of attainment than heretofore. It is therefore the ray on which approximation is possible, and in the use of ceremonial and of set forms, coupled to regulated rhythmic movement, will be found a meeting place for the two allied evolutions. In the use of ritual this will be apparent, and psychics are already bearing witness to the fact that both in the ritual of the Church and in that of Masonry this has been evidenced. More and more will this be the case, and it carries with it certain risks that will inevitably work themselves into common knowledge and thus affect in various ways the unwary sons of men.

As you know, a definite effort is being made at this time by the Planetary Hierarchy to communicate to the devas their part in the scheme of things, and the part the human family must likewise play. The work is slow, and certain results are inevitable. It is not my purpose to take up with you in these letters the part that ritual and set mantric forms play in the evolution of devas and of men. I only desire to point out that danger for human beings lies in the unwise use of forms for the calling of the devas, in experimenting with the Sacred Word with the object in view of contacting the Builders who are so largely affected by it, and in endeavouring to pry into the secrets of ritual with its adjuncts of colour and of sound. Later on, when the pupil has passed the portal of initiation, such knowledge will be his, coupled with the necessary information that teaches him to work with the law. In the following of the law, no danger lurks.

b—The race is possessed of a strong determination to penetrate within the veil, and to find out what lies on the other side of the unknown. Men and women everywhere are conscious within themselves of budding powers which meditation enhances. They find that by the careful following of certain rules they become more sensitive to the sights and sounds of the inner planes. They catch fleeting glimpses of the unknown; occasionally and at rare intervals, the organ of inner vision temporarily opens and they hear and see on the astral or the mental plane. They see devas at a meeting in which ritual has been employed; they catch a sound or a voice that tells them truths that they recognise as true. The temptation to force the issue, to prolong meditation, to try out certain methods that promise intensification of psychic faculty is too strong. They unwarily force matters and dire disaster results. One hint here I give:—*In meditation it is literally possible to play with fire.* The devas of the mental levels manipulate the latent fires of the system and thus incidentally the latent fires of the inner man. It is woefully possible to be the plaything of their endeavour and to perish at their hands. A truth I speak here; I give not voice to the interesting chimeras of a fanciful brain. Beware of playing with fire.

c—This transition period is largely responsible for much of the danger. The right type of body for the holding and the handling of the occult force has not yet been built, and in the interim the bodies now in use but spell disaster to the ambitious student. When a man starts out to follow the path of occult meditation, it takes well-nigh fourteen years to rebuild the subtle bodies, and incidentally the physical. All through that period it is not safe to tamper with the unknown for only the very strong refined physical body, the controlled stable and equalised emotional body and the properly striated mental body can enter into the subtler planes and literally work with Fohat, for that is what the occult does. Therefore is the emphasis laid by all wise Teachers everywhere on the Path of Purification, which must precede the Path of Illumination. They lay the emphasis on the building in of spiritual faculty before psychic faculty can be safely permitted; they demand service to the race every day throughout the scope of life before a man may be permitted to manipulate the forces of nature, to dominate the elementals, to co-operate with the devas, and to learn the forms and ceremonies, the mantrams and the keywords, that will bring those forces within the circle of manifestation.

August 4, 1920.

Danger from the Dark Brothers.

I think I gave you earlier practically all that I can as

yet impart anent the Brothers of Darkness, as they are sometimes termed. I only want at this point to lay emphasis upon the fact that no danger need be feared by the average student from this source. It is only as discipleship is approached and a man stands out ahead of his fellows as an instrument of the White Brotherhood that he attracts the attention of those who seek to withstand. When through application to meditation, and power and activity in service, a man has developed his vehicles to a point of real achievement, then his vibrations set in motion matter of a specific kind, and he learns to work with that matter, to manipulate the fluids, and to control the builders. In so doing he encroaches on the domain of those who work with the forces of involution and thus he may bring attack upon himself. This attack may be directed against any of his three vehicles and may be of different kinds. Let me briefly point out some of the methods employed against a disciple which are the ones which alone concern the student of these letters:

a—Definite attack on the physical body. All kinds of means are employed to hinder the usefulness of the disciple through disease or the crippling of his physical body. Not all accidents are the result of karma, for the disciple has usually surmounted a good deal of that type of karma and is thus comparatively free from that source of hindrance in active work.

b—Glamour is another method used, or the casting over the disciple of a cloud of emotional or mental matter which suffices to hide the real, and to temporarily obscure that which is true. The study of the cases wherein glamour has been employed is exceedingly revealing and demonstrates how hard it is for even an advanced disciple always to discriminate between the real and the false, the true and the untrue. Glamour may be either on the emotional or mental levels but is usually on the former. One form employed is to cast over the disciple the shadows of the thought of weakness or discouragement or criticism to which he may at intervals give way. Thus cast, they loom in undue proportion and the unwary disciple, not realising that he is but seeing the gigantic outlines of his own momentary and passing thoughts, gives way to discouragement, aye even to despair, and becomes of little use to the Great Ones. Another form is to throw into his mental aura suggestions and ideas purporting to come from his own Master but which are but subtle suggestions that hinder and help not. It takes a wise disciple always to discriminate between the voice of his real Teacher and the false whispers of the masquerading one, and even high initiates have been temporarily misled.

Many and subtle are the means used to deceive and thereby curtail the effective output of the worker in the field of the world. Wisely therefore have all aspirants been enjoined to study and work at the development of *viveka* or that discrimination which safeguards from deception. If this quality is laboriously built in and cultivated in all events, big and little, in the daily life, the risks of being led astray will be nullified.

c—A third method frequently employed is to envelop the disciple in a thick cloud of darkness, to surround him with an impenetrable night and fog through which he stumbles and often falls. It may take the form of a black cloud of emotional matter, of some dark emotion that seems to imperil all stable vibration and plunges the bewildered student into a blackness of despair; he feels that all is departing from him; he is a prey to varied and dismal emotions; he deems himself forsaken of all; he considers that all past effort has been futile and that naught remains but to die. At such times he needs much the gift of *viveka*, and to earnestly weigh up and calmly reason out the matter. He should at these times remind himself that the darkness hides naught from the God within, and that the stable centre of consciousness remains there, untouched by aught that may betide. He should persevere until the end,—the end of what? The end of the enveloping cloud, the point where it merges itself into sunlight; he should pass through its length and out into the daylight, realising that nothing can at any time reach to and hurt the inner consciousness. God is within, no matter what transpires without. We are so apt to look out at environing circumstances, whether physical, astral or mental, and to forget that the inmost centre of the heart hides our points of contact with the Universal Logos.

d—Finally (for I cannot touch on all the methods used), the means employed may be to cast a mental darkness over the disciple. The darkness may be intellectual, and is consequently still more difficult to penetrate, for in this case the power of the Ego *must* be called in, whereas in the former frequently the calm reasoning of the lower mind may suffice to dispel the trouble. Here, in this specific case, the disciple will be wise if he not only attempts to call his Ego or Higher Self for the dispelling of the cloud, but calls likewise upon his Teacher, or even upon his Master, for the assistance that they can give.

These are but a few of the dangers encircling the aspirant, and I hint at them solely for the purpose of warning and guidance, and not to cause alarm. You can here interpolate the earlier letter with the rules that I there give for the assistance of the disciple.

September 25, 1919.

The Dark Brotherhood.

Today I seek to speak to you on the powers of the Dark Brotherhood. Certain laws that govern their actions, certain methods employed by them in work need to be realised and certain methods of protection apprehended and utilised. As before I have told you the danger is as yet inappreciable to the majority, but more and more as time elapses shall we find it necessary to teach you, the physical plane workers, how to shield and guard yourselves from attack.

The Dark Brothers are—remember this always—*brothers*, erring and misguided yet still sons of the one Father though straying far, very far, into the land of distances. The way back for them will be long, but the mercy of evolution inevitably forces them back along the path of return in cycles far ahead. Anyone who over-exalts the concrete mind and permits it continuously to shut out the higher, is in danger of straying on the left-hand path. Many so stray . . . but come back, and then in the future avoid like errors in the same way as a child once burnt avoids the fire. It is the man who persists in spite of warning and of pain who eventually becomes a brother of darkness. Mightily fights the Ego at first to prevent the Personality so developing, but the deficiencies of the causal body (for forget not that our vices are but our virtues misused) result in a lop-sided causal body, over-developed in some direction and full of great gulfs and gaps where virtues should be.

The dark brother recognises no unity with his species, only seeing in them people to be exploited for the furtherance of his own ends. This then, on a small scale, is the mark of those who are being used by them wittingly or unwittingly. They respect no person, they regard all men as fair prey, they use everyone to get their own way enforced, and by fair means or foul they seek to break down all opposition and for the personal self acquire that which they desire.

The dark brother considers not what suffering he may cause; he cares not what agony of mind he brings upon an opponent; he persists in his intention and desists not from the hurt of any man, woman or child, provided that in the process his own ends are furthered. Expect absolutely no mercy from those opposing the Brotherhood of Light.

On the physical plane and on the emotional plane, the dark brother has more power than the Brother of the Light,—*not* more power *per se* but more *apparent power*, because the White Brothers choose not to exert Their power on those two planes, as do the Dark Brothers. They could exert Their authority but They choose to refrain, working with the powers of evolution and not of involution. The elemental forces to be found on these two planes are manipulated by two factors.

a—The inherent forces of evolution that direct all on to eventual perfection. The White Adepts co-operate in this.

b—The Dark Brothers who occasionally employ these elemental forces to wreak their will and vengeance on all opponents. Under their control work sometimes the elementals of the earth plane, the gnomes and the elemental essence as found in evil form, some of the brownies, and the fairy folk of colours brown, grey and sombre-hued. They cannot control the devas of high development, nor the fairies of colours blue, green and yellow, though a few of the red fairies can be made to work under their direction. The water elementals (though not the sprites or sylphs) move on occasion to their assistance, and in the control of these forces of involution they at times damage the furtherance of our work.

Oft too the Dark Brother masquerades as an agent of the light, oft he poses as a messenger of the gods, but for your assurance I would say that he who acts under the guidance of the Ego will have clear vision, and will escape deception.

At this time their power is ofttimes mighty. Why? Because so much exists as yet in the Personalities of all men that respond to their vibration, and so it is easy for them to affect the bodies of men. So few of the races, comparatively speaking, have as yet built in the higher vibration that responds to the key-note of the Brotherhood of Light, who move practically entirely on the two highest levels (or the atomic and sub-atomic subplanes) of the mental, emotional and physical planes. When moving on these subplanes the attacks of elementals on lower planes may be felt but effect no harm, hence the necessity of pure living and controlled pure emotions and elevated thought.

You will notice that I said that the power of the Dark Brotherhood is dominant apparently on the physical and emotional planes. Not so is it on the mental, which is the plane on which the Brothers of the Light work. Mighty dark magicians may be located on the lower mental levels, but on the higher, the White Lodge dominates, the three higher subplanes being the levels that They beg the evolving sons of men to seek; it is Their region, to which all must strive and aspire. The Dark Brother impresses his will on human beings (if analogous vibration exists) and on the elemental kingdoms of involution. The Brothers of Light plead as pleaded the Man of Sorrows for an erring humanity to rise upward to the light. The Dark Brother retards progress and shapes all to his own ends; the Brother of Light bends every effort to the hastening of evolution and—foregoing all that might be His as the price of achievement—stays amid the fogs, the strife, the evil and the hatred of the period if, in so doing, He may by all means aid some, and (lifting them up out of the darkness of earth) set their feet upon the Mount, and enable them to surmount the Cross.

And now what methods may be employed to safeguard the worker in the field of the world? What can be done to ensure his safety in the present strife and in the greater strife of the coming centuries?

1—A realisation that purity of all the vehicles is the prime essential. If a Dark Brother gains control over any man it but shows that that man has in his life some weak spot. The door whereby entrance is effected must be opened by the man himself; the opening whereby malignant force can be poured in must be caused by the occupant of the vehicles. Therefore the need of scrupulous cleanliness of the physical body, of clean steady emotion permitted in the emotional body, and of purity of thought in the mental body. When this is so, co-ordination will be present in the lower vehicles and the indwelling Thinker himself permits no entrance.

2—The elimination of all fear. The forces of evolution vibrate more rapidly than those of involution and in this fact lies a recognisable security. Fear causes weakness; weakness causes a disintegration; the weak spot breaks and a gap appears, and through that gap evil force may enter. The factor of entrance is the fear of the man himself, who opens thus the door.

3—A standing firm and unmoved, no matter what occurs. Your feet may be bathed in the mud of earth, but your head may be bathed in the sunshine of the higher regions. Recognition of the filth of earth involves not contamination.

4—A recognition of the use of common-sense and the application of this common-sense to the matter in hand. Sleep much and, in sleeping, learn to render the body positive; keep busy on the emotional plane and achieve the inner calm. Do naught to overtire the body physical, and play whenever possible. In hours of relaxation comes the adjustment that obviates later tension.

LETTER VI

THE USE OF FORM IN MEDITATION.

a—The Use of Form in raising the consciousness.
b—The Use of Form by the mystic and the occultist.
c—Specific Forms.
d—The Use of Form collectively.

LETTER VI

THE USE OF FORM IN MEDITATION.

August 6, 1920.

Your very natural desire to have me give you in this sixth letter certain specific forms to achieve certain results cannot be fully acquiesced in. I do not propose to outline for you any forms for careful following. The risks, as before I have pointed out, are too great apart from the supervision of a teacher at hand to watch reactions. These forms may later be given. The work is duly planned out for the coming generation of students, this series of letters having its place within that outline. What I intend to do today is something different. I purpose to do four things which we will separately take up and elucidate. These things, if duly assimilated and acted upon, will lead to further enlightenment. In the occult method of teaching step by step is given, point by point slowly laid before the pupil, and only as each step is taken and each point is grasped, will the next in order become clear. The teacher gives an indication, drops a hint, and touches some high light. The pupil follows the point emphasised, and finds on thus acting that further light pours in, another stage appears and other hints are dropped. In joint action and reaction therefore the occult student is trained by the occultist.

In studying the topic, "The use of *form* in meditation," the four divisions under which I seek to place the intended data are as follows:—

1—The use of Form in raising the consciousness.
2—The use of Form by the mystic and the occultist.

3—The use of specific forms for specific ends.
4—The use of Form collectively.

In the exposition of these subjects you will see that what I am endeavouring to produce is a just apprehension of the value of forms in meditation and not the imparting of any definite method. I seek to show the essential nature of proceeding *under law* in this the most important means of bringing about union with the divine, and of producing that at-one-ment between the higher and the lower that is the aim of all evolution. I desire to leave in the minds of those who read these words a just apprehension of the relationship between spirit and matter which is the basis of all work of this nature.

The method employed by the Logos in this the second solar system is definitely the use of form for purposes of manifestation, as a medium of expression and as the vehicle whereby the indwelling life may grow, expand, experience and find itself. This is the case whether the form is an entire solar system, whether it is a human being in his complexity, or whether it is a form built by that human being in his endeavour to realise and know,— a form built for the very purpose of providing a vehicle whereby the consciousness may, by set stages, raise itself step by step to some visualised point. This brings us to our first point:

1—*The use of form in raising the consciousness.*

We have under this heading to consider three things:

a—The Consciousness itself.
b—The goal towards which it seeks to rise.
c—The steps whereby it succeeds.

Each unit of the human race is a part of the divine consciousness, and is that which is conscious of, or is aware of something without itself,—something which knows itself to be differentiated from the vehicle which encloses it or the forms which environ it.

At this particular stage in evolution the average man is simply conscious of differentiation, or of being separated off from all other members of the human family, thus forming in himself a unit among other units. He acknowledges this and acknowledges the right of all other separated units so to consider themselves. He adds to this a recognition that somewhere in the universe there exists a supreme Consciousness, Whom he theoretically calls God, or Nature. Between this purely *selfish* point of view (I use the term "selfish" in the scientific sense and not as a belittling adjective) and the nebulous theory of God immanent there are to be found numerous stages, at each of which occurs an expansion of consciousness, or an enlargement of the point of view, that leads that self-recognising unit, step by step, from self-recognition to the recognition of superior selves, to the fitting of himself to be likewise recognised as a superior self, and eventually to the occult recognition of his own superior Self. He comes to recognise his Higher Self or Ego as his true Self, and from that stage passes on into that of the group consciousness. Here he realises first his egoic group and then other egoic groups.

This stage is succeeded by the recognition of the universal principle of Brotherhood; it involves not just a theoretical recognition, but a merging of the consciousness into that of the human consciousness, in its entirety; this is really that development of consciousness which enables a man to realise not only his egoic group affiliations but his place in the human Hierarchy on its own plane. He knows himself in fact as a part of one of the great Heavenly Men. This expands later into an almost inconceivably vast point of view—that of his place in the Grand Heavenly Man, as represented by the Logos Himself.

This is as far as we need go for our purpose, for this series of letters, aims not at the development of cosmic consciousness.

It will therefore be apparent to you that all these stages have to be taken systematically and that each one has to be mastered step by step. It is necessary first to grasp that the place where the expansion takes place, and the realisation has to be felt, has to be finally in the *thinking, waking consciousness*. The Ego on its own plane may be well aware of the unity of its consciousness with all other consciousnesses, and be realising his group as one with himself, but until the man (in physical plane consciousness) has raised himself to that same plane and is likewise aware of his group consciousness, and likewise regards himself as the higher Self within the egoic group and not as a separated unit, it is of no more use than a recognised theory is of use when not carried out in experience.

The man has to experience these stages in his physical consciousness and to know experimentally and not just theoretically that whereof I speak before he is deemed ready to pass on into the succeeding stages. The whole matter resolves itself into the expansion of the mind until it dominates the lower, and into the faculty of abstract conception which results eventually in physical plane manifestation. It means making your highest theories and ideals demonstrable facts and it is that blending of the higher and the lower and the equipping of that lower until it provides a fitting expression for the higher. It is here that the practice of meditation plays its part. The true scientific meditation provides graded forms whereby the consciousness is raised and the mind expanded until it embraces:

1—Its family and friends.
2—Its environing associates.
3—Its affiliated groups.
4—Its egoic group.
5—Other egoic groups.
6—That Man of the Heavens of which the egoic groups form a centre.
7—The Grand Heavenly Man.

To effect this certain forms will be laid down later, that (working along the line of a man's ray) will teach him in graded steps to do this. You will note that I have dealt with the consciousness itself and the goal it aspires to and have thus dealt with our first two points. This brings me to our last subsidiary heading, the steps whereby attainment eventuates.

Each man who enters upon occult development and who aspires toward the higher, has passed the stage of the average man,—the man who regards himself from the purely isolated standpoint and who works for what is good for himself. The aspirant is aiming at something different; he seeks to merge himself with his higher Self and with all that is entailed when we use that term. The stages beyond that, in all their intricacies, are the secrets of Initiation and with them we have naught to do.

Aspiration towards the Ego and the bringing in of that higher consciousness with the subsequent development of group consciousness very directly concern all who will read these letters. It is the next step ahead for those upon the Probationary Path. It is not achieved by simply giving thirty minutes a day to certain set forms of meditation. It involves an hour by hour attempt, all day long and every day, to keep the consciousness as near to the high pitch attained in the morning meditation as possible. It presumes a determination to consider oneself at all times as the Ego, and not as a differential Personality. Later, as the Ego comes more and more into control, it will involve also the ability to look upon oneself as part of a group, with no interests and desires, no aims or wishes apart from the good of that group. It necessitates a constant watchfulness every hour of the day to prevent the falling back into the lower vibration. It entails a constant battle with the lower self that drags down; it is a ceaseless fight to preserve the higher vibration. And—which is the point I am aiming to impress upon you—the aim should be the development of the habit of meditation all the day long, and the living in the higher consciousness till that consciousness is so stable that the lower mind, desire and the physical elementals, become so atrophied and starved through lack of nourishment that the threefold lower nature becomes simply the means whereby the Ego contacts the world for purposes of helping the race.

In so doing he is accomplishing something that is little realised by the average student. He is building a form, a definite thoughtform that eventually provides a vehicle whereby he steps out of the lower consciousness into the higher, a kind of *mayavirupa* that acts as his intermediate channel. These forms are usually, though not invariably, of two kinds:—

The student builds a form daily, with care and love and attention, of his Master, to him the embodiment of the ideal higher consciousness. He lays the outline of this form in meditation and builds in the fabric in his daily life and thought. The form is provided with all the virtues, scintillates with all the colours, and is vivified, first of all, by the love of the man for his Master, and later (when adequate for the purpose) it is vitalised by the Master Himself. At a certain stage in development this form provides the ground for the occult experience of entering into the higher consciousness. The man recognises himself as a part of the Master's consciousness and through that all embracing consciousness slips into the egoic group soul *consciously*. This form provides the medium for that experience until such a time as it can be dispensed with, and the man can at will transfer himself into his group, and later consciously dwell there permanently. This method is the one most largely used, and is the path of love and devotion.

In the second method the student pictures himself as the ideal man. He visualises himself as the exponent of all the virtues, and he attempts in his daily life to make himself what he visualises himself to be. This method is employed by the more mental types, the intellectuals, and those whose ray is not so coloured by love, by devotion or by harmony. It is not so common as the first. The mental thoughtform thus built up serves as the *mayavirupa* as did the other and the man passes from these forms into the higher consciousness. As you therefore see, in building these forms certain steps will have to be taken and each type will build the form somewhat differently.

The first type will start with some beloved individual, and from that individual, will rise through the various other individuals to the Master.

The other type will start with meditation on the virtue most desired, add virtue to virtue in the building of the form of the ideal self until all the virtues have been attempted and the Ego is suddenly contacted.

Tomorrow we will take up this same subject from a different angle and study the difference between the occultist and the mystic.

August 8, 1920.

2—Form as used by the occultist and the mystic.

The subject of this letter today will interest you for we are to take up form as used by the occultist and the mystic.

It might be of value to us if we first differentiated with care between the two types. I would begin by a statement of fact. The mystic is not necessarily an occultist, but the occultist embraces the mystic. Mysticism is but one step on the path of occultism. In this solar system—the system of love in activity—the path of least resistance for the majority is that of the mystic, or the path of love and devotion. In the next solar system the path of least resistance will be that which we now understand as the occult path. The mystic path will have been trodden. Wherein lies the difference between these two types?

The mystic deals with the evolving life; the occultist deals with the form.

The mystic deals with the God within; the occultist with God in outer manifestation.

The mystic works from the centre to the periphery; the occultist reverses the process.

The mystic mounts by aspiration and intensest devotion to the God within or to the Master Whom he recognises; the occultist attains by the recognition of the law in operation and by the wielding of the law which binds matter and conforms it to the needs of the indwelling life. In this manner the occultist arrives at those Intelligences Who work with the law, till he attains the fundamental Intelligence Himself.

The mystic works through the Rays of Love, Harmony and Devotion, or by the path of the second, the fourth and the sixth rays. The occultist works through the Rays of Power, Activity, and Ceremonial Law, or the first, the third and the seventh. Both meet and blend through the development of mind, or through the fifth Ray of Concrete Knowledge (a fragment of cosmic intelligence), and on this fifth ray the mystic is resolved into the occultist and works then with all the rays.

By finding the kingdom of God within himself and by the study of the laws of his own being, the mystic becomes proficient in the laws which govern the universe of which he is a part. The occultist recognises the kingdom of God in nature or the system and regards himself as a small part of that greater whole, and therefore governed by the same laws.

The mystic works as a general rule under the department of the World Teacher, or the Christ, and the occultist more frequently under that of the Manu, or Ruler, but when both types have passed through the four minor rays in the department of the Lord of Civilisation, then a completion of their development may be seen, and the mystic becomes the occultist and the occultist includes the characteristics of the mystic. To make it more simple for general comprehension:—after initiation the mystic is merged in the occultist for he has become a student of occult law; he has to work with matter, with its manipulation and uses, and he has to master and control all lower forms of manifestation, and learn the rules whereby the building devas work. Before initiation the mystic path might be expressed by the term, Probationary Path. Before the occultist can manipulate wisely the matter of the solar system he must have mastered the laws that govern the microcosm, and even though he is naturally on the occult path yet he will still have to find the God within his own being before he can safely venture on the path of occult law.

The mystic seeks to work from the emotional to the intuitional, and thence to the Monad, or Spirit. The occultist works from the physical to the mental, and thence to the atma or Spirit. One works along the line of love; the other along the line of will. The mystic fails in the purpose of his being—that of love demonstrated in activity—unless he co-ordinates the whole through the use of intelligent will. Therefore he has to become the occultist.

The occultist similarly fails and becomes only a selfish exponent of power working through intelligence, unless he finds a purpose for that will and knowledge by an animating love which will give to him sufficient motive for all that he attempts.

I have attempted to make clear to you the distinction between these two groups, as the importance of the matter is great when studying meditation. The form used by the two types is entirely different and when seen clairvoyantly is very interesting.

The mystic form.

The expression, "the mystic form," is almost a paradoxical remark, for the mystic—if left to himself—eliminates the form altogether. He concentrates upon the God within, brooding on that inner centre of consciousness; he seeks to link that centre with other centres—such as his Master, or some saint, or even with the supreme Logos Himself—and to mount by the *line of life*, paying no attention whatsoever to the environing sheaths. He works along the path of fire. "Our God is a consuming fire" is to him a literal statement of fact, and of realised truth. He rises from fire to fire, and from graded realisations of the indwelling Fire till he touches the fire of the universe. The only form that the mystic may be said to use would be a ladder of fire or a cross of fire, by means of which he elevates his consciousness to the desired point. He concentrates on abstractions, on attributes more than on aspects, and on the life side more than the concrete. He aspires, he burns, he harmonises, he loves and he works through devotion. He meditates by attempting to eliminate the concrete mind altogether, and aspires to leap from the plane of the emotions to that of the intuition.

He has the faults of his type,—dreamy, visionary, impractical, emotional, and lacking that quality of mind that we call discrimination. He is intuitive, prone to martyrdom and self-sacrifice. Before he can achieve and before he can take initiation he has three things to do:—

First, by meditation, to bring his whole nature under rule, and to learn to build the forms, and hence to learn their value.

Secondly, to develop appreciation of the concrete, and to learn clearly the place within the scheme of things of the various sheaths through which the life he so much loves has to manifest. He has to work at his mental body and bring it to the store house of facts before he can proceed much further.

Thirdly, to learn through the intelligent study of the microcosm, his little spirit-matter system, the dual value of the macrocosm.

Instead of only knowing the *fire that burns* he has to understand and work through *the fire that builds,* that fuses and develops form. He has, through meditation, to learn the threefold use of Fire. This last sentence is of very real importance and I seek to emphasise it.

August 10, 1920.

The occult form.

We studied, two days ago, the method whereby the mystic attains union, and outlined very briefly the path whereby he attempts to reach his goal. Today we will outline as briefly the course taken by the occultist, and his type of meditation, contrasting it with that of the mystic, and pointing out later how the two have to merge and their individual elements be fused into one.

The line of *form* is, for the occultist, the line of least resistance, and incidentally I might here interpolate a thought. The fact being admitted, we may therefore look with some certainty at this time for a rapid development of occult knowledge, and for the appearance of some true occultists. By the coming in of the seventh ray, the Ray of Form or Ritual, the finding of the occult path, and the assimilation of occult knowledge is powerfully facilitated. The occultist is at first occupied more with the form through which the Deity manifests than with the Deity Himself, and it is here that the fundamental difference between the two types is at first apparent. The mystic eliminates or endeavours to transcend *mind* in his process of finding the Self. The occultist, through his intelligent interest in the forms which veil the Self and by the employment of the *principle of mind* on both its levels, arrives at the same point. He recognises the sheaths that veil. He applies himself to the study of the laws that govern the manifested solar system. He concentrates on the objective, and in his earlier years may at times overlook the value of the subjective. He arrives eventually at the central life by the elimination, through conscious knowledge and control, of sheath after sheath. He meditates upon form until the form is lost sight of, and the creator of the form becomes all in all.

He, like the mystic, has three things to do:—

1—He has to learn the law and to apply that law to himself. Rigid self-discipline is his method, and necessarily so, for the dangers threatening the occultist are not those of the mystic. Pride, selfishness, and a wielding of the law from curiosity or desire for power have to be burnt out of him before the secrets of the Path can safely be entrusted to his care.

2—In meditation he has, through the form built, to concentrate upon the indwelling life. He has to seek the inner burning fire that irradiates all forms that shelter the divine life.

3—Through the scientific study of the macrocosm, "the kingdom of God without," he has to reach a point where he locates that kingdom likewise within.

Here, therefore, is the merging point of the mystic and the occultist. Here their paths become one. I spoke earlier in this letter of the interest to the clairvoyant in noting the difference in the forms built by the mystic and the occultist in meditation. I might touch on some of the differences for your interest, though until such vision is yours my point may be but words to you.

Occult and mystic forms clairvoyantly seen.

The mystic who is meditating has built before him and around him an outline nebulous, inchoate, and cloudy, and in such a way that he himself forms the centre of the form. Frequently, according to the trend of his mind, the nucleus of the form may be some favourite symbol such as a cross, an altar, or even his pictured idea of one of the Great Ones. This form will be wreathed in the mists of devotion, and will pulsate with floods of colour bespeaking aspiration, love and ardent longing. The colours built in will be of singular purity and clarity and will mount up until they reach a great height. According to the capacity of the man to aspire and to love will be the density and the beauty of the ascending clouds; according to his stability of temperament will be the accuracy of the inner symbol or picture around which the clouds of colour circulate.

The forms built by the man of an occult trend of thought, and who is more dominated by mind, will be of a geometrical type. The outlines will be clear, and will be apt to be rigid. The form will be more painstakingly built and the man, during meditation, will proceed with greater care and accuracy. He will (if I may so express it) take a pride in the manipulation of the material that goes to the building of the form. Matter of the mental plane will be more apparent and—though certain clouds of emotional matter may be added to the whole—matter of the emotional plane will be of secondary importance. The colours employed may be of equal clarity, but they are apportioned with specific intent, and the form stands out clearly and is not lost in the upward surge of emotional colours as the mystic form is apt to be.

Later, when the man in either case has reached a point of more rounded out development, and is both an occultist and a mystic, the forms built will combine both qualifications, and be things of rare beauty.

This will suffice for today, but I would like to outline for you the ideas that must be brought out later. We will deal with the use of forms in achieving specific results, and though it is not my intention to give or outline such forms, I wish to group them for you so that later when the Teacher moves among men He may find ready apprehension among students everywhere.

1—Forms used in work on the three bodies.

2—Forms on certain rays.

3—Forms used in healing.

4—Mantrams.

5—Forms used in one of the three Departments:—

    a—The Manu's Department.

    b—The Department of the World Teacher or the Christ.

    c—The Department of the Lord of Civilisation.

6—Forms for calling elementals.

7—Forms for contacting the devas.

8—Special forms connected with Fire.

August 11, 1920.

. . . Periods of physical weakness are of value only for the reason that they demonstrate the absolute necessity there is for the worker to build a strong body before he can accomplish much, and the importance of good health before the disciple can go forward on the Path. We cannot permit those we teach to do certain things, nor inform them along certain lines unless their physical vehicles are in good shape, and unless the handicap of ill health and disease is practically negligible, and the karma of accidental trouble almost completely obviated in the personal life. National or group karma occasionally involves a pupil, and upsets somewhat the plans, but this is unavoidable and can seldom be offset.

The use of specific forms for specific ends.

Until now we have dealt more with the personal aspects of meditation, and have considered the two types that are practically universal and fundamental, having studied briefly, (a) Meditation as followed by the mystic, and (b) Meditation as pursued by the occultist.

We have largely generalised and have not in any way attempted to enter into particulars. It is neither desir-

able at this stage nor proper. At a certain point in meditation, nevertheless, when the pupil has made the desired
progress and covered certain specific stages and attained
certain objectives (which attainment can be ascertained
by a review of the pupil's causal body) and when a
foundation of right living has been laid which neither
storms nor attack will be liable easily to upset or destroy,
the Teacher may impart to the earnest pupil instructions
whereby he can build in mental matter and under definite
rules, forms that will lead to specific actions and reactions. These forms will be imparted gradually, and at
times the pupil (this especially at first) may not be in the
least conscious of the results achieved. He will obey the
orders, say the imparted words, or work through the
outlined formulas, and the results attained may do their
work even though the pupil is unconscious of the fact.
Later—especially after initiation, as the subtler faculties
come into activity, and the centres are rotating in fourth
dimensional order—he may be aware of the effects of
his meditation on the emotional and mental planes.

Results never concern us. Strict obedience to the law,
and steady adherence to the rules laid down, with skill in
action aimed at are the part of the wise pupil. The effects
then are sure, and carry no karma with them.

. . . Let us take up each of the forms in order, but
first I would give a warning. I do not intend to outline
forms, or to give specific instructions as to how the results indicated may be achieved. That will be done later,
but when, it is not possible to say. So much depends
upon the work done during the next seven years, or on
the group karma, also on the progress made, not only by
the human hierarchy, but by the deva or angel evolution
as well. The secret of it all lies hid in the seventh Ceremonial Ray, and the hour for the next step onward will

be given by the seventh Planetary Logos, working in conjunction with three Great Lords, especially with the Lord of the third department.

Forms used in work on the three bodies.

These forms will be some of the first revealed, and already in the various meditations advocated by the wise Guides of the race you have some of the lesser foundation outlines designed for working on the *lower mind*. These forms will be based on the special need of any one body, and will seek through the manipulation of matter to build that which is needed to fill the gap, and thus to supply the deficiency. This manipulation will be begun first on the etheric matter of the physical body, by forms of breathing (respiration and inspiration), and by certain rhythmic currents set up on the mental plane and driving from thence to the lower ethers. The etheric body will thus be strengthened, purified, cleansed, and rearranged. Many of the diseases of the dense physical body originate in the etheric, and it will be an object of attention at as early a date as possible.

The emotional body likewise will be dealt with through special forms, and when the pupil has strenuously cultivated the quality of discrimination, and made it a working factor in his life, then these forms will be gradually imparted. But until he can distinguish somewhat between the real and the unreal, and until his sense of proportion is wisely adjusted, the emotional plane should be for him a battle ground, and not a field for experimentation. Let me illustrate the type of work that these forms which work on emotional matter will accomplish. The aim of the pupil who treads the Path is to build an emotional body that is composed of matter of the higher subplanes, is clear and sensitive, an accurate transmitter, and which

is characterised by a stable vibration, a steady rhythmic
motion, and is not prone to violent storms and the agi-
tating effects of uncontrolled emotion. When the idealism
is high, when the percentage of matter of the two higher
subplanes is approaching somewhat the desired figure,
and when the pupil recognises practically all the time
that he is not his vehicles, but is indeed the divine Dweller
within them, then certain things will be imparted to him,
which—when carefully followed out—will do two things:

They will act directly on his emotional body, driving
out foreign or lower matter, and stabilising his vibration.

They will build in emotional matter a body or form
that he can use for certain work, and can employ as his
agent to attain results that will be part of the purificatory and constructive work of the emotional body. This is
as much as can be said, but it will serve to show the
type of form aimed at.

Ray forms.

This is a profoundly interesting and vast subject, and
may only be indicated in general terms. Certain forms,
built up on the numerical aspect of the various rays, are
the special property of those rays and embody their geometrical significance, demonstrating their place in the
system. Some of these forms being on the concrete rays
or building rays are the line of least resistance for the
occultist, while other forms on the abstract or attributive
rays are more easily followed by the mystic.

These forms are for three objects:—

a. They put the pupil in direct contact with his own
ray, either the egoic or personality ray.

b. They link him up with his group on the inner
planes, either the group of servers, the group of invisible
helpers, or later with his egoic group.

c. They tend to merge the occult and the mystic paths in the life of the pupil. Should he be on the mystic path he will work at the forms upon the Rays of Aspect, and so develop knowledge of the concrete side of Nature—that side which works under law. You can reverse the case for the man of occult tendency, till the time comes when the paths merge and all forms are alike to the Initiate. You have to remember that at this point of merging a man works ever primarily on his own ray when he has transcended the personality and found the egoic note. Then he manipulates matter of his own ray, and works through his own ray-forms with their six representative sub-ray forms until he is adept, and knows the secret of synthesis. These forms are taught by the Teacher to the pupil.

You will find that though I have imparted but little on this subject, yet, if you brood over what I have given, it contains much. It may give those who wisely assimilate it the key they seek for their next step on. I may touch on this and somewhat enlarge when we take up the subject of access to the Masters through meditation.

Forms used in healing.

We must touch now on these forms, remembering first of all that they will be necessarily arranged in three groups, each with many subsidiary heads.

a. Forms for use in *physical healing*. You would be surprised how seldom these forms will be required, and how few in number therefore they are. The reason for this is that very few of the troubles of the dense physical body arise within that body itself. A few arise directly in the etheric body, but at this stage of evolution most of the troubles arise in the emotional body, and the remainder in the mental. We might generalise and say that:

25% of the ills flesh is heir to, arise in the etheric body.
25% in the mental body.
50% find their origin in the emotional body.

Therefore, though accidents may occur which lead to un-expected physical disaster and for which forms for heal-ing may be given, yet the wise student will find that the forms that affect the etheric body may be the first point of departure. These forms, built up in meditation, will act directly on the pranic channels that go to the make-up of the etheric—that intricate web which has its counterpart in the circulatory system of the dense physi-cal body. They are the seat of much of the present dis-ease in that body, either directly or through causes set up on the emotional plane and reacting on the etheric.

b. Forms for *healing the emotional body.* As said above, much of the present sickness is due to causes set up in the emotional body and these causes are mainly three. I would point out that I but outline broadly and give general indications.

Violent emotion and unstable vibration. This, if in-dulged in, has a shattering effect and reacts on the nervous system. If suppressed and inhibited it has an equally dangerous effect, and results in a diseased con-dition of the liver, in bilious attacks, in the poisons which are generated in the system and find their outlet in cer-tain cases of septic poisoning, in skin diseases, and in some forms of anemia.

Fear and forebodings, worry and despair. These types of emotion—which are so common—have a general debilitating effect on the system, leading to loss of vital-ity, to sluggish action of the organs, and to many forms of obscure diseases of the nervous system, of the brain and of the spine.

Sex emotions, covering a very large range of feeling, ranging from the suppressed sex emotion which is now beginning to be studied by our psychologists to the unclean criminal emotion that finds its expression in violent orgies and license.

Under all these heads many points may be gathered, but I write not letters on healing, but letters on meditation, so I must not further enlarge.

In the forms used in these three cases attention will be paid to the cause of the trouble, to the plane on which it originates, and to the effects on the lower bodies or body. In apportioning forms different aims will be in view. Where, for instance, the trouble is based on suppressed emotion, the effect of the form (when rightly followed) will be to transmute the emotion and turn it upward. When, by right use, the emotional body is cleared of the emotional congestion, the life-giving forces of the Ego, and of the pranic life everywhere available, will be set free. They can then circulate with facility, tuning up the entire system and cleansing all organs that were suffering from the inner congestion.

c. Forms for *mental healing*. These will be, for the majority of you, much more obscure, and in fact mental trouble is far more difficult to cure than either of the other two. This is due to two causes, one being that our polarisation as a race is not yet in the mental body. It is always much more easy to contact a body and to manipulate it when it is the seat of the centre of consciousness. The emotional body likewise, being more fluidic, is more easily impressed. I cannot enlarge upon the troubles of the mental body today save to point out that these causes may arise within the mental body itself as a karmic inheritance, or may originate on the emotional plane and work their way back into the mental body. For instance,

a person may be prone to some emotional storm. This—
if persisted in—may set up an analogous vibration in
the mental body. This vibration in its turn may become
practically permanent, and by the interaction of these
two bodies serious trouble may be set up. This trouble
may go all the way from simply causing a general sour-
ing of the Personality, so that the man is recognized as
an unhappy, unpleasant individual, to definite brain disease, resulting in lunacy, brain tumours and cancer in
the head.

For all these troubles forms of meditation may be
found which—if followed in time—will eventually dissipate them. The fundamental fact to be grasped here is
that only when the pupil has an intelligent appreciation
of the trouble or troubles affecting him, only when he has
the ability to conscientiously follow the imparted formulas, and only when his object is unselfish, will he be
trusted with these forms. When his object is to equip
himself for service, when he aims only at the acquirement of healthy vehicles for the better carrying out of
the plan of the Great Ones, and when he desires not to
escape disease for his own personal benefit, only then
will the formulas work in connection with the egoic consciousness. The downflow of life from the God within
results in sound vehicles, so that it is only as the Personality becomes merged in the Ego, and the polarisation
shifts from the lower to the higher that the work becomes
possible. That time is nearing now for many, and progress in the new medical school—based on thought—can
be looked for. Forms in meditation are but forms in
thought matter, so that it will be apparent to you that a
general beginning has been made.

One more hint on this matter I give:—Through the
various centres of the body—those seven centres with

which the pupil has to do—will come the power to heal the corresponding physical centre. As the centres are vitalised certain physical effects will be demonstrable, and in specific forms that work on and through the centres will come results that may throw light on this obscure matter of healing through the subtle bodies.

August 20, 1920.

Mantric forms.

We must today continue the discussion on the forms that will some day be in common use among the students of occult meditation. We have touched upon three of the forms, and five more remain to be dealt with.

Mantric forms are collections of phrases, words, and sounds which by virtue of rhythmic effect achieve results that would not be possible apart from them. These mantric forms are too numerous to study here; suffice it to indicate somewhat the types of mantrams there will be in use, or are now in use among those privileged to use them.

There are mantric forms based entirely on the Sacred Word. These, sounded rhythmically and on certain keys, accomplish certain results, such as the invoking of protective angels; they lead to certain effects, either objective or subjective. These forms or mantrams are much more in use among orientals and in the eastern faiths than at present among occidentals. As the power of sound is more completely understood and its effect studied, these mantrams will be adopted in the occident.

Some of them are very old and when enunciated in the original Sanskrit have unbelievably powerful effects. So powerful are they that they are not permitted to be known by the ordinary student and are only orally imparted during preparation for initiation.

There are a few very esoteric mantrams that exist in the original Sensa, and that have remained in the knowledge of the Brotherhood from the early days of the founding of the Hierarchy. They were brought by the Lords of Flame when They came to earth and are only thirty-five in number. They form the *key* that unlocks the mysteries of each subplane on the five planes of human evolution. The adept receives instruction on their use, and can employ them in the right place and subject to certain conditions. They are the most powerful known on our planet and their effects are far-reaching. As you know, each plane vibration responds to a different key and note, and its matter is manipulated, and its current tapped, by the sounding of certain words in a specific manner, and in a specific tone. When so sounded, the adept enters into the consciousness of that plane and of all contained therein. Mantrams in any tongue are founded on them, even though so far removed and unlike as to be practically useless.

Certain of these original mantrams are chanted in unison by the Brotherhood on great occasions, or when the united power of the Lodge is required to effect desired ends. Great events are inaugurated by the sounding of their key note with appropriate words employed; each root-race has its mantric chord known to those who work with races.

Again there are, as you know, certain mantrams in Sanskrit that are employed by students in meditation to call the attention of some one Master. These mantrams are communicated to Their disciples, and by their means the Master's attention is attracted, and His assistance called for.

Other and greater formulas are sometimes imparted by which the three Great Lords may be contacted, and Their attention drawn in any specific direction.

A mantram, when rightly sounded forth, creates a vacuum in matter, resembling a funnel. This funnel is formed betwixt the one who sounds it forth and the one who is reached by the sound. There is then formed a direct channel of communication. You will see therefore why it is that these forms are so carefully guarded and the words and keys concealed. Their indiscriminate use would but result in disaster. A certain point in evolution has to be reached, and a similarity of vibration somewhat achieved, before the privilege is afforded the pupil of being custodian of a mantram whereby he may call his Master.

There are also seven mantrams that are known to the three Great Lords and the Heads of the Hierarchy, whereby They can call the seven Planetary Logoi, or the seven "Spirits before the Throne" as They are called in the Christian Bible. One of these mantrams, which causes contact with the Logos of our planet, is known to the adepts as well. So the scale is mounted, and the Words are sounded forth, until we reach the mantram of our planet, which is based on the key of the Earth, and embodies a phrase which sums up our evolution. Each planet has some such note or phrase whereby its guides may contact their Planetary Logos. The seven Logoi in Their turn have Their available ritual or form whereby They can communicate with the threefold Lord of the Solar System. This is done always four times a year, or when urgent need arises.

Once a year the entire Hierarchy employs a composite mantram that creates a vacuum between the highest and the lowest members of that Hierarchy and on up—via the seven Planetary Logoi—to the Logos Himself. It marks the moment of intensest spiritual effort and vitalisation during the year, and its effects last throughout the intervening months. Its effect is cosmic, and links us up with our cosmic centre.

Ray mantrams. Each ray has its own formulas and sounds which have a vital effect upon the units gathered on those rays. The effect of sounding it by the student of meditation is threefold:

1. It links him and aligns him with his Higher Self or Ego.

2. It puts him in contact with his Master, and through that Master with one of the Great Lords,—dependent upon the ray.

3. It links him with his egoic group and binds all into one composite whole, vibrating to one note.

These mantrams are one of the secrets of the last three initiations and may not be sounded by the pupil before that time without permission, though he may participate at times in the chanting of the mantram under the Master's direction.

Mantrams, or formulas of words, sung by the pupil, which have direct effect on one of the three bodies. These mantrams are largely already in use—though in a much distorted degree—in the services of the religious bodies in all lands. Some light on them is being communicated in the ritual of the Church. . . . . The passwords as used in Masonry—though practically valueless now— are based on the use of mantrams and some day when there is an Initiate Head to all these organisations (such as Masonry, various esoteric societies, and religious bodies) the old mantrams will be given back in pure form to the peoples.

There are also mantrams for use in healing, and for the development of certain psychic faculties. Some mantrams have a direct effect on the centres of the body, and will later be used under the guidance of the Master for increasing vibration, for causing fourth dimensional movement, and for the complete vivification of the centre.

Still other mantrams act upon the hidden fire, but I will deal with them a little later. There are numerous oriental books on the subject, which is so vast a one that I caution the student from investigating much. It would but prove for the worker in the world a waste of time. I have touched upon the matter because no book on meditation would be complete without a reference to what will some day supersede all preliminary meditation. When the race has reached a certain point of development, and when the higher mind holds greater sway, these occult mantrams—rightly imparted and rightly enunciated— will be part of the ordinary curriculum of the student. He will start his meditation by the use of his ray mantram, thereby adjusting his position in the scheme; he will follow this with the mantram that calls his Master, and which puts him en rapport with the Hierarchy. Then he will begin to meditate with his bodies adjusted, and with the vacuum formed that may then be used as a medium of communication.

August 13th, 1920

Forms used in one of the three departments.

The interest of what I have to communicate today is very great, for we have to take up the matter of the forms used in the Departments of the Manu, the World Teacher and the Mahachohan, the Lord of Civilisation.

These three Departments represent in the Hierarchy the three aspects of the Logos as manifested in the solar system,—the Aspect of Will or Power, the Aspect of Love and Wisdom (which is the basic aspect for this system), and the Aspect of Activity or Intelligence. You know from your studies the work undertaken by these departments.

The Manu manipulates matter and is occupied with the evolution of form, whether it is the dense physical form of animal, mineral, flower, human being or planet, or the form of races, nations, devas or the other evolutions.

The Bodhisattva or World Teacher works with the evolving life within the form, with the implanting of religious ideas and with the development of philosophical concepts both in individuals and races.

The Mahachohan, who synthesises the four lower rays, deals with mind or intelligence, and, in collaboration with His Brothers, controls the evolution of mind whereby the Spirit or Self utilises the form or the Not-Self.

The synthetic work of the three Great Lords is inconceivably great. Form—Life—Intelligence, Matter—Spirit—Mind, Prakriti—Purusha—Manas, are the three lines of development, and in their synthesis comes completeness.

Each of these three lines works through formulas, or through set forms, which by graded steps put the man who employs the form in touch with the particular line of evolution represented by the Head of that line.

................What I seek to bring out here are the three clear lines whereby a man may mount to the Logos and find union with the *self* of the Solar System. He can mount by the line of the Manu, he can attain through the line of the Bodhisattva, or he can reach his goal via the path of the Mahachohan. But specially note, that on this planet the Lord of Love and Power, the first Kumara, is the focal point for all three departments. He

is the One Initiator, and whether a man works on the line
of power, or on the line of love, or on the line of intelligence, he must finally find his goal on the synthetic Ray of
Love and Wisdom. He must *be* love, and manifest it
forth, but it may be love working through power, it may
be love in harmony, or love working through knowledge,
through ceremonial or devotion, or it may be just pure
love and wisdom, blending all the others. Love was the
source, love is the goal, and love the method of attainment.

August 14th, 1920.

The three lines of approach.

As you will note (in continuation of that which we
studied yesterday) there are three direct lines of contact
between the higher and the lower, all finding their focal
point through the same Initiator, and all, at the same
time, quite distinct in their method of approach. If this
is borne in mind it will be apparent that each provides for
the man (whose egoic note is one of the three, or a department of the third) the line of least resistance and the path
whereby he may most easily approach the Ultimate. It
is fundamentally a matter dealing with various states of
consciousness, and here it is that the Great Ones so powerfully assist the student. Through meditation, adjusted to
the desired line, the student can control step by step the
various intermediate states that lie between him and his
goal. He rises by means of various focal points of force.
These focal points may be his Higher Self, they may be
his Master, they may be an ideal. . . . . . . But they are only
steps upon the ladder whereby expansions of consciousness are obtained, and the man is enabled to extend the
periphery of his consciousness until he gradually embraces all, and merges at last with the Monad, and later

with the All-Self, the Logos Himself.

For the sake of clarity and in order to satisfy the craving of the concrete mind for differentiation these three departments are pictured as distinct and separated the one from the other, though having their points of contact. In reality—apart from the illusion that mind always sets up—the three are one, and the seven are but blended parts of one synthetic whole. They all interlace and intermingle. All the three departments are but necessary parts of one organisation over which the Lord of the World rules. They are but the executives offices in which the business of our planet is handled, and each office is dependent upon the other offices, and all work in the closest collaboration. The man who finds himself on one line has to remember that in time and before perfection is achieved he must realise the synthesis of the whole. He must grasp it as a fact past all questioning and not just as a mental concept, and in his meditation there will eventually come a point when this realisation of the essential unity will be his and he will know himself as a fragment of a vaster whole.

In these three departments the method of approach to the Head of the Department is meditation, and the means whereby the student puts himself en rapport with the essential *Life* of that department (it is all a matter of terms) differ. The life within the form manifests—as a result of meditation—in three different ways. The results of meditation as demonstrated in terms of character, if I may so express it, are really the same aspects of manifestation under different terms or conditions. Let me tabulate them for you:—

Line of the Manu

Force, Strength, Power to rule.

Line of the Bodhisattva

Magnetism, Attraction, Healing.

Line of the Mahachohan

Electricity, Synthesis, Organisation.

I seek here to point out that the effect in the life of the student of meditation on one of these three lines will be as enumerated above, though all of course coloured and modified by his personality ray, and by the point attained in evolution. If you study the three words applied to the three lines you will find it very illuminating. (I seek not to enlarge the mental body but to train the intuition.) These words demonstrate the law as working through the three groups, and the working out into active expression in the three worlds of the due following of the desired line. Each line has its specific forms whereby those results are achieved, and the time is coming when the rudiments of these forms (the first fundamental formulas) will be given to students deemed ready and who have done the necessary preliminary work.

1. *The line of the Manu.*

We might here somewhat indicate the approximate method, and lay down certain rules which will serve to elucidate when the time comes.

This first line is specially the line of government, of racial development, of working in and with the matter of all forms on all the planes of human evolution. It is, as I have said before, the line of occultism. It emphasises the hierarchical method, it embodies the divine autocracy, and it is the line whereby our Solar Logos imposes His Will on men. It is closely linked to the Lords of Karma, and it is through the Manu's department that the Law of Cause and Effect is wielded. The four Lords of Karma work closely with the Manu, for They impose the Law, and

He manipulates the forms of men, of continents, of races, and of nations so that that law may be duly worked out.

The man therefore who attempts through meditation to contact these powers, to rise to union by these means, and to attain the consciousness of the Will aspect, works under set rules, rises from point to point under due forms, and broods ever on the Law and its workings. He seeks to understand, he discriminates and studies; he is occupied with the concrete and its place in the divine plan. He admits the fact of the indwelling life but concentrates primarily on its method and form of manifestation. The basic rules of expression and of government occupy his attention, and by studying the rules and laws, and by seeking to comprehend, he necessarily contacts the Ruler. From stage to stage he rises—from the ruler of the microcosm in the three worlds, to the group egoic and its focal point, a Master; from the ruler of the group he rises to the Manu, the Ruler of the department wherein he has his place, thence to the Ruler of the World, later to the Planetary Logos, and thence to the Solar Logos.

2. *The line of the Bodhisattva.*

This is the line of religion and of philosophy, and of the development of the indwelling life. It deals with consciousness within the form more than with the form itself. It is the line of least resistance for the many. It embodies the wisdom aspect of the Logos, and is the line whereby His love is manifested in a predominant fashion. The solar system being in itself a direct expression of the Logos, and of His love aspect, all in manifestation is based upon it—love in rule, love abounding, love in activity,— but in this second line the above manifestation is supreme, and will eventually absorb all the others.

The man who meditates on this line seeks ever to enter into the consciousness of all that breathes, and by graded expansions of consciousness to arrive eventually at the All-Consciousness, and to enter into the life of the Supreme Being. Thus he enters into the life of all within the Logoic Consciousness.

He broods not so much upon the Law as upon the life that is governed by that Law. Through love he comprehends, and through love he blends himself first with his Ego, then with his Master, next with his group egoic and then with all groups, till finally he enters into the consciousness of the Deity Himself.

3. *The line of the Mahachohan.*

This is the line of mind or intelligence, of knowledge and of science. It is the line of abstract mind, and of archetypal ideas. The man broods not so much upon the Law, not so much upon the Life, as upon the effects of both in manifestation, and upon the reason why. The man on this fivefold line ever asks why, and how, and whence, and seeks to synthesise, to comprehend and to make the archetypes and ideals facts in manifestation. He broods on the ideals as he senses them; he aims at contacting the Universal Mind, at wresting its secrets from it, and giving them expression. It is the line of business organisation, the line also in which the artists, musicians, scientists and the workers of the world have their place. The Spirits of Love and Activity pass much time in each of its five departments before passing on to the lines of love and of power.

In meditation the man takes some ideal, some part of the divine plan, some phase of beauty and of art, some scientific or racial problem, and by brooding over it and by the employment of lower mind, finds out all that can be known and sensed. Then, having done all that, he seeks to raise the consciousness still higher till he taps the source of illumination, and gains the light and information required. He mounts likewise by entering into the consciousness of those greater than himself, not so much from the point of view of love (as in the second line) as from admiration and joy in their achievement, and gratitude for what they have given to the world, and devotion to the same idea that impels them to action.

Therefore you will see from even the most superficial study of the above three lines how apparent it is that all the sons of men are rising. Even the ones—so apt to be despised—who are the active workers of the world may, in their place and through their devotion to the ideals of work or science or even of business organisation, be just as far advanced as the more highly considered ones who demonstrate more patently the love aspect of the divine Self. Forget not that activity is just as divine and just as fundamentally an expression of the All-Father as love in sacrifice, and even more so than what we now know as power, for the power aspect is as yet not comprehended by any of you, nor will it be until a further manifestation.

August 14th, 1920.

Forms used in calling devas and elementals.

In taking up the two points that you have enumerated six and seven, we shall be able to deal with them as one, for the mantrams and forms used in contacting the devas, angels or builders, and in calling the elementals or sub-human forms of existence, are practically the same, and should in these letters be counted as such.

As a preliminary step let us be quite clear wherein lies the distinction between these two groups.

The elementals are, in their essential essence, sub-human. The fact that they can be contacted on the emotional plane is no guarantee that they are on the evolution-

ary path. On the contrary, they are on the path of involution, on the downward arc. They are to be found on
all planes, and the etheric elemental forms—such as the
brownies, gnomes and pixies—are well known. They can
be roughly divided into four groups:—

1. The elementals of earth.
2. The elementals of water.
3. The elementals of air.
4. The elementals of fire.

They are the essence of things, if you could but realise it.
They are the elemental things of the solar system in their
four grades as we know them in this fourth cycle on the
fourth or earth planet.

The devas are on the evolutionary path, on the upward
way. They are, as you know, the Builders of the system,
working in graded and serried ranks. Devas are to be
found of the same rank as the Planetary Logoi, and the
Rulers of the five planes of human evolution hold rank
equal to that of a Master of the seventh Initiation.
Others are equal in development (along their own line)
to a Master of the fifth Initiation, and they work consciously and willingly with the Masters of the Occult
Hierarchy. They can be found on all the lesser grades
down to the little building devas who work practically
unconsciously in their groups, building the many forms
necessitated by the evolving life.

Earlier—prior to my dictating these letters to you—
you received one communication along the line of the
mantric invocation of the elementals and the devas. The
information given was correct, as far as it went, and you
may if you wish incorporate it here.

"Force in evolution and force in involution are two
different things. That is a preliminary statement.

In the one you have destruction, violence, blind elementary powers at work. In involution it is the elementals who do most of the work, working blindly along as controlled by the Builders. The work is constructive, cohesive, a gradual growing together, harmony out of discord, beauty out of chaos. The lower kingdoms of the devas work, guided by the great Building Devas, and all move upward in ordered beauty from plane to plane, from system to system, universe to universe. Therefore in studying occult lore you need to remember two things:—

a. You control elemental forces.

b. You co-operate with the devas.

In one you dominate, in the other case you endeavour to work with. You control through the *activity aspect,* by the definite doing of certain things, by the preparation of certain ceremonies, for instance, through which certain forces can play. It is a replica on a tiny miniature scale of what the third Logos did in world making. Certain activities had certain results. Later on, revelations can be made as to the rites and ceremonies through which you can get in touch with the various elementals, and control them. The Ceremonial Ray—by coming into incarnation at this time, is making things much easier along this particular line.

Fire elementals, water sprites, and the lower elementals can all be harnessed by rites. The rites are of three kinds:—

1. Protective rites, which concern your own protection.

2. Rites of appeal, which call and reveal the elementals.

3. Rites that control and direct them when summoned.

In working with the devas you use the *wisdom or love* aspect, the second aspect of the Logos, the building aspect. Through love and longing you reach them and your first step (as you are on the path of evolution, as they are) is to get in touch with them, for together you must work in the future for the guidance of the elemental forces and the helping of humanity. It is not safe for human beings, poor foolish things, to tamper with the forces of involution until they themselves are linked with the devas through purity of character and nobility of soul.

Through rites and ceremonies you can sense the devas and reach them, but not in the same manner nor for the same reason that you can the elementals. The devas attend ceremonies freely and are not summoned; they come, as you do, to tap the power. When your vibrations are pure enough the ceremonies serve as a common meeting-ground.

............I want to say in closing that when you have learned to use the activity aspect in work with the involutionary powers, and the wisdom aspect in co-operating with the devas, you will then *unitedly* pass on to use the first aspect, that of will or power."

Before proceeding further I seek to sound a note of warning as to the danger that lies in the calling and the contacting of these groups of builders, and more especially in the contacting of the elemental forces. Why especially the latter? Because these forces at all times find a response in one of the three lower bodies of men, these bodies (regarded as separated sheaths) being composed of these involutionary lives. Therefore he who unwittingly lays himself open to direct contact with any elemental, runs a risk, and may bitterly rue the day. But, as a man approaches adeptship and has achieved mastery over himself, and can consequently be trusted with the mastery of other forms of life, certain powers will be his. These powers—based as they are on law—will put into his hands the rule over lesser lives, and will teach him that co-operation with the deva hosts which will be so essential towards the latter end of evolution.

Mantrams of power.

The mantrams that hold the secret of power are, as you know and have been told above, of different kinds, and are primarily four:

a. Of prime importance are the protective mantrams.

b. The mantrams that call the elementals and lesser devas, and bring them into the magnetic radius of the one who calls.

c. The mantrams that impose upon the elementals and lesser devas the will of the one who calls.

d. Mantrams that break the charm, if I may put it so, and place the elementals and devas again outside the magnetic radius of the caller.

These four groups of mantrams refer especially to the calling and contacting of the lesser grades and are not much used, except in rare cases by initiates and adepts, who, as a general rule, work through the instrumentality of the great guiding devas and builders. The Dark Brotherhood work with the forces of involution and bend to their will the unwitting lesser forms of life. The true procedure—as followed by the Brotherhood of Light—is to control these involutionary groups and low grade devas through their own superior ranks, the cohorts of the building devas with their Deva Lords.

This brings me to another group of mantrams used in connection with the devas themselves.

a. Rhythmic mantrams, that put the one who uses them in contact with the deva group he seeks. These mantrams are, of course, forms of Ray Mantrams, for they call the devas on some one ray. These mantrams again will vary if the man himself is on the same ray as the group he calls. You ask why protective mantrams are not used first as in the case of calling elementals. Principally for the following reason. The mantrams calling elementals are more easily found and used than those calling the devas. History is full of instances of where this has been done, and all over the world (even at this time) are people who hold the secret that will put them in touch with elementals of one kind or another. Everyone in Atlantean days knew how to do this, and among savage peoples and by some individuals in civilised countries the art is still known and practised. Secondly, the average man, even if he knows the mantram, will probably fail in calling a deva, for it involves something more than just chanting the words and sounds. This something is one of the secrets of initiation. When a man is an initiate or an adept he needs not the protective rites, for it is a law in the occult world that only those of pure life and unselfish motive can successfully reach the deva evolution, whereas in connection with the elementary lives it works the other way.

b. Mantrams that permit of intercourse with the devas once they have been called. Speech, as we know it, is not understood by the devas, but impulses, forces, vibrations can be set up by the use of specific forms that lead to the desired result and obviate the need of speech.

These forms open the avenues of mutual comprehension.

c. Mantrams that influence groups, and others that influence specific devas. I would like to point out here that as a rule devas are handled in *groups* and not as individuals until you contact devas of a very high order.

d. Mantrams that directly call the attention of one of the deva lords of a subplane, or the mighty Deva Lord of a plane. They are known to very few and are only used by those who have taken high initiation.

August 17th, 1920.

The comprehension of force.

......The tension today is great, and the force pouring in on all the different centres is apt—unless duly regulated—to cause a feeling of fatigue, of tension, of excitement and of restlessness. The secret of regulation which lies in non-resistance is known to very few, and consequently the intensity of emotion, the violent reactions, and present widespread era of crime are the results, very largely, of force misused and misapplied. This can be seen demonstrating in all ranks of life, and only he who knows the secret of being naught but a channel, and who abides *still* within the secret place, can pass through the present crisis without undue shattering and pain. Stimulation —such as is at present abroad—leads to pain and consequent reaction and must be guarded against with as much care as its opposite, loss of vitality—guarded against, not in the sense of shutting oneself off from stimulating force but of receiving that force, passing it through one's being, and only absorbing as much of it as one can carry. The residue will then pass out from one as a healing agency on its return to the general reservoir. The true and occult significant of force in nature, of the elec-

trical currents of the universe, and of the latent heat
stored in all forms is little understood as yet by your
exoteric scientists, or your would-be occult students.
......approached the study of occultism from this angle,
and therefore, he attained a profound knowledge of law.

I have touched on this matter as it lies back of all
instruction along occult lines. If you can grasp somewhat its meaning, and understand how the law is but the
adaptation of the form to some one or other of these great
streams of force, you will illuminate your whole life and
be carried on those streams of force, those magnetic currents, that vital fluid, those electrical rays (no matter
what the terms used) right to the heart of the unknown.

This same idea of force and of the magnetic currents
of the solar system governs all I have imparted on meditation in all its branches—specific, individual and collective, based on form or formless; it is the medium
through which the mantrams work, from those that touch
the elemental lives up to the great Words chanted in
rhythm that call the Lord of a Ray, the Deva of a Plane,
or the Lord of a Solar System Himself. The sounding of
these Words, the ascent through graded forms to some
specific point, and the chanting of mantrams but put the
one who is thus working into the line of some one stream
of force. It is the finding of the line of least resistance
whereby to reach some goal, to communicate with some individual Intelligence, to control some involutionary life,
and to contact and co-operate with some group of devas.
The above digression may serve somewhat to sum up what
I have lately imparted anent forms, mantric or otherwise,
as used by the student of occult meditation.

As may be imagined, the calling of either the devas
or the elementals can only be safely undertaken by one
who has the power to utilise them wisely when called,

hence the mantrams we have enumerated above are only put into the hands of those who are on the side of the constructive forces of the system, or who can constructively control the destructive elements, bending them into line with the disintegrating forces that are themselves part of the great constructive scheme. Should anyone—not thus capable—be able to contact the devas, and, through the use of mantrams gather them to him, he would find that the force they carry would descend on him as a destructive one, and serious consequences might result in one or other of his bodies.

Think this out, therefore, remembering that those dangers would lie along the line of over-stimulation, of sudden shattering, and of disintegration through fire or heat. Should he gather involutionary lives around him the dangers would be different or rather would demonstrate in the opposite effect,—such as loss of vitality due to vampirism, a sucking out of the forces of one or another of his bodies, an abnormal building in of material into some one body (due to the action of such involutionary lives as the physical or desire elementals), and death through water, earth or fire, understood in an occult sense.

I have dealt here with the risks run by anyone who calls within his magnetic radius either of these two groups, without possessing the necessary knowledge to protect, to control and to use. Why have I dealt with this subject at all? Because these magic forms exist, and will be used and known when the student is ready, and the work requires it. Some day the lesser forms will be gradually given out to those who have prepared themselves, and who unselfishly work for the helping of the race. As I said earlier, they were known in Atlantean days. They led to dire results at that time, for they were used by those of unclean life, for selfish ends and evil purpose. They called the elemental hosts to perpetuate their vengeance on their enemies; they called the lesser devas, and utilised their powers to further their ambitions; they sought not to co-operate with the law, but to wield that law for physical plane schemes which originated in their desires. The ruling Hierarchy deemed the danger too great, for the evolution of men and devas was threatened, so They withdrew gradu-ally from the human consciousness the knowledge of the formulas and Words until such a time as the reason was developed somewhat, and the spiritual mind showed signs of awakening. In this way the two great evolutions, and the latent third evolution (composed of involutionary lives) were separated and shut off from each other. Tem-porarily the whole scale of vibration was slowed down, for the original purpose had been a parallel development. The secret of this apparent setting back of the plans of the Logos lies hid in the remnants of active cosmic Evil that had found their way into manifestation,—a remnant of the first or activity solar system, and the basis of this, the love system. Evil is but the sediment of unfinished karma and has its root in ignorance.

This separation on a threefold scale of the evolving and the involving lives has continued up to date. With the coming in of this seventh Ray of Ceremonial Magic, a tentative approximation of the two evolving groups is to be somewhat permitted, though not as yet with the involv-ing group. Remember this statement. The deva and human evolution will, during the next five hundred years, become somewhat more conscious of each other, and be able therefore more freely to co-operate. With this grow-ing consciousness will be found a seeking after methods of communication. When the need of communication for constructive ends is sincerely felt, then, under the judi-cious guidance of the Masters, will certain of the old mantrams be permitted circulation. Their action, interaction and reaction will be closely studied and watched. It is hoped that the benefit to both groups will be mutual. The human evolution should give strength to the deva, and the deva, joy to the human. Man should communicate to the devas the objective point of view, while they in turn will pour in on him their healing magnetism. They are the custodians of prana, magnetism and vitality, just as man is the custodian of the fifth principle, or manas. I have given several hints here and more is not possible.

Tomorrow we will take up perhaps the most vitally interesting division on forms connected with fire. Today the matter imparted suffices.

August 19th, 1920.

Mantric forms connected with fire.

Perhaps it would be of value if I touched somewhat upon the part fire plays in evolution and on the various departments connected with fire that may be found within our solar system. I especially emphasise it because in meditation the domain of fire is entered, and because of its prime importance. The departments in which fire plays its part are five. Let us therefore enumerate them. I will deal first with fire in the Macrocosm, and later show its microcosmic correspondence.

1—The vital fire that animates the objective solar system. For instance, as evidenced in the internal economy of our planet, and the central ball of fire, the sun.

2—That mysterious something called by H. P. B. Fohat, of which some of the manifestations are electricity, certain forms of light, and the magnetic fluid wherever encountered.

3—The fire of the mental plane.

4—The fire elementals who, in their essence, are fire itself.

5—The vital spark we call the "divine flame," latent in each human being, which distinguishes our Solar Logos from all other Logoi, and which is the sum of all His characteristics. "Our God is a consuming Fire."

All these differentiations of fire are practically differentiations of one and the same thing; they are basically the same though in manifestation they are diverse. They originated fundamentally from cosmic fire found on the cosmic mental levels. In the Microcosm you find this fivefold differentiation again, and it is in the recognition of this correspondence that illumination comes, and the purpose of meditation is achieved.

1—The vital fires that keep the internal economy of the human being,—the microcosmic system—in full manifestation. At the cessation of that inner burning, death ensues, and the physical objective system passes into obscuration. So it is in the Macrocosm. Just as the sun is the centre for our system, so the heart is the focal point for the microcosmic heat; similarly, as the earth is vitalised by the same heat and is, for our chain, the point of densest matter, and of greatest physical heat, so the lower generative organs are the secondary centre in the majority of cases for the internal fire. The correspondence is accurate, mysterious and interesting.

2—The correspondence in the Microcosm to Fohat is found in the pranic currents that, through the etheric body, keep the dense physical vitalised and magnetised. The resources of the pranic fluid are illimitable and little understood, and in their proper comprehension lies the secret of perfect health. We will touch upon this later.

3—The correspondence to the fire of the mental plane is easily demonstrable. For the work of the Lords of Flame in implanting the spark of mind has so developed and grown, that now the fire of intellect is to be seen burning in all civilised peoples. All energies are turned to the feeding of that spark and the turning of it to the greatest profit.

4—The fire elementals are known in some measure in the microcosm by the thoughtforms conjured up and vitalised by the man whose thought power suffices to do so. These thoughtforms, built by the man who can think strongly, are vitalised by his life or capacity to *heat,* and last as long as he has the power so to animate them. This is not for long at this time as the real power of thought is little comprehended. In the fifth great cycle, which for this chain will see the culmination of the fifth principle of mind, this correspondence will be more understood. At present the connection is necessarily obscure.

5—The vital spark latent in each human being which marks him out as of the same nature as the Solar Logos.

Here you have fire as it may be seen in the greater and the lesser systems. I would here sum up for you the purpose of fire in the microcosm, and what must be aimed at. You have the three fires:

1—The vital divine spark.

2—The spark of mind.

3—Kundalini, the twofold blending of the internal heat and of the pranic current. The home of this force is the centre at the base of the spine and the spleen as a feeder of that heat.

When these three fires—that of the quarternary, of the triad and of the fifth principle—meet and blend in proper geometrical manner, each centre is adequately vitalised, every power is sufficiently expressing itself, all impurity and dross is burnt away, and the goal is reached. The spark has become a flame, and the flame is part of the great egoic blaze which animates all of the objective universe.

Therefore, we are brought logically to the position that there will be for these three types of mantrams another mantram which will bring about their union and merging. You have in fact:—

Mantrams that affect kundalini, and arouse it in the right manner. By the power of the vibration they send it circulating through the centres according to their natural, geometrical progression. A secondary branch of these mantrams deals with the spleen, and the control of the pranic fluids for the purpose of health, for vitalisation, and for affecting the fire at the base of the spine.

Mantrams that work on the matter of the mental plane, on one or other of its two main divisions,— abstract and concrete,—and which work there in a twofold manner, producing an increased capacity to think, wield or manipulate mental matter, and, acting as a stimulant to the causal body, fit it more rapidly as a vehicle of consciousness, and prepare it for the final disintegration which is effected by fire.

Mantrams that evoke the God within, and work specifically on the Ego. From thence they set up a strong vibration within the higher Triad, and so cause a downflow of the monadic force into the causal body. All these mantrams can be used separately, and achieve their own result.

There are seven great mantrams, one for each ray, that (when used by the Master or by a member of the Hierarchy) combine all the three effects. They arouse kundalini, they work on the causal vehicle on the mental plane, and they set up a vibration in the Triad and thus effect an at-one-ment of the lower, the higher and the fifth principle. This is a reflection of what occurred at the coming of the Lords of Flame. It leads to complete unification, and marks the man out henceforth as one in whom love demonstrates in action by the aid of illuminated mind.

These are the four most important mantrams as regards individual evolution and development, and are well-known to all those who train pupils for initiation. But by themselves, even if discovered by the unready, they could accomplish little, for their use must be accompanied by the power that comes from the application of the Rod of Initiation. This Rod, through its surmounting diamond, focuses the three fires in the same way that a burning-glass reacts to the sun, and causes a conflagration.

I have here given you a lot of information in very few words. The matter is much condensed. It has a special significance for the man who nears the Path of Initiation. Ponder carefully on this which is imparted, for, by brooding upon it in the silence of the heart, light may come, and the inner fire glow with greater heat.

Other mantrams connected with fire can be further enumerated. There are two groups that are contacted by the use of certain rhythmic sounds.

The fire elementals and their various hosts in the
bowels of the earth, on the surface of the earth,
and in the air above the earth.

The devas of the mental plane, who are essentially
the devas of fire.

With the mantrams affecting the elementals of fire
there is nought to be said or imparted. They are, in many
ways, the most dangerous and the most powerful of the
elementals who attend to the earth economy. For one
thing, they far outnumber all the other elementals, and
are found on every plane from the highest to the lowest.
The elementals of water or earth are found only in certain
localities or spheres in the solar system, whilst the next
most numerous elementals are those of air.

Mantrams calling them, controlling and dismissing
them, were in common use among the Atlanteans. The
dangers aroused, and the menace stalking the land
through the indiscriminate use of elementals, so disturbed
the accurate working of the logoic plans, and so displeased
the Guides of the race that the knowledge was withdrawn.
The Atlantean root race passed away through disasters
by water, by floods, by submergings; when you remember
that water is the natural enemy of fire, and that the two
groups of elementals have no point of at-one-ment at this
stage, you may be able to understand an interesting point
about the Atlantean cataclysms.

Mantrams calling the fire devas are equally well
guarded, not only because of the dangers involved but
because of the obstructions in *time* that are caused when
these devas are heedlessly called and held by mantric
charm from pursuing their necessary vocations. Under
these two groups of mantric forms will be found many
lesser groups which work specifically with different bands
of elementals and devas.

We have here enumerated six groups of mantrams connected with fire. There are still a few more which I might briefly enumerate.

Purificatory mantrams that awaken a fire that purifies, and burns on one of the three lower planes. This is effected through the activity of elementals, controlled by fire devas, and under the direct guidance of an initiate or disciple for some specific purificatory end. The end may be to cleanse some one of the bodies or to purify a locality, a house or a temple.

Mantrams that call down fire for the magnetisation of talismans, of stones and of sacred spots.

Mantrams that bring about healing through the occult use of flame.

The mantrams used :—

    a—By the Manu, in manipulating that which is necessary in the moving of continents, and the submerging of lands.

    b—By the Bodhisattva, in stimulating the inner flame in each human being.

    c—By the Mahachohan, in His work with the intelligence, or the fifth principle.

All these mantric forms and many others exist......
The first step towards the attainment of these mantrams is the acquirement of the faculty of occult meditation, for it is not the sounding of the words alone that bring about the desired end but the mental concentration that visualises the results to be attained. This must be accompanied by the will that causes those results to be dominated by the one who chants the sounds. These mantric forms are dangerous and useless apart from the concentrated mental equilibrium of the man, and his power to control and vitalise.

August 21, 1920.

We come now to the last division of our sixth letter.

The use of Form collectively.

I propose to take this up under three heads which for purposes of clarity we will call:—

1—The use of sound collectively in a meditation form.

2—The use of rhythm collectively in meditation.

3—Special occasions on which these forms are used.

. . . . . . We have rather exhaustively considered in this series of letters individual meditation and have taken up the subject from many and varied angles. In all our handling of the matter only enough has been communicated to arouse the interest of the student and to incite him to greater effort, closer study, and deeper investigation. Only that which is understood and grasped as a fact in experience by the inner consciousness avails aught in the hard path of occult development. Theories and mental concepts avail not. They but increase responsibility. Only when these theories are put to the test, and are consequently *known* to be facts in nature, and only when mental concepts are brought down and demonstrated on the physical plane in practical experience, can the student be in a position to point the way to other searchers, and to hold out a helping hand to those following behind. To say: "I hear" may prove helpful and encouraging; to add to that the words "I believe" may carry added assurance, but to sound forth a trumpet note and say "I know" is the thing needed in this one of the darkest hours of the Kali Yuga. The *knowers* are as yet few. Yet to know is fully possible and is subject only to the diligence, the sincerity, and the capacity of the pupil on the path to stand firm in suffering.

Now having some dim idea of the results to be achieved, and the methods to be employed in individual meditation, and having enlarged a little on the use of forms by individuals, we can now take up the consideration of the matter from the collective standpoints.

Some of the most important things to note about the collective use of forms are that it has a universal vogue, is very effective, and can also be very dangerous. The collective worshipping of the Deity and the performance of religious rites in unison is so much a part of the public life of all peoples that its raison d'etre, and the results achieved, are apt to be overlooked. Every religion—Christian, Buddhist, Hindu, Mohammedan, down to the distorted fetish worship of the most degraded race—has emphasised the value and efficiency of a united attempt to contact the Divine. Results are inevitably achieved, ranging all the way from the calm and peaceful feeling that rests upon the participant in the Christian mysteries, to the frenzy and gyrations of the wildest dervish or the most benighted Zulu. The difference lies in the ability of the worshipper to assimilate force, and in his capacity to hold and carry it. These points are decided by his place on the ladder of evolution, and by the emotional and mental control of which he may be possessed.

The first postulate to remember in considering the collective use of form in meditation is that those forms, in employing sound and rhythm, should open up a funnel of communication between those taking part in them and the Intelligences or Powers they are seeking to approach. By the means of this funnel which penetrates from the physical to the emotional, or still higher to one or other of the mental levels, the Intelligences or Powers are enabled to pour forth illuminating light or power of some kind or other into those who thus approach Them. The funnel forms a channel whereby the contact can be made. The whole process is purely scientific and is based on vibration, and on a knowledge of dynamics. It is dependent upon the accurate formation, through occult knowledge, of a vacuum. The occult statement that "Nature abhors a vacuum" is entirely true. When through the correct intoning of certain sounds, this vacuum or empty funnel between the higher and the lower is formed, force or power of some manifestation of fohatic energy pours into the funnel under the inevitable working of the law, and, via that funnel, reaches its objective.

It is on the misuse of this knowledge that much of what we call black art or evil magic is based. By means of invocation and forms the Dark Brothers (or those who tamper with what you ignorantly term the powers of evil) tap forces connected with dark intelligences in high places. Thus they set in motion happenings on the physical plane that have their origination in the dark mysterious caves of cosmic evil as found within our solar system. Equally so, it is possible to tap the still greater forces of light and good and to make application of them on the side of evolution.

The use of sound collectively in meditation forms.

We will now take up the matter specifically from the standpoint of sound. In the study of the Sacred Word and its use we found that it had a triple effect, destructive, constructive and personal,—if I might so express it—or acting directly in a stimulating sense on the centres of the body. These three effects may be seen in the use of all sound collectively and by a large body of persons. We might enumerate still further for the sake of clarity a fourth effect, that of the creation of a funnel. This fourth effect is but a synthesis of the others in actuality, for ad-

justments in the matter of the three lower planes have to
be made in this creation of a funnel of communication.
Those adjustments result first of all in the destruction of
obstructing matter, and then in the construction of a
funnel for use. This is very definitely effected through the
instrumentality of the centres. This latter point is of
fundamental interest, and holds hid the secret of the most
potent use of sound. That use is its projection in mental
matter by means of one or other of the major centres. The
effects achieved by a group of persons who have the power
to work on mental levels, and to employ simultaneously
one of the major centres (either entirely the head centre
or one of the other major centres in connection with its
corresponding head centre) can be unbelievably powerful.
It is well for the race that as yet that power is not theirs.
Only when united purity of motive and an unselfish adherence to the good of all can be found, will this power be
permitted to return to the common knowledge of men. As
yet it is practically impossible to get a sufficient number of
people at the same stage of evolution, at the same point on
the ladder, employing the same centre and responding to
the same ray vibration to meet in unison, and sound together the same note or mantram. They must also be
animated by pure love, and work intelligently for the
spiritual uplift of all.

Part of the power of the Hierarchy is based on Their
ability to do just this very thing. As evolution progresses,
and the matter is more fully comprehended, meditation
groups will change from their present status, which is that
of bands of earnest aspirants seeking illumination, to
bands of workers constructively and intelligently working
together for certain ends. You have in the Christian Bible
the remnant of a tale which has descended to us from
Atlantean days. In those days the use of sound on physi-

cal and emotional levels was understood and practised, being utilised for selfish ends in most of the cases. You read that at the sound of trumpets, sounded a certain number of times after a rhythmical circuit of the walls of Jericho those walls collapsed. This was made possible by the occult knowledge of the leaders of the people who—being versed in the science of sound and having studied its destructive and creative effects,—knew just the moment to apply that science and effect the desired end.

These sounds can be grouped under three heads:—

The united sounding of the Sacred Word.

This is one of the most usual methods, and the most direct way of forming a funnel for the transmission of power. If it is so effective in the case of the individual, as has been again and again demonstrated, surely its united use will be tremendously effective, and even dangerously patent. It is the loss of the use of this Word that has crippled and hindered the efficiency of all the present exoteric faiths, but this loss has been deliberately brought about owing to the dangers incident to the low point of evolution of the human hierarchy. When the use of this word is restored collectively, and when congregations of men can sound it correctly on the right note and in the right cadence or rhythm, then the downflow of force from above (the quality of that force depending on key and tone) will be such that the vivification of the microcosm will affect the surrounding country and environment. It will cause corresponding stimulation in all the kingdoms of nature, for the human kingdom forms a link between the higher and the lower, and, in conjunction with the deva kingdom, provides a meeting ground for the forces of life.

These effects upon the different centres will be definitely felt on one or other plane in the three worlds. Let me illustrate, for clarity is desired. I must warn you however to bear in mind that no importance must be attached to the order specified here. The time is not ripe for the opening up of accurate information on this matter.

We will presume that a congregation of people is desirous of linking up with that channel of force that works through the emotions, and so stimulates to greater aspiration and love. In united silence they will stand until, at a given word from the leader, each unit in the group will deliberately withdraw his consciousness into the heart centre, and then from that heart centre (keeping the consciousness steadily there) he will drive forth the sound of the Sacred Word, pitched in the key to which the majority of the group respond. This key will be ascertained by the clairvoyant group leader reviewing rapidly the auras gathered before him. This sound will create the necessary funnel, and the result will be an immense temporary extension of the peripheries of the emotional bodies of the participants, and an intense vitalisation of their heart centres. By means of this the people will be enabled to reach heights and receive blessings otherwise not separately possible. You can for yourself think out other conditions. The use of the imagination in these matters is of real importance and develops a connection between that faculty and its higher counterpart, the intuition. Students of meditation must learn to imagine more.

The united sounding of certain mantrams which will be employed for specific purposes. Instances of such purposes are:—

a. The purification of a city.
b. The magnetisation of grounds that are to be employed as healing centres.

c. The clarification of the minds of the congregation in order that they may be able to receive the higher illumination.

d. The healing of people gathered together for that purpose.

e. The controlling of the forces of nature so that physical plane occurrences may be brought about.

f. The initiating of people into the Lesser Mysteries.

In this paragraph, as you rightly think, lies material that enlarged would fill a volume. It is part of that white magic that again will be restored to the race and by means of which a glory and a civilisation will be attained that was hinted at in Atlantean days, and is one of the dreams of the visionaries of the race.

Mantrams or words sounded forth collectively by which the deva, or angel kingdom, will be communicated with. These are a pecular set of mantrans connected with the Mahachohan's department and I will take them up more specifically later......

August 22, 1920.

The use of Rhythm Collectively in Meditation.

Rhythm might be expressed as that cadenced movement which automatically sways those who employ it into line with certain of Nature's forces. It is that directed action, followed in unison by a body of people, which results in certain alignments and effects upon one or other of the bodies or on all. It has for its objects therefore:

a. The swinging of a body, or a concourse of bodies, into the radius of action of a stream of force.

b. It causes an adjustment of the matter of one of the various bodies or of all the bodies that go to the make-up of the personnel of a group.

c. It blends—under certain geometrical balances and arrangements—the auras of the differentiated units in a group, and causes these auras to form one united group aura, thereby permitting of the rhythmic flow of force in certain specified directions, for certain specified ends.

This has been well understood right down the ages, even though the methods, procedure and results have not been scientifically comprehended or tabulated, except by various occult and esoteric bodies. In the old, so-called pagan rites the value of rhythm was well understood and even David, the psalmist of Israel, danced before the Lord. The swaying of the body to a certain tempo, and the swinging of the framework of the physical vehicle in various directions, subject at times to the musical sound of instruments, has a peculiar and definite effect upon the matter of the two subtler vehicles. By this rhythmic movement:

1. The force that is tapped in this manner is directed (according to the rhythm) to some one or other centre in the body.

2. The matter of the emotional and mental bodies is entirely re-adjusted and re-blended, resulting in certain effects having probably a physical manifestation.

3. The alignment of the vehicles is affected, and may be distorted or misplaced, or they may be correctly aligned and put in touch with the causal.

This is one of the main objects of the true rhythmic movement, distortions of which come down to us through the centuries, and have their apotheosis in the low type of modern dance. In the modern dance is found the corruptest manifestation of rhythmic movement, and the main effect of the rhythm is the direction of the force tapped by its means to the emotional vehicle, and to the lowest type of matter in that vehicle. This results on the physical plane in a most undesirable stimulation of the sex organs. In the true use of rhythmic movement the effect is to align the three lower vehicles with the causal vehicle, and this lining up—when coupled with intensest aspiration and ardent desire—results in a downflow of force from above. This causes a vivification of the three major centres and a definite illumination.

When an entire concourse of people is thus animated by a single high desire, when their auras blend and form one united channel for the downflow, the effect is tremendously intensified and can be world-wide in its radius. You have an instance of this in the wonderful Wesak festival, kept so universally in India to this day, when the Hierarchy forms itself into a channel for the transmission of power and blessing from the levels on which the Buddha may be found. He acts as a focal point for that power, and—passing it through His Aura—pours it out over mankind by means of the channel provided by the assembled Lords, Masters, graded initiates and disciples. This channel is formed by the use of sound and rhythm simultaneously employed. By the chanting of a certain mantram by means of the slow, measured movements that accompany that chanting, the funnel is formed that reaches upwards to the desired locality. The geometrical figures formed in the matter of the plane higher than the physical (which are the result of the geometrical movement of the concourse gathered in that Himalayan centre) form themselves into wonderful avenues of approach to the centre of blessing for the inhabitants, deva or otherwise, from any particular plane. For those who can clairvoyantly view the scene, the beauty of the geometrical forms is unbelievable, and that beauty is enhanced by the radiant auras of the Great Ones Who are gathered there.

In time to come the value of the combination of music, chanting, and rhythmic movement will be comprehended, and it will be utilised for the achieving of certain results. Groups of people will gather together to study the creative effects, or the purificatory efficacy of ordered sound joined to movement and unity; the constructive effect on the three bodies will be clairvoyantly studied; the eliminative effect on the matter of those bodies will be scientifically tabulated and all knowledge gained will be definitely applied to the improvement of those bodies. The quality of the force tapped, and its exhilarating, vivifying and stimulating effects will be closely watched. The centres will be studied in their relation to the streams of force contacted, and their culture and the intensification of the rotary movement will be definitely undertaken.

Another angle of the whole matter resolves itself into work in the world, and though dependent on the status and personnel of the group, it is not primarily for group purposes. Groups will apply themselves to the work of contacting certain types of logoic force, of passing it through the group funnel, and of sending it out through the world for certain constructive ends. This work is closely allied to that undertaken by the Nirmanakayas or Distributors of Force, and will be largely under their direction, for—when the right time comes—They will be able to use these groups as focal points for Their activities. Their work now has its focal point primarily on the mental plane and somewhat on the emotional. When the secret of causal alignment is better grasped, and when groups of people in physical incarnation can work in real co-operation (an impossibility at present, for the personality looms as yet too large) then the Nirmanakayas will be able to directly contact the physical plane, and so act with great force upon the evolutions found thereon.

Healing groups will work as follows. The circle of workers, with the unit to be healed placed in their midst, will definitely apply themselves to the healing of that unit by the use of set mantrams, and by the following of certain movements they will cause the focal point of the downpouring force to be the sick member in their midst. By the stimulating power of that force, by its re-building quality, or by its capacity to destroy and eliminate, what you call miracles will be matters of everyday occurrence. The subject is too vast to be more than hinted at here. But as the race progresses and the secret of making the at-one-ment is more comprehended, when many people tread the Probationary Path, when the percentage of initiates is greater than it is now, and when large numbers of the human race are more directly aligned with the egoic body, you will see the scientific application of the laws of sound and rhythm.

At the same time you will see the misuse of those powers—a misuse that will herald in one of the final struggles between the Lords of Light and the Lords of Darkness. Great will be the cataclysm and terrific the disaster, but ever the Light shines in darkness, and He Who reigns above all, and Who holds all within the circumference of His Aura knows the hour of opportunity, and knows too how to utilise that which can protect.

Special occasions on which these forms will be employed.

The great event on the planet in direct relation to the human race is the Wesak festival. There is one still greater moment in the calendar when a funnel is created directly between the earth and the supreme Ruler himself, the Logos of our system. This is accomplished through the power of certain mantrams and the united efforts of the Hierarchy and the Deva Lords of the planes. These Deva Lords are aided by the deva evolution, and the Hierarchy by those of the human race who are steady. They focus through the Lords of the Rays then in manifestation as well as through the Planetary Logos of this planet. The date of this event is not yet for exoteric communication.

On all the three main lines of approach—that of the Manu, or Ruler, the Bodhisattva, or World Teacher, and the Mahachohan, or Lord of Civilisation—their own specific groups will be found, subject to certain mantrams and words, and moving under certain rhythmic laws. One hint only can I give here but I think you will find it interesting. The time is coming when those who work under the Manu, manipulating nations, directing their attention to government and politics, sitting in the assemblies of the people, giving out the laws and apportioning justice, will begin all their work with great rhythmic ceremonies. By means of their united rhythm and chanted words, they will seek to put themselves in touch with the consciousness of the Manu and with His great governing department, so bringing more clearly into practice the working out of His plans and the formulation of His intentions. Having aligned their bodies and made the necessary funnel, they will proceed with business after having placed in their midst as a focal point of illumination one or two men who will give their entire attention to finding out the intention of the Manu and His subordinates upon the matter in hand.

So in the department of the Bodhisattva will a similar procedure be followed, for which the construction is already organised. The priest will be the focal point, and, after due ceremony and rhythm on the part of the united congregation, they will be the transmitters of information from on high. But here is a momentous point of interest: The priesthood will not in those days be a separated body of men. All will then be priests and a layman can hold that office when duly chosen at the beginning of the ceremony. The only qualification required will be the capacity to align with the higher, and to cooperate with all the other units in the concourse.

In the department of the Mahachohan, the Lord of Civilisation and Culture and the head of the third line of evolution, you will see again similar action. No university or school will start its sessions without the ceremony of alignment, the teacher this time being the focal line of information from the department controlling the activity of the mind. In this way the stimulation of the mental bodies of the students, and the strengthening of the channel between higher and lower mind will be greatly aided. The intuition will also be developed and contacted. In the above statements I have by no means covered the ground. I have but indicated the broad outlines of what will some day be facts in physical plane demonstration. The thought conveys much matter for consideration and for speculation and is full of helpfulness for the wise student. Aught that enlarges his horizon and increases the range of his vision is to be welcomed, even though his apprehension of these facts may be at fault and his capacity to assimilate leaves much to be desired.

LETTER VII

THE USE OF COLOUR AND SOUND

1. Enumeration of the colours and some comments.
2. Colours and the law of correspondences.
3. Effects of colours.
4. Application of colours and their future use.

LETTER VII

THE USE OF COLOUR AND SOUND.

August 27th, 1920.

There is no question that those who break the law perish by the law, whilst those who keep it live by it. The true study of occultism is the study of the why and how of phenomena. It is the finding out of the method whereby results are achieved, and it involves close analysis of events and circumstances in order to discover their governing laws. I have been led to make these preliminary remarks today because I saw with clarity the questions that are controlling your mind. These questions are of great value, if you continue to apply yourself to the search for the right answer. Certain definite laws govern the life of the disciple. They are the same laws that control all life. The difference consists in the partial realisation—on the part of the disciple—of the purpose of those laws, their raison d'etre, and their conscious judicious application to the circumstances met in daily living. By conformance to the law is the personal life transmuted. . . Take for instance *the Law of Substance*. This law puts the disciple in the position of wisely utilising the universal storehouse. It is the manipulation of matter, and its adaptation to the interacting forces of supply and demand. . . Blind faith is right for the mystic. It is one of the means whereby the Divine storehouse is entered, but to understand the method whereby that storehouse is kept replenished, and to comprehend the means whereby the bounteous supply of the All Father is brought in contact with the children's need is better still. One of those maxims I can here give anent supply and demand. *It is only as a skilful use is made of the supply for the needs of the worker and the work* (I choose these words each one with deliberation) *that that supply continues to pour in.* The secret is: use, demand, take. Only as the door is unlocked by the law of demand is another and higher door unlocked permitting supply. The law of gravitation holds hid the secret. Think this out.

Some remarks on colour.

Now we must go to work. The subject for our consideration this evening is of profound and complicated interest. This seventh letter of mine has to do with the use of colour and sound in meditation.

We have, as you know, dealt a good deal with the subject of sound in our earlier letters, both in studying the use of the Sacred Word, and in the study of forms and mantrams. It is a truism to say that sound is colour and colour is sound, yet so it is, and the topic I really seek to bring to your attention is not so much sound *as* sound, but the colour effects of sound. I seek to emphasise especially the colour aspect in this letter, begging you to remember always that all sounds express themselves in colour.

When the Logos uttered the great cosmic Word for this solar system, three major streams of colour issued forth, breaking almost simultaneously into another four, so giving us the seven streams of colour by which manifestation becomes possible. These colours are:—

1. Blue.
2. Indigo.
3. Green.
4. Yellow.
5. Orange.
6. Red.
7. Violet.

Not unwittingly have I placed them in this order but the exact significance is left for you to discover.

I want to emphasise a second thought:—These seven streams of colour were the product of logoic meditation. The Logos meditated, brooded, conceived mentally, formed an ideal world, and built it up in thought matter. Then our objective universe flashed into being, radiant with the seven colours, with the deep blue or indigo for synthetic undertone. Therefore certain things can be posited about colour:—

1. It has to do with objective meditation, therefore it has to do with form.
2. It is the result of sound uttered as the culmination of meditation.
3. In these seven colours, and their wise comprehension, lies the capacity of man to do as does the Logos and build.
4. Colours have certain effects on the different vehicles, and on the planes on which those vehicles function. When it is known by the occultist which colour is applicable to which plane, and which colour therefore is the basic hue for that plane, he has grasped the fundamental secret of microcosmic development, and can build his body of manifestation by means of the same laws that that Logos employed in building His objective solar system. This is the secret that ray meditation will eventually yield up to the wise student. These four points lay the foundation for all that follows.

I would here seek to put your mind at rest on the point as to whether the colours enumerated by me conflict with those enumerated by H. P. B. You will not find they

do, but both of us use *blinds,* and both of us use the same
blinds as those who have eyes can see. A blind is not a
blind when recognised, and I offer not the key. One or
two hints however I may give:—

Complementary colours may be spoken of in occult
books in terms of each other. Red may be called green
and orange may be called blue. The key to the accurate
interpretation of the term employed lies in the point of
attainment of the unit under discussion. If speaking of
the Ego one term may be used; if of the Personality, another; whilst the Monad or higher auric sphere may be
described synthetically or in terms of the monadic ray.

The colours of higher or lower mind are at times
spoken of in terms of the plane and not in terms of the
ray involved.

Blue-indigo, being cosmically related, and not simply
analogous, may be used interchangeably for purposes of
blinding. Let me illustrate:—

The Lords of the Flame, in their work in connection
with this planet, may be spoken of in terms of four
colours:—

    a. *Indigo,* as They are in the line of the Bodhisattva
       in connection with the Love or Wisdom Ray. The
       Lord of the World is a direct reflection of the
       second Aspect.
    b. *Blue,* because of its alliance with indigo and its
       relationship to the auric egg; just as the Solar
       Logos is spoken of as the ''Blue Logos'' (literally
       indigo), so the colour of the perfected man, and
       of the auric envelope through which he manifests,
       will be predominantly blue.
    c. *Orange,* which is the complementary to blue and
       which has direct connection with man as an intelli-
       gence. He is the custodian of the fifth principle

of manas in its relation to the totality of the personality.

d. *Yellow,* being the complement of indigo, and also the colour of buddhi, and on the direct line of the second Aspect.

I give the above illustration to demonstrate to you the great complexity involved by the use of blinds, yet also to show you that for those who have the seeing eye even the choice of these blinds is not arbitrary, but subject to rule and law.

It is therefore obvious to you why it is so often emphasised that in dealing with esoteric matters lower manas helps not. Only he who has the higher vision in process of development can hope to attain any measure of accurate discrimination. Just as the green of the activity of Nature forms the basis of the love aspect, or the indigo vibration of this love system, so will it be found upon the mental plane. More may not be said, but food for thought lies here. Orange also holds the secret for the Sons of Mind, and in the study of *flame* (which even exoterically blends all the colours) comes illumination.

In studying this question of colour and sound in meditation how best shall we divide our vast subject? Let us consider it under the following heads:—

1. Enumeration of the colours and certain comment thereon.
2. Colours and the Law of Correspondences.
3. The effects of colours:—
    a. On the bodies of the pupil.
    b. On groups and on group work.
    c. On the environment.
4. The application of colour:—
    a. In meditation.

    b. For healing in meditation.

    c. In constructive work.

5. The future use of colour.

Under these five heads we should be able to sum up all that has to be said at present. Perhaps little that I may say will be fundamentally new, for I give not aught which may not be found in that foundation book of H. P. B.'s. But in a newer presentation, and in the aggregation of material under one head may come enlightenment, and a further wise adjustment of knowledge. We will take up these five divisions later. Tonight I will only add a few further points to those already given.

Colours as manifested on the physical plane show at their crudest and harshest. Even the most exquisite of shades as seen by the physical eye is hard and harsh compared to those on the emotional plane, and as the finer matter of the other planes is contacted, the beauty, the softness and the exquisite quality of the different hues grow with each transition. When the ultimate and synthetic colour is reached the beauty transcends all conception.

Colours—such as we have now to do with in evolution—are the *colours of light*. Certain colours, which are the left-overs from the previous solar system, have been seized upon as modes of expression by that mysterious something which we call "cosmic evil" (in our ignorance so we term it). They are involutionary colours, and are media for the force of the Dark Brotherhood. With them the aspirant to the Path of Light has naught to do. They are such hues as brown, grey, the loathsome purple, and the lurid greens that are contacted in the dark places of the earth, on the emotional plane, and on the lower level of the mental plane. They are negations. Their tone is lower than the note of Nature. They are the offspring of night, esoterically understood. They are the basis of glamour, of despair, and of corruption, and must be neutralised by the pupil of the Great Ones by the admission of the colours connected with light.

6. The synthesis of all the colours, as aforesaid, is the synthetic ray of indigo. This underlies all and absorbs all. But in the three worlds of human evolution the orange of flame irradiates all. This orange emanates from the fifth plane, underlies the fifth principle, and is the effect produced by the esoteric sounding of the occult words "Our God is a consuming Fire." These words apply to the manasic principle, that fire of intelligence or reason which the Lords of the Flame imparted, and which stimulates and guides the life of the active personality. It is that light of reason which guides a man through the Hall of Learning on into the Hall of Wisdom. In the latter hall its limitations are discovered, and that structure which knowledge has built (the causal body or the Temple of Solomon) is itself destroyed by the consuming fire. This fire consumes the gorgeous prison house which man has erected through many incarnations, and lets loose the inner light divine. Then the two fires merge, mount upwards and are lost in the *Triadal Light*.

Certain colours belong more exclusively to the human Hierarchy, others to the deva. In their ultimate blending and intermingling comes eventual perfection. . . .

August 29th, 1920.

1. *Enumeration of the Colours.*

Tonight we must continue our study on colour and take up our first point.

In doing this I will make certain comments and give you certain data, impressing upon you nevertheless again the fact that I use the exoteric terms, and that the discussion is but for suggestive purposes. The very use of the word "Colour" shews the intention, for, as you know, the definition of the word conveys the idea of concealment. Colour is therefore "that which does conceal." It is simply the objective medium by means of which the inner force transmits itself; it is the reflection upon matter of the type of influence that is emanating from the Logos, and which has penetrated to the densest part of His solar system. We recognise it as *colour*. The adept knows it as differentiated force, and the initiate of the higher degrees knows it as *ultimate light*, undifferentiated and undivided.

We enumerated the colours yesterday and in a certain order. I seek again to enumerate them thus, only this time reminding you that the one Ray of which all the others are but sub-rays, might be regarded as a circle of sevenfold light. Too apt is the student to picture seven bands, striking down athwart the five lower planes till they contact the earth plane and are absorbed into dense matter. Not so is it in fact. The seven colours may be regarded as a band of seven colours circling and continuously shifting and moving through the planes back to their originating source....... These seven bands of colour emanate from the synthetic Ray. The indigo sub-ray of the indigo Ray forms the path of least resistance from the heart of densest matter back again to the source. The bands of colour form a circulating ring which, moving at different rates of vibration, passes *through* all the planes, circling down and up again. What I seek to bring out specially here is that these seven bands do not all move at the same rate, and herein lies hid the key to the complexity of the matter. Some move at a swifter rate of vibration than do some of the others. Hence—as they carry their corresponding monads with them—you have here the answer to the question as to why some egos seem to make more rapid progress than do some others.

These coloured rings do not follow a straight unimpeded course, but interweave in a most curious manner, blending with each other, absorbing each other in stated cycles, and grouping themselves in groups of threes or fives, yet ever moving onwards. This is the real foundation to the diamond pattern upon the back of the serpent of wisdom. Three major lines of colour should be portrayed as forming the lattice work on the serpent's skin, with the four other colours interweaving. Some day some student of colour and of the Divine Wisdom should compile a large chart of the seven planes, and superimposed upon those planes should be placed a seven-coloured serpent of wisdom. If correctly drawn to scale some interesting geometrical patterns will be found as the circles cut across the planes, and some impression will be conveyed occularly of the complexity of the matter of the seven rays. . . . . . .

Certain brief statements seem to be in place:—

The true *indigo* is the blue of the vault of heaven on a moonless night. It is the culmination, and at the attainment by all of synthesis, the solar night will supervene. Hence the colour corresponds to what the sky nightly proclaims. Indigo absorbs.

Green is the basis of the activity of Nature. It was the synthetic colour for system 1, and is the foundation for the present manifested system. The note of Nature is green, and each time a man reviews the robe in which the earth is clad he is contacting some of the force that reached its consummation in system 1. Green stimulates and heals.

I seek to call your attention here to the fact that it is not yet permissible to give out the esoteric significance of these colours, nor exact information as to their order and application. The dangers are too great, for in the right understanding of the laws of colour and in the knowledge (for instance) of which colour stands for a particular ray lies the power the adept wields.

Comments on the colours.

Certain colours are known and it might be well if we here enumerated them. The synthetic ray is indigo, or a deep blue. It is the Ray of Love and Wisdom, the great fundamental ray of this present solar system, and is one of the cosmic rays. This cosmic ray divides itself, for purposes of manifestation, into seven sub-rays, as follows:

1. Indigo...............and a colour not disclosed.

2. Indigo-indigo... The second sub-ray of Love and Wisdom. It finds its great expression on the second monadic plane, and its major manifestation in the monads of love.

3. Indigo-green....... The third sub-ray, the third major Ray of Activity or Adaptability. It is the basic ray of the second system. It is the great ray for the deva evolution.

4. Indigo-yellow...............The Harmony Ray.

5. Indigo-orange.. The Ray of Concrete Knowledge.

6. Indigo. ...and a colour not disclosed. The Ray of Devotion.

7. Indigo-violet..... The Ray of Ceremonial Order.

Now you will note that I do not name the two colours, indigo-red and indigo-blue, nor do I apportion them to certain rays or planes. It is not that it is not possible to do so, but it is the withholding of this information that creates the puzzle. Certain things you must always remember in dealing with these colours:

That I have given their exoteric names and application, and that of all I have given only two correspond with their esoteric application,—*indigo and green*. The Synthetic Ray and the Activity Ray are at this stage the only two of which you can be absolutely assured. One is the goal of endeavour, and the other is the foundation colour of Nature.

That the other five colours with which our fivefold evolution is concerned, change, intermingle, blend, and are not esoterically understood in the same sense as you might imagine from the use of the words, red, yellow, orange, blue and violet. Esoterically they scarcely resemble their names, and the names themselves are intended to blind and mislead.

That each of these three colours and the other two are only understood as yet through four of their lesser sub-rays. This is the fourth round and only four sub-rays of these colours have as yet been glimpsed. By remembering these three points undue emphasis will not be laid upon apparent information, and the student will wisely reserve his opinion.

Yellow is another of the colours that have come to us from system 1. The blending of blue and of yellow in that system had much to do with the production of activity. Yellow harmonises, it marks completion and fruition. Note how in autumn, when the processes of Nature have run their course and the cycle is complete, the yellow of the autumn is spread upon the landscape. Note also that when the sun pours unimpeded down the yellow of the harvest is also to be seen. So it is in the life of the spirit. When the fourth plane of harmony or of buddhi is achieved, then is consummation. When the work of the personality is completed, and when the sun of the microcosm, the Ego, pours unimpeded down into the personal life, then comes fruition and harvest. The at-one-ment, or the harmonising has been made, and the goal has been reached. Blue and yellow blended result in green, and the synthetic blue or indigo (the love and wisdom aspect) dominates when the plane of harmony is reached. It leads then to the third plane of atma whereon the green of activity predominates......

August 31st, 1920.

In continuing our study of colour and meditation, and our particular division in that study, I would—for your encouragement—point out that the part that falls to you is the reception and publication of these letters and of the imparted data, whereas the responsibility for that data rests with me. Even if you understand them not, and even if it seems to you that some of the data may be contradictory, I would suggest for your consideration that in the esoteric interpretation lies hid half the mystery, and the other half is concealed by the fact that all interpretation depends upon the standpoint of the interpreter, and the plane whereon his consciousness is working. The value of what I impart now consists in this:—that in the study of colour (which is one form of the study of vibration) comes the ability to understand personal vibration, to attune that vibration to the egoic one, and to synchronise it later with that of the Master. One of the main methods of effecting this synchronisation is meditation. When the intelligence grasps the scientific facts anent this subject, then comes the utilisation of these facts for the advancement of vibration, and the wise development of the colours necessitated.

We dealt in my last letter with the four colours —blue, indigo, green, and yellow,—and in this primary grouping lies much of interest. We now come to a different group of colours, and one that falls naturally together, orange, red, and violet.

Orange. This colour is for our purpose the colour of the mental plane, the colour that marks burning; it is the symbol of flame, and curiously enough the colour that epitomises separation. But I would have you note that the occult orange is not exactly the colour that you understand by the term. Exoteric orange is a blend of yellow and red; esoteric orange is a purer yellow, and the red scarcely is seen at all. This orange comes in as a vibration set up by a cosmic ray, for you have to remember that this fifth ray (just as the fifth plane and the fifth principle) is closely allied to the cosmic ray of the intelligence, or to that activity aspect that found its great expression in the first solar system. The synthetic ray of that time was the green ray, and it found one of its closest alliances in the ray of orange, or mind or intelligence demonstrating through form. You get a correspondence in this solar system in the synthetic Ray of Love and Wisdom, and its close relationship to the fourth Ray of Harmony. It finds a demonstration in the triangle formed by their interaction, as follows:—

FIRST SOLAR SYSTEM

Green Ray

Third Aspect

Activity or Intelligence

Third sub-ray
Activity
Green-green

Fifth sub-ray
Manas, mind
Green-orange

SECOND SOLAR SYSTEM

Indigo Ray

Second Aspect

Love and Wisdom

Second sub-ray
Love and Wisdom
Indigo-indigo

Fourth sub-ray
Harmony
Indigo-yellow

In the activity system you have the third aspect of universal mind or activity, demonstrating through the orange of the concrete sub-ray......adaptability through form—form which perfectly expresses that latent activity. Similarly in the second system of love, you have the love aspect demonstrating through the yellow of the ray of harmony or beauty—love expressing itself perfectly through unity, harmony or beauty. Note here the fact that I again use terms that are dependent for their correctness upon their exoteric or esoteric interpretation.

Therefore to return to what I earlier said, this orange comes in as a vibration set up by the earlier cosmic ray of activity in the earlier solar system; the force of orange (which is scientific apprehension by the intelligence) comes in to perfect the link between spirit and form, between life and the vehicles through which it is seeking expression.

We might apportion the great basic colours between the various terms that we use to express the totality of the manifested universe:—

1. *Life Aspect*	2. *Form Aspect*	3. *Intelligence Aspect*
Spirit..........Matter...........Mind		
Consciousness.. Vehicle..........Vitality		
Self........... Not-Self........ Relation between		

Ray	*Ray*	*Ray*
2. Love and Wisdom.	1. Power or Will......	3. Activity or Adaptability
4. Harmony.........	7. Ceremonial Law....	5. Concrete Knowledge
6. Devotion.........	5. Concrete Knowledge	

This is but one of the ways in which the rays may be apportioned and considered as influences having direct effect upon the evolving life, or upon the form in which it evolves by means of that third factor, the intelligence. These three divisions make the three points of a cosmic triangle:—

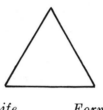

Intelligence

Life   *Form*

and the current of the rays playing macrocosmically between the three has its microcosmic correspondence in the fire of kundalini (awakened through meditation) playing in accurate geometrical form between the three major centres:—

Head

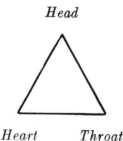

Heart   *Throat*

All the seven rays interact between the life, the form and the inner mind, and are in their essence themselves those three. They are life, they are form, they are intelligence, and their totality is the manifested universe. All seven at different times play on the different aspects.

The most important interaction exists between:—

a. The Love-Wisdom Ray and the Harmony Ray, as it does between the monadic plane and the buddhic.

b. The Power Ray and that of Ceremonial Law, just as it does between the first and the seventh planes.

c. The Activity or Adaptability Ray and that of Concrete Knowledge or Science, just as it does between the third plane of atma and the fifth plane of mind. Green and orange were allied in the first solar system, and continue their alliance here. I have opened up for all true students vast realms of thought.

In the relationship between indigo, blue and yellow lies hid a secret.

In the relationship between green, orange and red another is revealed.

In the relationship between blue, red, and violet lies still another mystery.

The student, who, by using his intuition, apprehends these three mysteries has found the key to the greater cycle and holds the key to evolutionary development. Remember, therefore, when studying the microcosm that the same relationship will be found, and will open the portal to the "Kingdom of God within."

Red is for all apparent purposes one of the most difficult colours to consider. It ranks as undesirable. Why? Because it has been considered as the colour of kama, or evil desire, and the picture of the dark and lurid reds in the emotional body of the undeveloped man rises ever to one's vision. Yet—at some distant time—red will be the basis of a solar system, and in the perfect merging of red, green and blue will come eventually the completed work of the Logos and the consummation of the pure white light.

> The activity system was green.
> The love system is blue.
> The power system will be red.

The result of merging red, blue, and green is—as you know—white, and the Logos will then have esoterically "washed His robes and made them white in the blood," just as the microcosm, in a lesser sense, does in process of evolution.

Violet. In a curious way the violet Ray of Ceremonial Law or Order is a synthetic ray when manifested in the three worlds. Just as the synthetic Ray of Love and Wisdom is the synthesis of all the *life* forces, so in the three worlds the seventh ray synthesises all that has to do with *form.* On the first plane, life in its purest, highest, undifferentiated synthetic aspect; on the seventh plane, form in its densest, grossest, most differentiated aspect; one is summed up in the synthetic Ray of Love, whilst the other is worked upon by the seventh.

A synthesis too is found in the fact that through the medium of violet the deva and human kingdoms can find a place of contact. Esoterically violet is white. In the blending of these two kingdoms the seven Heavenly Men attain perfection and completeness, and are esoterically considered to be white, the synonym of perfection.

Another point of synthesis is the fact that through the dominance of this seventh ray comes a point of merging between the dense physical and the etheric bodies. This is of paramount importance in the macrocosm, and to the student of meditation. It is necessary to effect this merging and alignment before the transmission of the teaching to the dense physical brain can in any way be considered accurate. It has a close bearing upon the alignment of the centres.

I have sought in the above remarks solely to indicate lines of thought which, if followed closely, may lead to surprising results. By the study of colours and the planes, by the study of colour and its effect and relationship to the life side, and by the study of the form side of the mind, will come much of value to the student of meditation, provided always he does three things:—

1.   That he seeks to find the esoteric colours and their right application to the planes and centres, to the bodies through which he manifests, and to the bodies through which the Logos manifests (the seven sacred planets); to the rounds and to the races, and to the cycles of his own individual life. When he can do this he holds in his hands the key to all knowledge.

2.   That he endeavours to make practical application of all indicated truth to his personal life of service in the three worlds, and that he tries to conform in his methods of work to the methods demonstrated by the Logos through the seven rays or influences. By this I mean that, through meditation, he brings his life systematically and in ordered occult cycles under those seven great influences, and so produces an ordered beauty in his manifestation of the Ego.

3. That he remembers ever that perfection, as we know it, is only partial and not real, and that even perfection itself—as grasped by the mind of man, is but illusion, and that only the next logoic manifestation will reveal the ultimate glory in view. As long as there is differentiated colour there is imperfection. Remember, colour as we know it is the realisation by the man using a fifth root-race body in the fourth round on the fourth chain, of a vibration that contacts the human eye. What then will

colour be as visioned by a man of the seventh round in a seventh root-race body? Even then a whole range of colours of wondrous beauty will be outside and beyond his comprehension. The reason being that only two great aspects of logoic life are being thoroughly demonstrated and the third will be but partially revealed, waiting for the still greater "Day be with us" to flash forth in perfect *radiance*. This word "radiance" has an occult meaning worthy of your consideration.

                                    September 3rd, 1920.

In the steady adherence to the next duty and the planting of the foot firmly on the next step ahead lies the open road to the Master, and the incidental clearing away of all difficulties. In the formulating of high mental concepts, and the expressing of them on the physical plane lies that development of the mental body that permits of an ever greater influx of the life from above. In the stabilising of the emotions, and in the transference of desire from that plane to the buddhic comes the ability to reflect truly the higher point of view. In the disciplined, purified physical body comes the capacity to work out that which the inner man knows. If these three things are attended to, the law can then work and emancipation be hastened. People ask themselves, how does the law work? What is our part in the carrying out of action that sets the law loose in the individual life? Simply adherence, as stated above, to the highest duty and an ordering of the personality life so that that duty may be perfectly achieved.

The Esoteric and Exoteric colours.

Today our subject is the second one in our letter on the use of colour and deals with the law of correspondences and of colour...... The esoteric meaning of the exoteric colours is not yet wholly imparted, as I have already told you. Some of these meanings have been given out by H.P.B. but their significance has not been sufficiently apprehended. One hint I give for your wise consideration. Some of the information given in The Secret Doctrine anent colour and sound concerns the first solar system and some concerns a portion of the second solar system. The distinction has naturally not been apprehended, but as a key fact for studying in the newer school, the revelation will be great. In this statement as to the esoteric significance of the colours I would have you now tabulate (even though it can be found in The Secret Doctrine), in order to form the basis of such later communications as I may seek to impart.

Exoteric	*Esoteric*
Purple	Blue
Yellow	Indigo
Cream	Yellow
White	Violet

Only four as yet can be communicated, but if rightly understood they hold the key to the present fourth round, and to its history. This being the fourth chain and the fourth round you will note therefore how in the number four lies the history of the present. Especially would I urge you who are the teachers and students of the coming generation to ponder upon the significance of white being esoterically violet. It has special application now in the coming in of the violet ray, the seventh ray being one of the three major rays *in this round;* it wields power in ratio to the four, on the four and under the four.

The esoteric colours of the exoteric red, green and orange may not yet be imparted to the general public, though students and accepted chelas, whose discrimination can be trusted, can attain the necessary knowledge with effort.

I would here like to point out certain other considerations which can be best dealt with by a brief consideration of the law of analogy and correspondence. We might therefore consider the following points:—

a. Wherein the microcosm and the macrocosm correspond.
b. The basic correspondences.
c. Colour in the microcosm and in the macrocosm.

Let us briefly take up each point, for in the right apprehension of the law lies the ability to think esoterically, and wrest the inner meaning out of the external happenings.

Microcosmic and macrocosmic correspondence.

The relationship between the microcosm and the macrocosm is accurate, and exists not only broadly but likewise in detail. This is a fact to be grasped and worked out. As knowledge increases and progress is made, and as the ability to meditate results in the faculty of transmitting from the higher Triad to the Personality, via the causal, then these facts will be ever more clearly demonstrated in detail, and perfect comprehension will ensue. "As above, so below" is a truism glibly repeated but little realised. What is found above and what will consequently be developing below?

Above will be found Will, Love and Activity, or Power, Wisdom and Intelligence, the terms that we apply to the three aspects of divine manifestation. Below will be found these three in process of appearing:—

a. The Personality expresses active intelligence.

    b. The Ego expresses love or wisdom.

    c. The Monad expresses power or will.

You have in the three worlds of the Personality:—

    a. The physical, expressing a reflection of the activity aspect.

    b. The astral, expressing a reflection of the love or wisdom aspect.

    c. The mental, expressing a reflection of the will or power aspect.

What have you for the colours of those three bodies, exoterically described?

    a. The violet of the physical as expressed by the etheric.

    b. The rose or red of the astral.

    c. The orange of the mental.

What have you in the Triad, or the world of the threefold Ego?

    a. Higher manas, expressing the activity or intelligence aspect.

    b. Buddhi, expressing the love or wisdom aspect.

    c. Atma, expressing the will or power aspect.

What again are the colours of those bodies exoterically described?

    a. The blue of the higher manasic levels.

    b. The yellow of the buddhic level.

    c. The green of the atmic level.

They are in the process of transmutation. You have to effect the corresponding change of colour from the lower to the higher. Couple up this information that I have here imparted with that given in an earlier letters on the transference of polarisation.

    There is a direct correspondence between:—

    a. The violet of the etheric level and the blue of the higher mental.

b. The rose of the astral and the yellow of the buddhic.

c. The orange of the mental and the green of the atmic.

The secret of it all is to be found in the application of the occult laws of meditation.

Again you can shift the whole range of colour higher, and in the Monad work out the correspondence.

a. The green of the third aspect.

b. The synthetic blue or indigo of the second aspect.

c. The red of the first aspect.

I would point out here that as you return to the centre of systemic evolution the nomenclature of these colours is most misleading. The red, for instance, has no resemblance to that termed red or rose on the lower plane. The red, the green and the indigo of these high levels are to all intents and purposes new colours of a beauty and translucence inconceivable. If justly interpreted, you have here a hint of the correspondence between the microcosm and the macrocosm.

The colours exoterically have to do with the form. The forces or qualities which those colours conceal and hide have to do with the life, evolving within those forms. By the use of meditation the bridge is formed which connects these two. Meditation is the expression of the intelligence that links life and form, the self and the not-self, and in time and in the three worlds the process of this connection eventuates on the plane of mind which links the higher and the lower. The correspondence will always be found perfect. Therefore through meditation will come that knowledge which will effect three things:—

1. Give the inner significance of the exoteric colour.

2. Build in the qualities that those colours veil.

3. Effect the necessary transmutation of the colours from the Personality to the Triad, and later from the Triad to the Monad.

The causal body acts as a synthesis of these colours in the life of the reincarnating Ego, just as the synthetic ray blends all the colours in logoic manifestation. Endeavour to keep clear in your own mind......that colours are the expressions of force or quality. They hide or veil the abstract qualities of the Logos, which qualities are reflected in the microcosm in the three worlds as virtues or faculties. Therefore, just as the seven colours hide qualities in the Logos, so these virtues demonstrate in the life of the personality and are brought forward objectively through the practice of meditation; thus each life will be seen as corresponding to a colour. Ponder on this.

The basic correspondences.

It is in the study of these correspondences in the different departments of the manifested universe, and the application of these colours to their adjusted portion that the beauty of the synthetic whole and the illuminating of the microcosmic life ensues. Let us enumerate or tabulate in broad general fashion, leaving the detailed working out to the student of meditation. More at this juncture is not possible.

1. The threefold solar system.
   The threefold evolving jiva.
   The three aspects of the Logos.
   The threefold Monad.
   The spiritual Triad, the Ego.
   The threefold Personality.
   The three worlds of human evolution.
   The three persons of the Deity.

2. The four Lipika Lords.
   The four Maharajahs.
   The fourfold lower man, the quaternary.

3. The five planes of human evolution.
   The five senses.
   The fivefold department of the Mahachohan.
   The five kingdoms of nature.
      a. The mineral kingdom.
      b. The vegetable kingdom.
      c. The animal kingdom.
      d. The human kingdom.
      e. The spiritual or superhuman kingdom.
   The fifth principle of manas.

4. The seven rays or hierarchies.
   The seven colours.
   The seven planes of manifestation.
   The seven Kumaras.
   The seven principles of man.
   The seven centres.
   The seven sacred planets.
   The seven chains.
   The seven globes.
   The seven rounds.
   The seven root-races and subraces.
   The seven initiations.

What I seek to emphasise in the above table is that to the adept the correspondence of all these is perfectly known and exists in terms of consciousness, in terms of form, and in terms of intelligence. He knows it,—if I may so express it,—in terms of colour when dealing with form; in terms of sound when dealing with the life side, and in terms of vitality when dealing with intelligence, or the activity aspect. The above statement will repay much earnest thought; it contains a statement of occult fact. According to the three lines of approach as dealt with in our preceding letter, will be the use of the terms as above described.

Colour in the microcosm and in the macrocosm.

Here lies much of difficulty owing to the process of constant mutation. Colour in the microcosm is subject to the following factors:—

1. The factor of the ray of the Ego.
2. The factor of the ray of the Personality.
3. The factor of the point in evolution.

One hint may here be given. At a low point in evolution the colours are largely based on the activity aspect. Later comes the working in the love, or wisdom aspect, which has three effects:—

a. The dropping out of colours from the lower sheaths which are the left-overs from a previous system. It involves the elimination of such hues as brown and gray.

b. The transmutation of certain colours into those of higher tone.

c. An effect of transluscence, or an underlying radiance or brilliance, which is the result of the greater purity of the bodies and the dimensions of the ever-growing inner flame.

4. The factor of the ray, or rays, that are manifested passing out of manifestation or coming into manifestation. These rays necessarily affect the egos in incarnation; they cause a change of vibration somewhat or a consequent change of colouring or of quality. If a man, for instance, is on the Ray of Science, and comes under the influence of the incoming Ray of Harmony, the effect on his trend of thought, and consequently on the colour he

will be demonstrating, will be quite noticeable. All these factors cause the blending and merging and mixing that is practically inextricably confusing to the man from the standpoint of the three worlds.

......I appreciate your feeling that even these hints but lead apparently to greater confusion. But by constant application to the subject in hand, by frequent brooding and meditation on the colours, and by an endeavor to attain their esoteric significance, and their microcosmic application, will gradually appear the thread that will lead the student out of his confusion into the clear light of perfect knowledge. Have, therefore, courage, a broad elasticity of view, and an ability to reserve opinion until further facts are demonstrated, and also an avoidance of dogmatic assertion. These will be your best guides in the early days of your search. Many have, through meditation and a receptiveness to the higher teaching, found their way out of the Hall of Learning into the Hall of Wisdom. Only in the Hall of Wisdom can the esoteric interpretation of the colours be truly known. That Hall is entered through the meditation which prepares the student for that initiation which opens to him the door. Therefore, hold fast to meditation and falter not in purpose.

September 4th, 1920.

We have for discussion today, something of real spiritual application in a practical sense. Much that I have imparted to you has provided food for thought and for speculation. It tends to the development of the higher mind and by stimulation of imagination it somewhat develops the intuition. Much of it has been in the nature of prophecy, and of the holding forth of an ideal some day to be attained. Only by pointing out the goal and by emphasising that point will man be induced to make the

necessary effort and thereby approximate in some measure the desired position. But today we come down to practical living and the imposing upon the personality of a
certain rate of rhythm. We do this in our study of the
third point upon the effect of colour:—

    a. On the bodies of the student.
    b. On the groups with which he is affiliated.
    c. On his environment.

The point I seek specially to emphasise is the *life side*
and not the form side of colour. As I wrote earlier, *colour
is but the form assumed by force, of some kind, when that
force is moving at a certain measure, and when its action
and movement is impeded or unimpeded by the material
through which it plays.* In this sentence lies the key to
the solution of the problem as to the colour differences on
the higher planes and on the lower. The resistance of matter to the downflow of force or life, and its relative density
or rarity accounts for much of the colour distinction. One
of the distinctions has, necessarily, a cosmic basis and is
consequently difficult of apprehension by three-dimension-
al man in this, the fourth round. But the basic reason of
the difference can be apprehended sufficiently to permit
the pupil to realise the absolute necessity of steadily refining his vehicles so that the force may radiate through
with greater facility. It is therefore on the three lower
planes a question of practical living and a bringing of all
the three bodies under definite rules of refinement.

These forces in terms of spiritual development, and
not so much in terms of form, demonstrate through the
virtues, as you call them, through magnetism and through
vitality and intelligence. To put it quite briefly, as the
student builds a pure physical body and a refined etheric,
as he develops the emotional virtues and as he co-ordi-

nates and enlarges his mental body, he is continuously altering its rate of vibration, and changing its rhythm, which change demonstrates to the eye of the clairvoyant as mutation in colour. As you have been taught, the colours as seen in the aura of a savage and in those of the average developed man are extraordinarily dissimilar. Why? Because one is moving or vibrating at a slow rate and the other with greatly increased rapidity. One has a rhythm slow, sluggish and heavy, the other is pulsating and moving with a tremendous velocity, permitting consequently a more rapid play of the material of which those bodies are constructed.

Therefore, I would like to point out that as the race progresses as a collective unit, Those Who gaze upon it from a higher plane are aware of the steady improvement in the colours seen, and of a greater purity and clarity of hue in the aura of the race, which aura is composed of the composite auras of the units of the race. For instance, the aura of the Atlantean root-race and that of the Aryan are widely diverse, and radically different. We have, therefore, demonstrated our first point that, as the units evolve, the colours change and this is brought about by the tranmutation of what you term vices, into virtues. *A vice is dominance of an involutionary quality of the same force which at a later period will show forth as a virtue.*

The second point I seek to make is that these influences (which show forth as colours when they contact matter) move in their own ordered cycles. These cycles we describe as the coming in or the going out of a ray. In this fourth round usually four rays are in flux at any one given time; by this I seek to impress upon you that though all rays manifest in the solar system, at certain stages of manifestation more or less of them will be dominating simultaneously. These rays, forces, influences, or co-ordinations of qualities, when expressed in terms of light, colour the matters they impinge upon with certain recognisable hues, and these give the *tone* to the life of the personality or to the Ego. They are recognized by you as the composite character and are seen by the clairvoyant as colour.

Groups, therefore, of units who converge through similarity of vibration will be seen as having approximately the same basic hue, though with many lesser differentiations in colour and tone. As stated before, the colour of large masses of people can be gauged and judged. It is in this way that the members of the Hierarchy in Whose Hands is placed evolutionary development in the three worlds, judge of the stage attained and the progress made.

Different rays come in bearing units coloured by that ray. Other rays pass out carrying with them units of a different basic hue. In the period of transition the blending of colour is of deep complexity, but of mutual helpfulness and benefit. Each ray imparts somewhat to the other rays in incarnation at the same time, and the rate of rhythm will be slightly affected. This from the standpoint of the present and of time in the three worlds, may be almost inappreciably small, but through the frequent meeting and interplay of the forces and colours, and their constant action and interaction upon each other, will come a steady, general levelling up, and an approximation in vibration. You will see, therefore, how synthesis is achieved at the end of a greater maha-manvantara. The three rays absorb the seven and lead eventually to a merging in the synthetic ray.

In the microcosm the three rays of the Monad, the Ego, and the Personality will likewise dominate and absorb the seven, and in time also lead to a merging in the synthetic ray of the Monad. The correspondence will be found perfect.

These forces, or virtues, or influences (I reiterate synonymous terms because of the need of clear thinking on your part) are gradually received into the bodies of the personality with ever greater facility and fuller expression. As the bodies are refined they provide better mediums for incoming forces, and the quality of any particular force,—or, to reverse it, the force of any particular quality—becomes more perfectly expressed. Here comes in the work of the student in meditation. Early in evolution these forces played through and on the bodies of a man with little understanding on his part, and small ability to profit thereby. But as time proceeds, he comprehends more and more the value of all that eventuates, and seeks to profit by the sum of the qualities of his life. Herein comes opportunity. In the intelligent apprehension of quality, in the striving after virtue, and in the building-in of God-like attribute, comes response to those forces and a facilitating of their action. The student of meditation ponders on those forces or qualities, he seeks to extract their essence, and to comprehend their spiritual significance; he broods on his own lack of response, he realises the deficiencies in his vehicle as a medium for those forces; he studies the rate of his rhythmic vibration, and he strenuously endeavors to bend every opportunity to meet the need. He concentrates on the virtue, and (if he is so situated that he is aware of the incoming ray or of the ray in dominance at that time), he avails himself of the hour of opportunity and co-operates with the force extant. All this he does through the ordered forms of the true and occult meditation.

As time progresses—yes, again I prophesy—occult students will be given certain facts anent the dominating rays which will enable them to avail themselves of the opportunity any particular ray affords.

Effect on the Environment.

As regards our third point, the effect of all the above on the environment, it will be obvious at once to the careful student that the effect upon the environment will be noticeable, especially as more and more of the human race come under the *conscious* control of their higher self and in line with the law. Certain things will then be possible:—

a. Direct contact with the deva or angel evolution will come about, though it is impossible now through instability of vibration.

b. Many very highly developed souls will come in who are at present hindered by the low rate of vibration and consequent heaviness of colour of the majority of the human race. There are, in the heaven world and on the causal level, some great, and, to you, incomprehensible units of the fourth Creative Hierarchy, awaiting opportunity of expression, just as some of you awaited a period in the Atlantean race before taking incarnation on this planet. When the rate of the vibration of a larger percentage of the race has reached a certain measure, and when the colour aspect of the co-ordinated auras of the groups is of a certain tone, they will return, and bring to the earth much of value past your realisation.

c. Another interesting point upon which we have not time to dwell is that the rhythmic effect on even the two kingdoms beneath the human will be objectively demonstrable. It was no idle boast of the prophet of Israel when he said "The leopard shall lie down with the lamb" or that "the desert shall blossom like a rose". It will be brought about by the domination of certain vibrations and the bringing in of certain colours veiling certain virtues or influences.

September 7th, 1920.

Today we will take up the subject of the application of colour. If colours are but the veil cast over an influence, and if you can, by use of the intuition, find out which colours thus shroud a virtue you have the key to the matter in hand. You will have noted two facts that stand out in these letters:—

That the subject touched upon is so vast that only its outline has in any way been attempted.

That each sentence written in these letters aims at an exact impartation of a complete thought and is full of matter for consideration. Why have I not dealt with the matter in greater detail, and why have I not entered into lengthy explanations and sought to expand the sentences into paragraphs? For the sole reason that if the preliminary work has been done in the meditation of the past years by the student he will find the material of these letters conducive to the development of abstract thought, and to the widening of the channel that communicates with the intuition. I but seek to be suggestive. My aim is but to indicate. The usefulness of the teaching I give depends upon the intuition of the pupil. Therefore, when I say that colour has certain effects when applied I would warn you that it will be necessary to interpret the above in terms of life, in terms of form, and in terms of mind.

The application of colour.

      a. In meditation.
      b. In healing.
      c. In constructive work.

Colour may be used in many ways, and the above three ways do not cover the subject. They but indicate three ways that are of immediate and practical use to the student. Colour may be employed in contacting other evolutions, subhuman or superhuman; in definite work of destruction or of shattering; it may be used in conjunction with other methods such as music or movement, or in connection with stated mantrams, thereby bringing about certain results, but with all these we need not, in this series of letters, concern ourselves. The growth of the individual and his increased capacity to be of service are all brought about by the wise use of occult meditation. Let us therefore consider our first point.

Use of Colour in Meditation.

All colours emanate from one source or one primary colour—in this solar system the cosmic ray of indigo veiling cosmic love or wisdom,—and then split into three major colours and thence into the four minor, making the seven colours of the spectrum. You will expect to see the same effect in the life of the individual, for always the macrocosm affects the microcosm. His primary colour will be his monadic ray, manifesting next in the three colours of the Triad and in the four colors of the Quaternary. These colours on the path of return are resolved into the three and thence again into the one.

The path of manifestation, of differentation, is the path of acquisition. It is the homogeneous becoming the many or the heterogeneous. It is the breaking up of the one basic colour into its many component parts. This is the *form side,* the expression of that which veils the life. On the *life side* it is the development from the one basic quality of the many inherent virtues; it is the latent possibility of divinity demonstrating as the many attributes of the divine; it is the one life manifesting its many qualities through diversity of form. It is the self, with the inherent capabilities of the All Self, utilising forms for the demonstration of its all-including perfections. On the *intelligence side* it is the method whereby the life utilises the form and develops its thorough comprehension, analysis and intellect. It is the relation between life and form, the self and the not-self, between spirit and matter, manifesting as modes of expression whereby the indwelling divinity imposes his characteristics upon the material provided for his using. The God within expresses all his latent virtues through forms by the use of activity or intelligence. The life shows colour and the form perfects those colours, as the intelligence aspect (which forms the energising link) becomes more evolved and comprehension is developed.

On the path of return, renunciation is the rule, in contradistinction to the earlier method. The indwelling life renounces the forms, hitherto regarded (and necessarily so) as essential. By the use now of the intelligence which has linked these two pairs of opposites, spirit and matter, consciousness and form, the forms built of matter by the aid of the intelligence are one after another repudiated by the aid of that same intelligence, or reasoning faculty transmuted into wisdom. The forms go, but the life remains. The colours are gradually reabsorbed, but the divine virtues persist, stable now and enduringly of use by reason of experience. Not potential are these attributes divine, but developed into powers for use. Inherent faculty has become active characteristics carried to the nth power. The veils are discarded one by one; the sheaths are dropped and superseded; the vehicles are dispensed with and the forms are no longer required, but the life ever remains and returns to its parent ray. It is resolved back into its primary, plus activity and expression, plus experience and the ability to manifest; plus all that constitutes the difference between the ignorant savage and the solar Logos. This has been consummated by the utilisation of many forms by the life, the intelligence constituting the means whereby that life employed those forms as a mode for learning. Having manifested as an aspect of this primary ray, having through many incarnations differentiated that ray into its many component parts, having veiled himself under all the seven colours that compose that ray, the reincarnating jiva takes the path of return and from the seven becomes the three and from the three again becomes the one.

When the man does this *consciously,* when he willingly and with full comprehension of what he has to do endeavours to set the indwelling life free from the veils that hide, and from the sheaths that imprison, he discovers that the method whereby this is accomplished is by the subjective life of occult meditation, and the objective life of service. In service is renunciation, and, under the occult law, therefore, in service the subjective finds liberation, and is set free from objective manifestation. Think this out, for it has much hidden under the veil of words.

The occult student, therefore, from the standpoint of colour has two things to do in meditation.

1. To discover his three major colours as manifested in the Personality, the Ego, and the Monad.

2. To resolve then the lower quaternary into the three, the first stage of which is consciously to withdraw into the Ego and so atrophy the lower self. The student begins by eliminating the colours that are not desirable, killing out all low or coarse vibration and eventually so

refining his vehicles that the three major colours—of which he is the expression—shine out with perfect clarity. This leads him up to the third initiation. After that, he seeks to resolve the three into the one until he has withdrawn all his consciousness from the lower vehicles into the monadic sheath.

It was not my intention, as you erroneously supposed, to give you information as to the effect of colours playing on the bodies in meditation. I have sought only to give you some idea of colour as a veil that must eventually be set aside. Under the heading of the "Future use of colour," I may touch upon that which interests you, but to understand fundamentals is far better than to have formulas for experimenting given to you.

September 10th, 1920.

We will, today, scarcely do more than touch upon our second point, which is the application of colour for healing purposes, the reason for this brevity being that the subject, in order to be handled correctly and therefore safely, should be dealt with at length, and the old adage will consequently prove true in this connection that "a little knowledge is a dangerous thing". Unless the matter of healing with colour is dealt with in correct fashion and with technical knowledge and at length, the results achieved might prove more disastrous than beneficent. The subject will later be fully eluciated if the future brings that which is intended, and in the meantime I can, for your information, outline certain features of this work, point out certain conditions incident to success, and foretell for you somewhat the trend the matter will probably take.

Application of colour in healing.

We are dealing with the subject now from the standpoint of meditation. It is essential therefore that we consider the subject from that angle. In meditation the work of healing is handled entirely from the mental standpoint. The direction of any force supplied will be from the mental body of the patient and will work from thence to the physical via the emotional.

This involves on the part of the person or group that undertakes this work the ascertaining of certain facts. Let us briefly enumerate them in order to clarify the mind of the reader:—

1. The work will be largely subjective and will deal with causes and not with effects. The primary aim of the healing group will be to discover the originating cause of the trouble and having located that cause in either the emotional or the mental body the members of the group will then proceed to deal with the effect as demonstrated in the physical or the etheric. Should the trouble be entirely physical, such as is the case in an accident of any kind, or in some affliction which is purely the result of heredity or of congenital trouble, the ordinary high class physical plane scientific methods will be applied at first, and the work of the healers will be to aid those methods through concentration on the subtler bodies. This applies during the transition period into which the race is now entering. Later, when the knowledge of occult healing is more familiar, and the laws which govern the subtle bodies are more known, physical plane science will be superseded by the preventive science of the subtler planes, that science which aims at the provision of right conditions and the building of bodies that are both self-protecting and neutral to all attack. It will be found that the comprehension

of the law of vibration, and the effect of one vibration upon another vibration holds the key to the establishing of better conditions of living, and of sound bodies on all planes.

But as things are now, disease, corruption of different kinds and trouble in all the bodies is everywhere contacted, and when conditions are thus recognised, means of aiding must be earnestly sought. This leads us on to our next point:

2. The ascertaining by the group that practises healing of full information as to the patient, based on the following questions:—

a. What are his basic lines of thought?
By what thoughtforms is he principally surrounded?

b. What is the predominant hue of his emotional body? What is its rate of vibration?
Is the patient subject to sudden turmoils that throw the entire emotional body into disorder?

c. What are his most ordinary topics of conversation? What are his principal interests?
What literature does he study?
What are his favourite pursuits?

d. What is the condition of the centres in his body?
Which centres are awakened?
Are any centres rotating in fourth dimensional order? Which centre is the major one in any particular case?

e. What is the state of the etheric body?
Does it show symptoms of devitalisation or of congestion?
Is the patient lacking in vitality?
What is the value of his magnetic action on other people?

Having studied the patient from all these angles, and not at any earlier time, will the group who purpose healing study the physical vehicle itself in detail. Then—with some idea of the inner conditions that underly the trouble —they will study as follows:—

f. The condition of the nervous system, giving particular attention to the spine, and to the state of the inner fire.

g. The state of the various organs of the body, and especially the organ, or organs, that are causing distress.

h. The structure itself, studying the bones and the flesh, and the condition of the vital fluid, the blood.

Higher vision and health.

This, as you can see, necessarily involves either direct scientific knowledge, or else it involves the faculty of inner vision, that *sees* the trouble wherever it may be, and can clairvoyantly view the entire frame and organs, so locating instantaneously any trouble. This capacity presupposes the development of those inner powers which give knowledge in the three worlds, and so obviates the disastrous mistakes that so oft eventuate in the modern practice of medicine, as you call the art of healing. There will not be so much danger of error in the future day of healing, but what I seek to point out is that although those errors will be obviated in the case of the physical body, yet much time must elapse before full comprehension of the emotional body has reached the point where modern science has placed the physical. The healing of the physical body and its due comprehension and study can be carried on by the man who has the inner vision. With his ability to see on emotional levels he can co-operate with the modern enlightened medical man, and thus safeguard him from error, enabling him to judge truly of the extent of the trouble, the seat of distress, its assistance, and the progress of the cure.

Emotional trouble that is working out in the physical body, as is the case in the majority of physical ills today, can usually be located and eliminated by judicious treatment. But emotional trouble that is deepseated in the subtle body, has to be dealt with from mental levels, so that it requires a mental psychic to deal with and eliminate it. All these methods of course entail *the active conscious co-operation of the patient himself.*

Similarly, mental trouble has to be dealt with directly from the causal level, and necessitates therefore the assistance of the Ego, and the help of someone who has causal vision and consciousness. This latter method, and the major part of these types of trouble, lie far ahead for the race, and therefore little concern us at this time. Nevertheless the curing of physical ailments that have their seat in the emotional body is already beginning to be known and slightly studied. In the study of psychology and in the comprehension of nervous diseases and troubles and their linking together will come the next step ahead in medical science. The link between the body of the emotions and physical body is the etheric body. The next immediate step is to consider the etheric body in two ways, either as a transmitter of prana, the life force, vitality or magnetism, or as the vehicle which links the emotional nature to the dense physical. The physical invariably follows the behests of that nature as transmitted via the etheric.

In forming groups for healing under ideal conditions you would have at the head of the group a person with causal consciousness, who can deal with any trouble in the mental body, and who can study the alignment of all the bodies with the Ego. The group will also include:—

   a. A person, or persons who can clairvoyantly view the subtle body of the emotions.

   b. A number of people who know somewhat the rudiments of the law of vibration, and can definitely, by the power of thought, apply certain waves of colour to effect certain cures, and bring about, through scientific comprehension, the desired results.

   c. Some member of the group will also be a member of the medical profession, who will work with the physical body, under the direction of *conscious* clairvoyants. He will study the resistance of the body, he will apply certain currents, and colours, and vibrations, which will have a direct physical effect, and by the co-operation of all those units in the group, results will be achieved that will merit the name of miracles.

   d. In the group, also, will be a number of people who can meditate occultly, and can, by the power of their meditation, create the necessary funnel for the transmission of the healing forces of the higher self and of the Master.

   e. Besides this, in each group will be found some person who can *accurately* transcribe all that takes place, and so keep records that will prove to be the literature of the new school of medicine.

I have here touched on the ideal group. It is not as yet in any way possible, but a beginning can be made by the utilisation of any knowledge and powers that may be found amongst those who seek to serve their race and the Master.

As you will note from the above, colours will be applied in two ways:—

1. On the subtler planes by the power of thought, and

2. By means of coloured lights applied to the physical body.

On the physical plane the exoteric colour will be applied, whilst on the subtler the esoteric. The work therefore will be (until the esoteric becomes the exoteric) largely in the hands of the occult students of the world, working in organised groups under expert supervision.

You ask, just what is the point at which these groups may now begin to work with colour? The thing that now lies ahead to be mastered and done is to develop the knowledge necessary anent the etheric, to inculcate the building of pure bodies, and to study the effect of different colours on the dense physical. It has been but little studied as yet. It will be found that certain colours will definitely affect certain diseases, cure certain nervous troubles, eradicate certain nervous tendencies, tend to the building of new tissues, or to the burning out of corruption. All this must be studied. Experiments can be made along the line of vitalisation and magnetisation, which involve direct action on the etheric, and this again will be found hid in the law of vibration and of colour. Later....... we can take up with greater detail the work of these healing groups, when gathered for meditation. Here I would but add that certain colours have a definite effect, though I can only as yet enumerate three, and them but briefly :—

1. *Orange* stimulates the action of the etheric body; it removes congestion and increases the flow of prana.

2. *Rose* acts upon the nervous system and tends to vitalisation, and to the removal of depression, and

symptoms of debilitation; it increases the *will to live*.

3. *Green* has a general healing effect, and can be safely used in cases of inflammation and of fever, but it is almost impossible as yet to provide the right conditions for the application of this colour, or to arrive at the adequate shade. It is one of the basic colours to be used eventually in the healing of the dense physical body, being the colour of the note of Nature.

This seems to you sketchy and inadequate? So it is, even more so than you can grasp. But forget not that which I have often told you, that in the following up of brief hints lies the path that leads to the source of all knowledge.

September 11, 1920.

We come now to the final part of our thoughts on the use of colour in meditation. We have dealt with the matter in such a way that if the hints that are scattered throughout the communication are adequately followed up they will form the basis of certain inevitable conclusions. These conclusions will eventually prove to be the postulates upon which the newer schools of medicine or science will base the continuance of their work. We might sum up the imparted data under definite statements:—

1. That the basic colours of the Personality must be transmuted into the colours of the Triad, or the threefold Spirit. This is effected by the truly occult meditation.

2. That the colours with which the beginner will be primarily concerned are orange, rose and green.

3. That the violet ray holds the secret for this immediate cycle.

4. That the next point of apprehended knowledge will be the laws governing the etheric body.
5. That in the development of the intuition comes cognisance of the esoteric colours which the exoteric veil.
6. That colour is the form and force of virtue (in the occult sense) in the inner life.

I have summed up the practical points requiring immediate attention for the purposes of clarification. With this as the basis of study the student may expect eventually to see the complete transformation of the type of work done both by the schools of medicine and by chairs of psychology. Certain prophecies I may here make which you can note down for the benefit of those who may come after.

Forecasts anent the future.

1. The phraseology of the medical schools will more and more become based on vibration and be expressed in terms of sound and colour.
2. The religious teaching of the world and the inculcation of virtue will be likewise imparted in terms of colour. People will eventually be grouped under their ray-colour, and this will be possible as the human race develops the faculty of seeing auras. The number of clairvoyants is already greater than is realised, owing to the reticence of the true psychic.
3. The science of numbers, being in reality the science of colour and sound, will also somewhat change its phraseology and colours will eventually supersede figures.
4. The laws that govern the erection of large buildings and the handling of great weights will some

day be understood in terms of sound. The cycle returns, and in the days to come will be seen the re-appearance of the faculty of the Lemurians and early Atlanteans to raise great masses,—this time on a higher turn of the spiral. Mental comprehension of the method will be developed. They were raised through the ability of the early builders to create a vacuum through sound, and to utilise it for their own purposes.

5. Destruction, it will be shewn, can be brought about by the manipulation of certain colours, and by the employment of united sound. In this way terrific effects will be achieved. Colour can destroy just as it can heal; sound can disrupt just as it can bring about cohesion; in these two thoughts lie hid the next step ahead for the science of the immediate future. The laws of vibration are going to be widely studied and comprehended and the use of this knowledge of vibration on the physical planes will bring about many interesting developments. They will be partially an outgrowth of the study of the war and its effect, psychological and otherwise. More was effected by the sound of the great guns, for instance, than by the impact of the projectile on the physical plane. These effects are as yet practically unrecognised, and are largely etheric and astral.

6. Music will be largely employed in construction, and in one hundred years from now it will be a feature in certain work of a constructive nature. This sounds to you utterly impossible, but it will simply be the utilisation of ordered sound to achieve certain ends.

You will ask, what place has all this in a series of letters on meditation? Simply this:—that the method employed in the utilisation of colour and sound in healing, in promoting spiritual growth, and in exoteric construction on the physical plane, will be based on the laws that govern the mental body, and will be forms of meditation. Only as the race develops the dynamic powers and attributes of thought—which powers are the product of meditation, rightly pursued—will the capacity to make use of the laws of vibration be objectively possible. Think not that only the religious devotee or mystic, or the man imbued with what we call higher teaching, is the exponent of the powers attained by meditation. All great capitalists, and the supreme heads of finance, or organised business, are the exponents of similar powers. They are personifications of one-pointed adherence to one line of thought, and their evolution parallels that of the mystic and the occultist. I seek most strongly to emphasise this fact. *They are the ones who meditate along the line of the Mahachohan, or the Lord of Civilisation or Culture.* Supreme concentrated attention to the matter in hand makes them what they are, and in many respects they attain greater results than many a student of meditation. All they need to do is to transmute the motive underlying their work, and their achievement will then outrun that of other students. They will approach a point of synthesis, and the Probationary Path will then be trodden.

The Law of Vibration will gradually, therefore, be more and more understood, and be seen to govern action in all of the three departments of the Manu, the World-Teacher and the Mahachohan. It will find its basic expression and its familiar terminology in those of colour and sound. Emotional disorder will be regarded as discordant sound; mental lethargy will be expressed in terms of *low* vibration, and physical disease will be numerically considered. All constructive work will eventually be expressed in terms of numbers, by colours, and through sound.

This suffices on this matter and at this juncture I have nought further to communicate. The subject is abstruse and difficult, and only by patient brooding will the darkness lighten. Only when the ray of the intuition strikes athwart the pall of darkness (which pall is the ignorance that hides all knowledge) will the forms that veil the subjective life be irradiated and known. Only when the light of reason is dimmed by the radiant sun of wisdom will all things be seen in their just proportions, and will the forms assume their exact colours, and their numerical vibration be known.

LETTER VIII.

ACCESS TO THE MASTERS VIA MEDITATION.

1. Who are the Masters?
2. What access to a Master entails:—
    a. From the standpoint of the pupil?
    b. From the standpoint of the Master?
3. Methods of approach to the Master in meditation.
4. The effect of this access on the three planes.

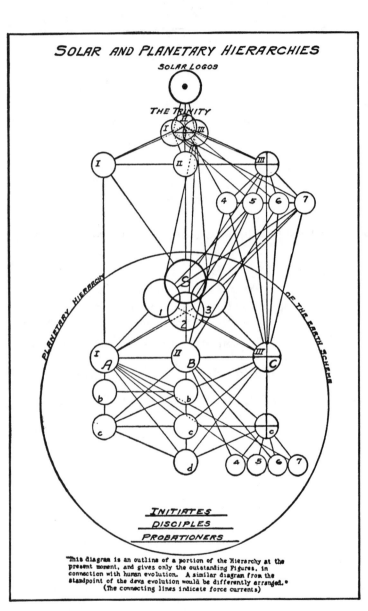

SOLAR AND PLANETARY HIERARCHIES

SOLAR LOGOS

THE TRINITY

PLANETARY HIERARCHY

OF THE EARTH SCHEME

INITIATES

DISCIPLES

PROBATIONERS

"This diagram is an outline of a portion of the Hierarchy at the
present moment, and gives only the outstanding Figures, in
connection with human evolution. A similar diagram from the
standpoint of the deva evolution would be differently arranged."
(The connecting lines indicate force currents)

KEY TO DIAGRAM OF SOLAR AND PLANETARY HIERARCHIES
THE SOLAR HIERARCHY

The Solar Logos.

The Solar Trinity or Logoi

I The Father ....Will.
II The Son ....Love-Wisdom.
III The Holy Spirit....Active Intelligence.

The Seven Rays

Three Rays of Aspect.
Four Rays of Attribute.

1. Will or Power	II. Love-Wisdom	III. Active Intelligence
		4. Harmony or Beauty.
		5. Concrete Knowledge.
		6. Devotion or Idealism.
		7. Ceremonial Magic.

THE PLANETARY HIERARCHY

S. Sanat Kumara, the Lord of the World.
(The Ancient of Days.
The One Initiator).

The Three Kumaras.
(The Buddhas of Activity).
1 2 3

The Reflections of the 3 Major and 4 Minor Rays

The 3 Departmental Heads.

I. *The Will Aspect*	II. *The Love-Wisdom Aspect.*	III. *Intelligence Aspect*
A. The Manu.	B. The Bodhisattva. (The Christ. The World Teacher)	C. The Mahachohan. (Lord of Civilisation)
b. Master Jupiter.	b. A European Master.	
c. Master M—	c. Master K.H.	c. The Venetian Master.
	d. Master D.K.	4. The Master Serapis.
		5. Master Hilarion.
		6. Master Jesus.
		7. Master R—.

Four grades of initiates.

Various grades of disciples.

People on the Probationary Path.

Average humanity of all degrees.

LETTER VIII.

ACCESS TO THE MASTERS VIA MEDITATION.

September 12th, 1920.

The search for the goal.

Today it may be possible to touch somewhat upon the subject of the Masters and how They may be approached through meditation. This I know is a subject close and dear to your heart, as it is to the heart of all those who earnestly follow the light within. I seek to handle this subject with you in such a way that at the close of this letter the Masters will be more real to you than ever before; the significance of approach to Them be better comprehended and the method more simplified; and the effect of contact with Them will be so demonstrated in the life that its immediate and practical attainment will be earnestly pursued. Let us, therefore, as we have always done, divide our subject into certain heads and divisions:—

1. Who are the Masters?
2. What does access to Them entail:—
    a. From the standpoint of the pupil?
    b. From the standpoint of the Master?
3. Methods of approach to the Masters through meditation.
4. The effect of this access on the three planes.

Everywhere throughout the whole world is felt the urge that drives a man to seek out someone who, for him, embodies the ideal. Even those who do not admit the existence of the Masters seek some ideal, and then visualise that ideal as embodied in some form on the physical plane. They picture themselves, perhaps, as the exponents of ideal action, or visualise some great philanthropist, some superlative scientist, some notable artist or musician, as embodying their supreme conception. The human being,—simply because he is himself fragmentary and incomplete—has always this urge within himself to seek other and greater than himself. It is this that drives him back to the centre of his being, and it is this that forces him to take the path of return to the All-Self. Ever, throughout the aeons, does the Prodigal Son arise and go to his Father, and always latent within him is the memory of the Father's home and the glory there to be found. But the human mind is so constituted that the search for light and for the ideal is necessarily long and difficult. "Now we see through a glass darkly, but then face to face"; now we catch glimpses through the occasional windows we pass in our ascension of the ladder, of other and greater Beings than ourselves; They hold out to us helping hands, and call to us in clarion tones to struggle bravely on if we hope to stand where They are now standing.

We sense beauties and glories surrounding us that as yet we cannot revel in; they flit into our vision, and we touch the glory at a lofty moment only again to lose the contact and to sink back again into the murky gloom that envelopes. But we *know* that outside and further on is something to be desired; we learn also the mystery that that external wonder can only be contacted by withdrawing within, till the centre of consciousness is found that vibrates in tune with those dimly realised wonders, and with those radiant Souls Who call Themselves our Elder Brothers. Only by trampling on the external sheaths that veil and hide the inner centre do we achieve the goal, and find the Ones we seek. Only by the domination of all forms, and the bringing of those forms under the rule of the God within, can we find the God in all, for it is only the sheaths in which we move upon the plane of being that hide from us our inner God, and that shut us off from Those in Whom the God transcends all outer forms.

The great Initiate, Who voiced the words I quote, added still other words of radiant truth: "Then shall we know even as we are known." The future holds for each and all who duly strive, who unselfishly serve and occultly meditate, the promise of knowing Those Who already have full knowledge of the struggler. Therein lies the hope for the student of meditation; as he struggles, as he fails, as he perseveres, and as he laboriously reiterates from day to day the arduous task of concentration and of mind control, there stand on the inner side Those Who know him, and Who watch with eager sympathy the progress that he makes.

Forget not the earlier part of the Initiate's remarks where he points out the way whereby the darkness is dispelled, and knowledge of the Great Ones is reached. He emphasises that only by *love* is the path of light and knowledge trodden. Why this emphasis upon love? Because the goal for all is love, and therein lies the merging. To put scientifically what is oft a nebulous sentiment, we might express it as follows:—It is by the attainment of the vibration which is analogous to the Ray of Love-Wisdom (the Divine Ray) that the Lords of Love are contacted, that the Masters of Compassion are known, and that the possibility of entering into the consciousnesses of the Great Ones and of all our brothers of whatsoever degree, becomes a fact in manifestation.

This is the path to be trodden by one and all, and the method is meditation. The goal is perfect love and wisdom; the steps are the surmounting of subplane after subplane on all the three planes; the method is that of occult meditation; the reward is the continuous expansion of consciousnes that puts a man eventually en rapport with his own Ego, with other selves, with the waiting eager Master to Whom he is assigned, with fellow disciples and more advanced Initiates whom he may contact in that Master's aura, till he finally contacts the One Initiator, is admitted into the Secret Place, and knows the mystery that underlies consciousness itself.

September 14th, 1920.

Who are the Masters?

It might be of value to us in our consideration of the subject of access to the Masters via meditation if we started with a few fundamental statements, dealing with the Masters and Their place in evolution. We will therefore take up our first point. We shall thus bring before the readers of these letters some idea as to Their status, Their comprehensive development, and Their methods of work. Needless to say, much that will follow will carry nothing new in import. The things that concern us most closely and the things that are to us the most familiar are oft the most frequently overlooked, and the most nebulous to our reasoning faculty.

A Master of the Wisdom is One Who has undergone the fifth initiation. That really means that His consciousness has undergone such an expansion that it now includes the fifth or spiritual kingdom. He has worked His way through the four lower kingdoms:—the mineral, the vegetable, the animal and the human—and has, through meditation and service, expanded His centre of consciousness till it now includes the plane of spirit.

A Master of the Wisdom is One Who has effected the transfer of polarisation from the three atoms of the personal life—as included in the causal body—into the three atoms of the Spiritual Triad. He is consciously spirit-intuition-abstract mind, or atma-buddhi-manas, and this is not potentially but in full effective power, realised through experience. This has been brought about, as earlier said, through the process of meditation.

A Master of the Wisdom is One Who has found not only the chord of the Ego, but the full chord of the Monad, and can ring the changes therefore at will upon all the notes from the lowest to that of the monadic. This means occultly that He has now developed the creative faculty, and can sound the note for each plane and build thereon. This power—first to discover the notes of the monadic chord and secondly to use those notes in constructive building—is first realised through meditation occultly performed, balanced by service lovingly administered.

A Master of the Wisdom is He Who can wield the law in the three worlds and can dominate all that evolves on those planes. By learning the laws of mind through the practice of meditation, He expands the laws of mind till they embrace the laws of the Universal Mind as demonstrated in lower manifestation. The Laws of Mind are mastered in meditation. They are applied in the life of service which is the logical outcome of true knowledge.

A Master of the Wisdom is He Who has passed out of the Hall of Learning into the Hall of Wisdom. He has there graduated through its five grades and has transmuted lower mind into mind pure and unalloyed, has transmuted desire into intuition, and has irradiated His consciousness with the light of pure Spirit. The discipline of meditation is the only way in which this can be accomplished.

A Master of the Wisdom is He Who, through knowledge acquired by means of the five senses, has learnt that synthesis exists and has merged those five senses into the synthetic two, that mark the point of attainment in the solar system. Through meditation the geometrical sense of proportion is adjusted, the sense of values is clearly recognised, and through that adjustment and recognition, illusion is dispelled and reality is known. The practice of meditation and the inner concentration there brought about awakens the consciousness to the value and true use of form. Thereby reality is contacted and the three worlds can no more ensnare.

A Master of the Wisdom is He Who knows the meaning of consciousness, of life, and of spirit. He can pass—by the line of least resistance—straight to the "bosom of His Father in Heaven". The approach to the line of least resistance, the direct path, is found through the practice of meditation.

A Master of the Wisdom is He Who has resolved Himself from the five into the three, and from the three into the two. He has become the five-pointed star, and when that moment is reached He sees that star flash out above the One Initiator, and recognises it in those of equal place to His. He has sanctified (in the occult sense) the Quaternary, has used it as the foundation stone upon which to erect the Temple of Solomon. He has grown beyond that Temple itself and has come to recognise it as limitation. He has withdrawn Himself from its confining walls and has entered within the Triad. He has done this always by the occult method, that is, consciously and with full knowledge of each step taken. He learns the meaning of each confining form; then, He has assumed control and wielded the law upon the plane consistent with the form. He has then outgrown the form and has discarded it for other and higher forms. Thus He has progressed always by means of the sacrifice and death of the form. Always it is recognised as imprisoning; always it must be sacrificed and must die so that the life within may speed ever on and up. The path of resurrection presupposes crucifixion and death, and then leads to the Mount whence Ascension may be made. In meditation the value of the life, and the confines of the form, can be appreciated and known, and by knowledge and service can the life be set free from all that limits and trammels.

A Master of the Wisdom is One Who has chosen to stay upon our planet to help His fellowmen. . . . All Who attain the fifth Initiation are Masters of the Wisdom, but all stay not and work as servers of the race. They pass to other work of greater or equal importance. To the general public the significance of the term lies in the thought that They choose to stay and limit Themselves for the sake of men who are pressing forward on the wave of evolution. Through meditation has the Great One reached His goal and (which is a thing not so oft comprehended) through meditation, or the manipulation of thought matter, and by work on the mental bodies of the race, is the work carried on that aids the evolutionary process.

A Master of the Wisdom is He Who has taken the first initiation that links Him up with the greater Brotherhood on Sirius. As afore I have told you, He is an Initiate of the First Degree in the greater Lodge. He has attained an expansion of consciousness that has admitted Him into touch with the solar system in many of its departments. Now He has ahead of Him a vast reach of expansions that will eventually take Him beyond systemic consciousness into something far greater and wider. He has to begin to learn the rudiments of that cosmic meditation that will admit Him into a Consciousness past our conceivable surmise.

A Master of the Wisdom is He Who can *consciously* function as part of the Heavenly Man to Whose Body He may belong. He understands the laws governing groups and group souls. He governs a group soul consciously Himself (a group on the path of return and formed of the lives of many sons of men) and He knows His place in the body systemic. He realises the centre in the Body of the Heavenly Man by means of which He and His group are kept in sympathetic vibration, and conducts His relationship with other groups in the same Body under certain definite laws. The value of meditation as a preparation for this activity will be realised by all thoughtful students, for meditation is the one means whereby the sense of separateness is transcended, and unity with one's kind occultly comprehended.

A Master of the Wisdom is He Who has entrusted to Him, by virtue of work accomplished, certain Words of Power. By means of these Words He wields the law over other evolutions than the human, and through them He co-operates with the activity aspect of the Logos. Thus He blends His consciousness with that of the third Logos. Through these Words He assists with the building work, and the cohesive manipulating endeavor of the second Logos, and comprehends the inner working of the law of gravitation (or attraction and repulsion) that governs all the functions of the second aspect logoic. Through these Words He co-operates with the work of the first Logos, and learns, as He takes the sixth and seventh Initiations (which is not always done) the meaning of Will as applied in the system. These Words are imparted orally, and through clairvoyant faculty but must be found by the Initiate Himself, by the use of atma and as He attains atmic consciousness. . . . When atmic consciousness is developing by means of the intuition, the

Initiate can contact the stores of knowledge inherent in the Monad, and thus learn the Words of Power. This ability comes only after the application of the Rod of Initiation as wielded by the Lord of the World. Therefore by the higher stages of occult meditation does a Master of the Wisdom increase still further His knowledge. Not static is His consciousness, but daily embracing more. Daily does He apply Himself to further expansion.

A Master of the Wisdom is One Who has earned the right through similarity of vibration to work with the Heads of the Hierarchy of this planet, and in conjunction with analogous Heads on two other planets connected with our chain. When He has taken other initiations He can contact and work in conjunction with all the seven Planetary Logoi, and not just the three in control of allied chains. The whole system can be embraced by Him, and His consciousness has expanded to include the entire objective solar system.

I could enumerate still other definitions, and further elucidate the matter for you, but that imparted today suffices. The point reached by a Master is high, but only relatively so, and you must not forget that when attained by Him it seems low indeed, for He measures it up with the vista expanding before Him. Each expansion of consciousness, each step upon the ladder, but opens before the Initiate another sphere to be embraced, and another step ahead to be taken; each initiation achieved but reveals still higher ones to be mastered, and never comes the point where the aspirant (be he an average man, an initiate, a Master, a Chohan, or a Buddha) can remain in a condition static, and is incapable of future progress. Even the Logos Himself aspires, and even the One to Whom He aspires reaches up to a Greater.

What happens in the system transpires likewise on cosmic levels, and what is mastered here must be repeated on a vaster scale in the cosmos itself. In this thought lies inspiration and development and not despair or weariness. The reward that comes with each step forward, the delight that lies in increased comprehension, rewards the struggling aspirant in adequate fashion. . . . Tomorrow we will deal with the more practical side, that of the man who aims at this high calling.

September 16th, 1920.

What access to the Master entails.

We deal today with the second point in our eighth letter, and we have to look at the subject in two ways, briefly from the standpoint of the Master, and rather lengthily from the viewpoint of the pupil.

We have in these letters given a broad outline of the magnitude of the task that lies ahead of the man who proposes to attain. Much that has been written has no interest for the man who is only of average development, but chiefly concerns the man who has reached a specific point in evolution, and stands upon the Path of Probation. Much that might be said upon this matter has been covered in that earlier series I communicated to you. I seek not to cover the same ground here, but to deal more specifically with the internal relationship which exists between Master and pupil.

That relationship exists in four grades, in each of which a man progresses nearer to his Master. These four grades are as follows and cover the period wherein the man is under training until the time when he himself becomes an adept.
They are:—

a. The period wherein he is on probation.

  b. The period wherein he is an accepted disciple.
  c. The period wherein he is regarded as the Master's
      intimate, or—as it is esoterically termed—the
      "Son of the Master."
  d. The period wherein the final three initiations are
      taken, and he knows himself as one with the
      Master. He ranks then as the "Beloved of the
      Master," a position analogous to that which
      John, the beloved disciple, held in the Bible story.
All these stages are governed by two things:—
  a. Similarity of vibration.
  b. Karma,
and all are involved in the ability of the man to develop
group consciousness.

On the planes of the higher mind, on the second subplane you have a reflection of what can be seen on the
highest planes of our solar system. What have you there?
The seven Heavenly Men are there to be found, each of
Whom is composed (from the standpoint of form) of
group souls,—those group souls being made up of the individual human and angel units of consciousness. On the
second subplane of the mental plane you have the groups
belonging to the Masters, if so I may express it. These
groups are animated and vitalised from the atomic subplane where the Masters (when manifesting for the helping of the sons of men) have Their habitat,* just as the
Heavenly Men have Their originating source and the
cause of Their life on the atomic plane of the solar system, that which we call the plane of adi, or the first plane.
These groups are formed around a Master, are enclosed
within His aura, and are a part of His consciousness.
They include people whose egoic ray is the same as His,
or whose monadic ray is the same.

---

* Since 1920, great changes have occurred. Now (1949) there has been
a shift to the Buddhic Plane. (A. A. B.)

This means that two types of people are concerned:—

1. Those who are preparing for the first and second initiations, taken upon the ray of the Ego, and
2. Those who are preparing for the two next initiations, which are taken upon the ray of the Monad. You have here a cause of the transference of people from one ray to another. It is only an apparent transference, even though it entails passing into the group of a different Master. This takes place after the second initiation.

A Probationer's three objects.

During the period wherein a man is under probation, he is supposed to be developing three things:—

1. The ability to contact his group, or in other words, to be sensible of the vibration of the group of which some particular Master is the focal point. He contacts it at times and at rare intervals at first. During the early part of his probation, whilst he is under observation, he can only sense and hold the group vibration (which is the Master's vibration) for a very brief interval. He will at some high moment link up with the Master and with the group, and his whole being will be flooded with that high vibration, and surge upward in an outburst of his group colour. Then he will relax, drop back and lose the contact. His bodies are not refined enough and his vibration is too unstable to hold it long.

But, as time progresses (longer or shorter according to the earnestness of the pupil) the frequency of the times of contact increases; he can hold the vibration somewhat longer, and does not relax back to normal with so much ease. Then the time comes when he can be trusted to hold the contact fairly stably. He passes then to the second stage.

2. The second thing he is supposed to be developing on the probationary path is the faculty of abstract thought, or the power to link up with the higher mind, via the causal body. He must learn to contact the lower mind simply as an instrument whereby he can reach the higher, and thus transcend it, until he becomes polarised in the causal body. Then, through the medium of the causal body, he links up with the abstract levels. Until he can do this he cannot really contact the Master, for, as you have been told, the pupil has to raise himself from his world (the lower) into Their world (the higher).

Now both these things—the power to touch the Master and the Master's group, and the power to polarise himself in the causal body and touch the abstract levels—are definitely the result of meditation, and the earlier letters you have received from me will have made this clear. There is therefore no need to recapitulate the earlier imparted data, save to point out that by strenuous meditation, and the faculty of one-pointed application to the duty in hand (which is after all the fruit of meditation worked out in daily living) will come the increased faculty to hold steadily the higher vibration. Again and again would I reiterate the apparently simple truth, that *only similarity of vibration* will draw a man to the higher group to which he may belong, to the Master Who represents to him the Lord of His Ray, to the World Teacher Who administers to him the mysteries, to the One Initiator Who effects the final liberation, and to the centre within the Heavenly Man in Whose Body he finds a place. It is the working out of the Law of Attraction and Repulsion on all the planes that gathers the life divine out of the mineral kingdom, out of the vegetable and animal kingdoms, that draws the latent Deity from out of the limitations of the human kingdom, and affiliates the man with his divine group. The same law effects his liberation from subtler forms that likewise bind, and blends him back into his animating source, the Lord of the Ray in Whose Body his Monad may be found. Therefore the work of the probationer is to attune his vibration to that of his Master, to purify his three lower bodies so that they form no hindrance to that contact, and so to dominate his lower mind that it is no longer a barrier to the downflow of light from the threefold Spirit. Thus he is permitted to touch that Triad and the group on the subplane of the higher mental to which he—by right and karma—belongs. All this is brought about by meditation, and there is no other means for achieving these aims.

3. The third thing the probationer has to do is to equip himself emotionally and mentally, and to realise and prove that he has somewhat to impart to the group with which he is esoterically affiliated. Think upon this: too much emphasis is laid at times upon that which the pupil *will get* when he becomes an accepted disciple or probationer. I tell you here, in all earnestness, that he will not take these desired steps until he has somewhat *to give,* and something to add that will increase the beauty of the group, that will add to the available equipment that the Master seeks for the helping of the race, and that will increase the richness of the group colouring. This can be brought about in two ways that mutually interact:—

a. By the definite equipping, through study and application, of the content of the emotional and mental bodies.

b. By the utilisation of that equipment in service to the race on the physical plane, thereby demonstrating to the eyes of the watching Hierarchy that the pupil has somewhat to *give.* He must show that his one desire is to be a benefactor and to serve, rather than to grasp and acquire for himself. This life of acquisition for the purposes of giving must have for incentive the ideals touched in meditation, and for inspiration those downpourings from the higher mental levels and from the buddhic levels which are the result of occult meditation.

When these three results are brought about, and when the high vibration touched is more frequent and stable, then the probationer takes the next step forward and becomes an accepted disciple.

Accepted Discipleship.

The second period, wherein a man is an accepted disciple, is perhaps one of the most difficult in a man's whole period of lives. It is made so in several ways:—

He is definitely a part of the Master's group, and is within the consciousness of the Master at all times, being kept within His aura. This involves the steady holding of a high vibration. I would have you ponder on what the effect of this would be. To hold this vibration is at all times a difficult thing to do; it frequently involves an intensification of all that subsists within a man's nature, and may lead (especially at first) to curious demonstration. Yet, if ever a man is to be able to hold the force that is the result of the application of the Rod of Initiation, he has to demonstrate his ability to do so at an earlier stage, and be able to hold himself stably and to move steadily forward when subjected to the intensification of vibration that comes from the Master.

He has to discipline himself so that nothing can enter into *his* consciousness that could in any way harm the group to which he belongs, or be antagonistic to the Master's vibration. If I might so express it, so as to give you some conception of my meaning, when he first forms part of the group enclosed in the Master's aura, he is kept on the periphery of that aura until he has learnt to throw off automatically, and to reject immediately, every thought and desire unworthy of the Self and thus harmful to the group. Until he has learnt to do this he cannot advance into a closer relationship, but must remain where he can be automatically shut off. But gradually he purifies himself still more, gradually he develops group consciousness and thinks in group terms of service, gradually his aura takes on more and more the colouring of his Master's aura, till he *blends* and has earned the right to be gathered closer to his Master's Heart. Later I will explain the technical meaning of this phrase, when dealing with the work of the Master with the pupil. Suffice it to say, that as the term of "accepted disciple" progresses (and it varies in different cases) the disciple advances ever closer to the heart of the group, and finds his own place and functional activity in that body corporate. That is the secret: the finding of one's place,—not so much one's place upon the ladder of evolution (for that is approximately known), but in *service*. This is of more importance than is realised, for it covers the period which, at the end, will definitely demonstrate which path a man will follow after the fifth initiation.

Sonship to the Master.

We now come to the time when the disciple moves on to the much coveted position of a "Son of the Master." He is then a part *consciously* and at all times of the Master's consciousness. The interplay between the Master and disciple is being rapidly perfected, and the disciple can now consciously and at will link up with the Master and ascertain His thoughts. He can enter into His plans, de-

sires and will. This he has won by the right of similarity
of vibration, and because the shutting off process (necessitated earlier by discordant vibration) is practically
superseded; the disciple has so purified himself that his
thoughts and desires cause no disquietude to the Master,
and no contrary vibration to the group. He has been tried
and not been found wanting. His life of service in the
world is more concentrated and perfected, and he is daily
developing his power to give, and increasing his equipment. All this concerns his relationship to some Master
and to some one group soul. It is not dependent upon his
taking initiation. Initiation is a technical matter and can
be expressed in terms of esoteric science. A man can take
initiation and yet not be a "son of a Master." Discipleship is a personal relationship, governed by terms of
karma and affiliation, and is not dependent upon a man's
status in the Lodge. Keep this clear in your mind. Cases
have been known when a man has acquired—through diligence—the technical requisites for initiation before becoming affiliated with any particular Master.

This later relationship of "son" to some Master has
a peculiar sweetness all its own, and carries with it certain privileges. The disciple can then lift some of the bur-
den off his Master's shoulders, and relieve Him of some
of His responsibilities, thereby setting Him free for more
extended work. Hence the emphasis laid on *service, for it
is only as a man serves that he advances.* It is the key-
note of the vibration of the second abstract level. The
Master at this period will confer with His "Son" and plan
the work to be done upon their united point of view. In
this way He will develop His pupil's discrimination and
judgment, and lighten His own load along certain lines,
thus setting Himself free for other important work.

The final period of those under discussion can have but little submitted about it. It covers the period when a man is mastering the final stages of the Path and is entering into closer and closer touch with his group and with the Hierarchy. He is not only vibrating in tune with his group and with his Master, but is beginning now to gather out his own people, and form a group himself. This group will be at first only on emotional and physical levels and on the lower mental. After the fifth initiation he will enclose within his aura these groups and those on egoic levels who are his own. This in no way prevents his being one with his Master and group, but the method of interblending is one of the secrets of initiation.

All this, coupled with what has been earlier imparted, will give you some idea of the rights and powers acquired on the Probationary Path and on the Path of Initiation. The means of development are ever the same:—occult meditation and service; the inner life of concentration and the outer life of practice; the inner ability to contact the higher, and the outer ability to express that faculty in terms of holy living; the inner irradiation from the Spirit, and the outer shining before men.

September 17th, 1920.

...... The subject that we have for the past few days been studying, though not so technical as some of the earlier imparted data, yet carries with it a vibration that will make this eighth letter one of those with the most potent appeals in the series. We have dealt with the facts as to the Masters and Who They are, and Their place in the scheme of things, and we have touched briefly upon what access to a Master entails from the standpoint of a pupil. We have seen that that access is a gradual process and carries a man from an occasional outer contact with a Master and His group to a position of the closest intimacy, and to an attitude that places the pupil within the aura and close to the heart of his Teacher. Today we will consider for a while what this gradual changing of position has entailed on the part of the Master and what it has necessitated on His side.

The relationship of Master and pupil.

As you have frequently been told, the attention of a Master is attracted to a man by the brilliance of the indwelling light. When that light has reached a certain intensity, when the bodies are composed of a certain grade of matter, when the aura has attained a certain hue and when the vibration has reached a specific rate and measure, and when a man's life commences to *sound occultly* in the three worlds (which sound is to be heard through the life of service), some one particular Master begins to test him out by the application of some higher vibration, and by the study of his reaction to that vibration. The choice of a pupil by a Master is governed by past karma and by old association, by the ray on which they both may be found, and by the need of the hour. The Master's work (as much of it as may wisely be made exoteric) is varied and interesting, and is based on a scientific comprehension of human nature. What is it that a Master has to do with a pupil? By enumerating the chief things to be done we may get some idea of the scope of His work:—

He has to accustom the pupil to raise his rate of vibration till he can continuously carry a high one, and then assist him until that high vibration becomes the stable measure of the pupil's bodies.

He has to assist the pupil to effect the transfer of polarisation from the lower three atoms of the Personality to the higher ones of the Spiritual Triad.

He has to watch over the work accomplished by the pupil whilst making the channel between higher and lower mind, whilst he builds and employs this channel (the antahkarana). This channel eventually supersedes the causal body as a means of communication between the higher and the lower. The causal body is itself eventually done away with when the pupil takes the fourth initiation and can freely create his own body of manifestation.

He definitely assists at the vivification of the various centres and their correct awakening, and He later aids the pupil to work consciously through those centres, and to carry the circulating fire in right geometrical progression from the base of the spine to the head centre.

He superintends the work of the pupil on different planes and makes records of the extent of the work accomplished, and the far-reaching effect of the spoken word as enunciated by the pupil. This is (putting it occultly) the effect on the inner planes of the note of the pupil's exoteric life.

He enlarges the consciousness of the pupil in various ways, and develops his capacity to include and contact other rates of vibration than the human, to understand the consciousness of other evolutions than the human, and move with facility in other spheres than the earth sphere.

His immediate goal in working with the pupil is to prepare him for the first initiation. This takes place when the capacity of the pupil to hold a certain rate of vibration for a specific length of time is developed, the length of time being that wherein he must stand before the Lord of the first two initiations. This is accomplished by a gradual raising of the vibration at few and stated intervals, and later more frequently, until the pupil can vibrate with greater ease and comfort to the vibration of his Master, and can hold the vibration for an ever in-

creasing length of time. When he can hold it for this
period (the length of which is of course one of the secrets
of the first initiation) he is subjected to the application of
a still higher vibration which—when held—will enable
him to stand before the Great Lord for a length of time
sufficient to permit of the initiation ceremony. The application then of the Rod of Initiation effects something that
stabilises vibration, and makes it easier to progress in
the task of vibrating to the higher measure of the subtler
planes.

He develops the capacity of the pupil to work in
group formation. He studies his action and interaction
on his own affiliated group. He works with the pupil's
causal body and its expansion and development, and
teaches the pupil to understand the law of his own being
and through that understanding brings him to a comprehension of the macrocosm.

Now all these various aspects of the Master's work
(and these are but a few of the points which might be
considered) might be dealt with at length and would
prove of illuminating interest to the reader. All the above
paragraphs could be extended and prove of exceeding interest. But the main point I seek to make here is in connection with the earlier stages of this work, before the pupil is admitted into the later stages of close intimacy with
his Master. The Master during this period works with
his disciple principally:—

a. At night, when he is out of the physical body.
b. During the periods when the disciple is meditating.

According to the success of the meditation, according to
the ability of the student to shut off the lower and contact the higher, so will come the opportunity of the Master
to accomplish successfully the scientific definite work that

needs His attention. Students of meditation would be astounded and perhaps discouraged, could they realise how seldom they provide the right conditions through meditation which will enable their watching Teacher to bring about certain effects. By the frequency of the student's ability to do this comes indication of progress, and the possibility of carrying him on another step. Emphasise this point in teaching, for it carries with it an incentive to greater diligence and application. If the pupil himself on his side provides not the just conditions, the Master's hands are tied and He can do but little. *Self-effort is the key to progress, coupled to conscious comprehending application to the work laid down.* When that effort is made with perseverance, then comes the opportunity of the Master to carry out His side of the work.

As the pupil meditates with occult accuracy he brings his three lower bodies into alignment and—with emphasis I reiterate—only as alignment is effected is the Master able to work with the bodies of the pupil. If naught else is effected by the publication of these letters except the intensification of the desire to meditate with correctness, the object in view will be largely attained. In that effort the right conditions between pupil and Master, and a correct interrelation will be brought about. Meditation provides these conditions, when rightly followed. It prepares the field for labour and for work.

Let us briefly consider the various periods as enumerated yesterday when considering the pupil's relationship to a Master.

In the period when the man is under probation and supervision.........he is left almost entirely to himself and is only conscious of the attention of the Master at rare and irregular intervals. His physical brain is not often receptive to the higher contact, and though his Ego is fully aware of his position on the Path, not yet is the physical brain in a condition to know. But on this point no hard and fast rule can be laid down. When a man has been for several lives making contacts with his Ego or with his Master he may be aware of it. Individuals differ so much that no universal rule in detail can be formulated. As you know, the Master makes a small image of the probationer, which image is stored in certain subterranean centres in the Himalayas. The image is magnetically linked with the probationer, and shews all the fluctuations of his nature. Being composed of emotion and mental matter it pulsates with every vibration of those bodies. It shews their predominating hues, and by studying it the Master can rapidly gauge the progress made and judge when the probationer may be admitted into a closer relationship. The Master views the image at stated intervals, rarely at first, as the progress made in the beginning stages is not so rapid, but with ever increasing frequency as the student of meditation comprehends more readily and more consciously co-operates. The Master when inspecting the images works with them, and through their means effects certain results. Just as later the Rod of Initiation is applied to the bodies and centres of the initiate, so at certain times the Master applies certain contacts to the images and via them stimulates the bodies of the pupil.

A time comes when the Master sees, from His inspection of the image, that the needed rate of vibration can be held, that the required eliminations have been made, and a certain depth of colour attained. He can then take the risk (for risk it is) and admit the probationer within the periphery of His own aura. He becomes then an accepted disciple.

During the period wherein a man is an accepted disciple the work done by the Master is of very real interest. The pupil is assigned to special classes conducted by more advanced disciples under the supervision of the Master, and though he may attend still the larger general classes in the Ashram (the Master's hall for teaching) he is subjected to a more intensified training..........The Master works in the earlier stages in four main ways:—

a. At intervals, and when the progress of the pupil justifies it, He "gathers the pupil to His Heart." This is an esoteric statement of a very interesting experience to which the pupil will be subjected. At the close of some class in the ashram, or during some specially successful meditation wherein the pupil has reached a certain rate of vibration, the Master will gather him close to Himself, bringing him from the periphery of His aura to the centre of His consciousness. He thereby gives him a tremendous temporary expansion of consciousness, and enables him to vibrate at an unusual rate for him.

Hence the need for meditation. The reward of such an experience far outweighs any of the strenuous parts of the work.

b. The Master works upon the bodies of his pupil with colour, and brings about results in those bodies that enable the pupil to make more rapid progress. Now you will see why......so much emphasis is laid upon colour. It is not only because it holds the secret of form and manifestation (which secret must be known by the occultist) but the emphasis is laid thus in order that he may consciously co-operate in the work of the

Master on his bodies, and intelligently follow the effects brought about. Ponder on this.

c. At stated intervals the Master takes His pupils, and enables them to contact other evolutions, such as the great angels and devas, the lesser builders and the sub-human evolutions. This can be safely done by the pupil through the protective effect of the Master's aura. Later, when himself an initiate, the pupil will be taught how to protect himself and to make his own contacts.

d. The Master presides over the work of stimulating the centres in the pupil's bodies and the awakening of the inner fire. He teaches the pupil the meaning of the centres and their correct fourth dimensional rotation and in time He will bring the pupil to a point where he can consciously and with full knowledge of the law work with his centres, and bring them to a point where they can be safely stimulated by the Rod of Initiation. More on this subject is not yet possible.........

I have only touched in the briefest manner on a few of the things a Master has to do with His pupils. I take not up the later stages of the pupil's progress. We lead all on by gradual steps, and as yet even accepted disciples are rare. If by meditation, service, and the purifying of the bodies, those now on probation can be led to make more rapid progress, then will come the time for the communication of further information. What use is it to give facts of which the student cannot as yet make use? We waste not time in interesting intellectually those we seek to help. When the pupil has equipped himself, when he has purified himself and is vibrating adequately, naught can withhold all knowledge from him. When he opens the door and widens the channel, light and knowledge will pour in.

Tomorrow we will take up our third point, methods of approach to a Master via meditation; certain types of meditation will be slightly enlarged upon which will facilitate contact, but forget not that the life of objective service must keep pace with the subjective growth; only when the two are seen together and approved are the necessary steps for contact permitted. A Master is only interested in a man from the point of view of his usefulness in the group soul, and his capacity to *help*.

September 19th, 1920.

We can today take up our last two points practically simultaneously. They deal with methods of approach to the Masters and the objective effects on the three planes of human evolution. Some of the points touched upon are already well known. Others may not be so familiar to the general student.......In these letters we have dealt with the student himself and what he has to bring to the endeavour; we have indicated likewise his goal—and very sketchily—the forms and methods whereby success may be achieved. We have dealt also with those aids to meditation, the Sacred Word, Colour and Sound, and have indicated that which (brooded upon in silence) may lead to the student making some discoveries for himself. Lastly we have tried to bring the Masters and Their reality nearer to the student, and thereby facilitate his approach to Them.

What now remains to be done? To indicate five things that may be looked for with conviction by the student who has endeavoured to conform his life to the lines laid down by me in these letters. If the student but provides the right conditions, if he conforms to the necessary rules, if he aims always at regularity, at calmness, at that inner concentration that holds the mystery of the High Places, he will on certain occasions and with ever-increasing frequency awake to some definite realisations. These realisations will be the outer recognition of inner results, and will be the guarantee to him that he is on the right path. But I would here point out again that these results are only achieved after long practice, strenuous struggle, diligent disciplining of the threefold lower man, and consecrated service to the world.

Methods of approach and effects obtained.

The methods of approach are broadly three and we might indicate five results that will eventuate from the employment of these methods. The three methods are:—

1. Sanctified service.
2. Love demonstrating through wisdom.
3. Intellectual application.

They are all three but diverse methods of expressing one and the same thing,—active one-pointedness that expresses itself in service for the race through love and wisdom. But some individuals express this in one way and some in another; some carry the outer appearance of intellectuality and others of love, yet before the attainment is possible intellectuality must be based on love, whilst love without mental development and that discrimination that mind affords is apt to be unbalanced and unwise. Both love and mind must be expressed in terms of service before the full flower of either is attained. Let us consider each of these methods separately and indicate the meditation to be followed thereon:—

Sanctified Service. This is the method of the man who wields the law, the method of the occultist, and the rudiments of the method are laid down in raja-yoga

..............The word "sanctification," as you know, in the basic sense signifies the complete surrender of the whole being to one object, the Lord or Ruler. It means the giving wholly to the one the devotee aspires to. It means the consecration of the whole threefold man to the work in hand. It entails, therefore, the application of the entire time and self to the bringing of each body under the subjugation of the Ego, and the complete mastery of each plane and subplane. It involves the comprehension of each evolution and form of divine life as found on those planes and sub-planes, with one aim in view and only one—the furthering of the plan of the Hierarchy of Light. The method followed is that of the intensest application to the work of rounding out the bodies and of making them fit instruments for service. It is perhaps the hardest way that a man can tread. It leaves no department of the life untouched. All is brought under law. In meditation therefore the form of that meditation will be a threefold structure:—

a. The laws governing the physical body will be studied and brooded over. This brooding will find expression in a rigid disciplining of the physical body. It will be set apart wholly for service, and subjected consequently to a process that will attune and develop it more quickly.

b. The body of the emotions will be scientifically studied and the laws of *water* (occultly understood) will be comprehended. The significance of the term, "there shall be no more sea" will be known, and the sea of storm and passion will be superseded by the sea of glass, which directly reflects the higher intuition, and mirrors it with perfect accuracy, being unruffled and immovable. The emotional body will be set apart wholly for service, and its place in the threefold microcosm will be regarded as corresponding to that in the macrocosm, whilst the occult significance of its being the only complete unit in the threefold lower nature will be apprehended, and the fact made use of to effect certain results. Ponder on this.

c. The place of lower mind in the scheme of things will be studied, and the quality of discrimination developed. Discrimination and fire are occultly allied and just as the Logos by fire tries every man's work of what sort it is, so the microcosm on a lesser scale has to do the same. Just as the Logos likewise does this paramountly in the fifth round of judgment and of separation, so the microcosm on his lesser scale does the same in the last and fifth period of his evolution,—touched upon and described earlier in these letters. Every power of the mind will be utilised to the uttermost for the furtherance of the plans of evolution; first in the man's own development, then in the special field of work wherein he expresses himself, and lastly in his relationship with other units of the race, as he constitutes himself their guide and servant.

See you therefore the synthesis of it? First the strenuous one-pointedness that is the sign of the occultist blended with the wisdom and love which are reflected from the higher in the mirror of the emotional body, and then the intellect forced to act as the servant of the Ego through one-pointed effort animated by love and wisdom. The result will be the true Yogi.

I would point out here that the true Yogi is he who, after due carrying out of the set forms and times of meditation, merges that meditation in the everyday living, and will eventually be in the attitude of meditation all the day.

Meditation is the means whereby the higher consciousness is contacted. When the contact becomes continuous, meditation, as you understand it, is superseded. In this first method the occult student works from the periphery to the centre, from the objective to the subjective, from the form to the life within the form. Therefore through the emphasis laid in Raja Yoga on the physical body and its wise control the occultist realises the essential importance of the physical, and the uselessness of all his knowledge apart from a physical body whereby he can express himself and serve the race. It is the line of the first ray, and its affiliated or complementary ray.

Love and wisdom. This method is the line of least resistance for the sons of men. It is the sub-ray of the synthetic ray of an analogous vibration, of which our solar system is the objective manifestation. But I would seek to point out that the love achieved by the student of meditation who follows this line is not the sentimental conception that is so often discussed. It is not the non-discriminating love that sees no limitation, nor concedes a fault. It is not the love that seeks not to correct and that expresses itself in an ill advised attitude to all who live. It is not the love that sweeps all into service, suitable or unsuitable, and that recognises no difference in point of development. Much that is called love,—if logically followed out—would apparently dispense with the ladder of evolution, and rank all as of equal value. So potentially all are, but in present terms of service all are not.

True love or wisdom sees with perfect clarity the deficiencies of any form, and bends every effort to aid the indwelling life to liberate itself from trammels. It wisely recognises those that need help, and those that need not its attention. It hears with precision, and sees the thought of the heart and seeks ever to blend into one whole the workers in the field of the world. This it achieves not by blindness, but by discrimination and wisdom, separating contrary vibrations and placing them in position diverse. Too much emphasis has been laid on that called love (interpreted by man, according to his present place in evolution) and not enough has been placed on wisdom, which is love expressing itself in service, such a service that recognises the occult law, the significance of time, and the point achieved.

This is the line of the second ray and its affiliated and complementary rays. Later it is the all-inclusive one, and the solvent and absorber. It can be followed, being synthetic, on either the Raja Yoga line or the Christian Gnostic line, owing to its synthetic significance. . . .

Intellectual application. Here the order is reversed and the student, being frequently polarised in his mental body, has to learn through that mind to understand the other two, to dominate and control, and to utilise to the uttermost the powers inherent in the threefold man. The method here is perhaps not so hard in some ways, but the limitations of the fifth principle have to be transcended before real progress can be made. These limitations are largely crystallisation and that which you call pride. Both have to be broken before the student who progresses through intellectual application can serve his race with love and wisdom as the animating cause.

He has to learn the value of the emotions, and in so learning he has to master the effect of fire on water, occultly understood. He has to learn the secret of that plane, which secret (when known) gives him the key to the downpour of illumination from the Triad via the causal and thence to the astral. It holds the key also of the fourth etheric level. This will not as yet be comprehended by you, but the above hint holds for the student much of value.

This is the line of the third ray, and of its four subsidiary rays, and is one of great activity, of frequent transference, and of much mental display in the lower worlds.

Only when the student, who progresses by intellectual application, has learned the secret of the fifth plane, will he live the life of sanctified service, and so blend the three rays. Always synthesis must be attained, but always the fundamental colouring or tone remains. The next or fifth round will show the greatest exposition of this method. It will be the round of supreme mental development, and will carry its evolving Monads to heights undreamed of now.

This round marks the height of the second method, that through love or wisdom. It is the fourth round, that wherein the emotional reaches a high point of vibration, and there is direct connection between the fourth plane of harmony, between the emotional body, or the fourth principle, the quaternary, the fourth root-race or the Atlantean which co-ordinated the astral. I give you food for thought in these correspondences.

September 21st, 1920.

Five effects of Meditation in the three worlds.

Today we are to take up the five effects in the three bodies in the lower worlds that the student of meditation will be conscious of if he has duly followed the course laid down.

These effects are not specifically effects in the life as apparent to the onlooking world, such as greater love or spirituality or capacity to serve. What I seek today to bring out are the indications in the *physical brain consciousness* of the student that he *has* done some of the necessary work and is attaining somewhat the desired object. Keep this very clearly in mind. I do *not* seek to make clear all the many and various results achieved by the successful following of the occult laws of meditation. I deal here only with one phase of the matter, and that is, the realisation, in the physical brain consciousness, of certain results along the line of our immediate topic,—access to the Masters.

This narrows down our subject to that of a conscious realisation of the Masters and of some one particular Master by the student in his physical brain. This realisation is very largely independent of his place upon the Path, of his nearness to or distance from initiation. Some very advanced egos may be working at this problem, and be close indeed to their Master, without being able to bring through to the physical brain specific facts proving to them this nearness. Some effect this knowledge at earlier stages than others. It is dependent upon the type of body in use and the work done in previous lives, resulting in a physical vehicle that is a fairly just exponent of the inner man. Oft the man is of far greater calibre and attainment on the inner planes than he is on the physical. So many of our most earnest workers in this particular half century are working out evil karma through the possession of inadequate bodies. Through diligence, application, high endeavour, and the long and patient following of the rules laid down, there comes a time when the student is suddenly conscious—right within the physical brain—of certain unexpected events, an illumination or a seeing that has before been unknown. It is something that is so real yet so momentarily surprising that no amount of subsequent apparent disproving can take away from him the knowledge that he *saw,* he contacted, he felt.

As often I have told you, it is not possible in any way in this work to do more than widely generalise. Sixty thousand million souls in process of evolving, each following certain rounds of lives totally different from those of others, offer a wide field to choose from, and no one experience is exactly the same as another. But it might be generally laid down that there are five ways (out of the many possible) which are of such frequent occurrence, comparatively speaking, as to warrant our enumerating them. All have been hinted at, but I may somewhat enlarge the already imparted data.

Seeing the Master and the self within the cave of the heart. As you know, the student has often been told to visualise himself and the Master—about the size of a quarter inch—within the circumference of the etheric heart. He is told to picture, toward the close of his meditation the heart etheric, and therein build minute forms of the Master to Whom he is drawn and of himself. This he proceeds to do with due and elaborate care, with the aid of the imagination and loving effort, working daily on his figures till they become to him very real, and their building and forming becomes almost an automatic part of his meditation form. Then comes a day (usually when astrological conditions are fit and the moon approaches the full) when he becomes conscious *within his brain* that those figures are not the little puppets he thinks, but that he is within the figure representing himself, and that he stands literally and in all verity before the Master. This occurs at rare intervals at first, and the consciousness of the fact is held but for a few brief seconds; as progress is made, and every department of his nature and of his service develops, with greater frequency will come the experience, with longer periods will it be marked, until there comes a time when the pupil can link up as easily in this manner with his Master as earlier he formed his figures.

Just what did occur? The pupil had succeeded in doing three things:—

1. Identifying himself with the figure within the heart, and aspiring to the Master.

2. Making a definite channel between the heart centre (wherein he is endeavouring to focus his consciousness) and its corresponding head centre. Each of the seven centres in the body, as you know, has a counterpart within the head. It is in the linking up of the centre with its counterpart in the head that illumination comes. This, —in the case in point,—has been accomplished by the student. He has connected the heart with its head centre.

3. Not only has he accomplished the two above things but he has so purified that part of the physical brain that corresponds with the particular head centre that it *can* respond to the higher vibration necessitated, and therefore accurately record what has transpired.

Recognition of vibration. In this instance the method is not quite the same. The student becomes conscious during his moments of intensest aspiration in meditation of a certain peculiar vibration or sensation in his head. It may be in one of three places:—

        a. At the top of the spine.
        b. In the forehead.
        c. At the top of the head.

I speak not here of the sensation that comes when psychic faculty develops, though there is an alliance between the two, but I speak of a definite vibration that accompanies contact with one of the Great Ones. The student at first is only conscious of a feeling of momentary heightening, which takes the form of a ripple or movement in the head.

At first it may be attended with some discomfort, if felt in the forehead it may cause tears and weeping, if at the top of the spine or base of the skull exhilaration and even dizziness, and if at the top of the head a sense of expansion with a feeling of fulness, as if the limiting skull were too confining. This wears off with greater use. It is all caused by a contact, momentary at first, with some one Master. In time the student comes to recognise this vibration and to associate it with some particular Great One, for each Master has is own vibration which impresses itself upon His pupils in a specific manner. This method of contact is frequently attended by perfume. In time the pupil learns how to raise his vibration to a certain pitch. Having done this he holds the vibration steady until he senses the Master's answering vibration or the perfume. Then he endeavours to merge his consciousness with the Master's as far as may be, to ascertain the Master's will, and to understand what it is that the Master has to communicate. As time progresses and the response of the pupil grows, the Master on His side will attract his attention or signal to him approval (for instance by arousing this vibration within his head)....

September 23rd, 1920.

...... We have now our three remaining points to take up, having already dealt with the two that touched upon contact with the Master in the cave of the heart, and the recognition of His vibration There are still three other ways(out of many, forget not) whereby the earnest student may be conscious in his physical brain of having contacted his Master.

Bringing through into the physical brain consciousness the memory of the Master's ashram and the lessons imparted there.

As the student perseveres in his meditation, as he increases his facility to throw himself into the right vibration, he builds up a pathway (if so we may term it) that leads him direct to his Master. This is a literal statement of fact. Good work earns for the man in time the right to be with the Master at stated periods. This entails good work in meditation coupled with active service for the race. These intervals are rare at first but come more frequently as progress is made. He will then become aware of this contact through remembrance on awakening. He will see the room of the Master, and remember his associates in the work of the class. He will remember certain sentences, as spoken by his Master, and will bring back a recollection of work suggested or of admonition. This is one of the methods which are indicative to the pupil that he is succeeding, through the ability built up in meditation, in gaining access to the Master.

The attainment of a certain amount of causal consciousness. This is indicative of the pupil's having developed (mayhap in small degree, yet definitely realised) the power to enter somewhat into Their world. The faculty of abstract thought and contemplation, the power to transcend the limitations of time and space, are powers of the body egoic, and as all egoic groups are—as aforesaid —controlled by some one Master, the development of egoic consciousness (when consciously recognised) is indicative of contact and access. Many souls unconsciously contact their Ego, and temporarily have flashes of egoic consciousness but when the pupil can consciously raise himself, when he with deliberation intensifies his vibration, and transfers his polarisation into the body egoic, even if for a brief moment, then he can know that he is for that brief moment vibrating to the key of the Master of his group. He has made contact. He may not remember in his physical brain, at first, the details of that contact, he may not realise the appearance of the Master or the words that passed His lips, but having consciously conformed to rule, and entered within the silence of the high places, the law ever works, and he *has* made his contact. Some disciples know their Master intimately on the inner planes and work under His direction, but many lives may elapse before they comprehend the law and with deliberation can make the channel of access, through power developed in meditation.

As time elapses this ability to contact increases until the point is reached when the pupil can at any time find out what is the will of the Master and have access to His heart.

This fifth method is not so usual but it is known to some natures. *Through sound the aspirant is aware of success.* He follows his usual form of meditation. He perseveres from day to day and works on all the three planes over the work to be done. He continuously raises his vibration and aspires in the needed endeavour, coupling all interior effort to the external life of loving service. At some one meditation he will suddenly become aware of a note of music, that seems to be sounded within his head or to emanate from his heart. It will not be evoked by the sounding of the Sacred Word, which Word when sounded by the man on a certain key may call forth a musical response from the Ego, but it will come as a result or culmination of the meditation, and the sound of the note will vibrate within the centre so distinctly as never to be forgotten. It is again an indication of success. The Master has been contacted, and has responded by sounding the tone of the man's own Ego. This is really the basis of the custom of the doorkeeper responding to the would-be aspirant to the mysteries of the group. When the work is properly done, the aspirant will sound the admission word in his own key or tone, endeavouring to strike the note that will evoke the Ego. The doorkeeper will respond and chant forth the reply in the same full sonorous tone, thereby, through the power of sound, linking the man up with the Master of the coming ceremonies. This puts each member of the group—through his own effort and through the third factor, the doorkeeper—en rapport with the Master. In time this will be more fully understood and effort will be made to keep the tone reverberating between those who enter and those who guard the Threshold. When perfectly accomplished (a thing impossible now) it forms a perfect protection. Groups will be formed according to egoic formation and the particular Master. The note of the group will be known to the one who guards the entrance, and no one can get in who sounds not the note in either the higher or lower octave. This applies to groups consecrated to inner spiritual development, and that are directly concerned with the work of a Master with His affiliated pupils or disciples or probationers. Other groups, formed of units diverse and under different rays and Masters, will guard their door by another method, later to be revealed.

When, in meditation, a student hears this inner musical note, he should endeavour to register it, and cultivate the faculty of both recognising it and utilising it. This is not easy at first, as the sounding is both unlooked for and too brief to catch. But as time progresses, and the pupil succeeds in again and yet again getting a similar response, then he can begin to find out the method and watch the causes that set the vibration in motion.

As I have said before, many are the methods whereby a pupil becomes aware of success in the path of access. Above are but five out of these many. Later, when the

Schools are organised and watched over by a Master in physical plane consciousness, records will be kept of the times and modes of contact and in this manner much knowledge will accrue. I would in conclusion point out that always the calling forth of the response must be the work of the pupil, and that the hour of that response depends upon the earnestness of his work, the consecration of his service and his karmic liabilities. When he merits certain response it will be demonstrated in his stars, and naught can hinder or delay. Equally, naught can really hasten, so the pupil need not waste time in doleful ponderings upon the lack of response. His the part to obey the rules, to conform to the forms laid down, to ponder and wisely adhere to the prescribed instructions, and to definitely work and to ardently serve his fellowmen. When he has done all this, when he has built the necessary vibrating material into his three lower bodies, when he has aligned them with the body egoic (even if only for a brief minute) suddenly he may see, suddenly he may hear, suddenly he may sense a vibration, and then forever he may say that faith is merged in sight, and aspiration has become recognition.

LETTER IX

FUTURE SCHOOLS OF MEDITATION.

1. The one fundamental school.
2. Its national subdivisions.
3. The location, personnel, and buildings of the school.
4. The grades and classes.

LETTER IX

FUTURE SCHOOLS OF MEDITATION.

September 26th, 1920.

We take up today another of the series of letters on occult meditation, that dealing with "Future Schools of Meditation". In this letter I shall attempt somewhat to show how the training and development indicated in the other letters will be applied and I shall deal somewhat with prophecy, pointing out what will some day be possible and present, and not what is as yet in any way approachable. Always it is necessary to have high ideals, and ever the human mind leaps forward to some appointed goal. If I here outline what may seem a visionary impossibility it is but that I seek to hold up such an ideal, and to give to the race an objective well worth their highest endeavour.

Preliminary remarks.

Let us pause a moment and lay down certain postulates anent the present that will (so to speak) clear the ground for future action.

The value of meditation is becoming everywhere admitted. Schools for concentration and methods of mental development are commonly advertised in the daily papers.

True meditation is as yet little understood. Concentration is but the foundation upon which the future work is to be based.

As yet the future structure cannot be raised, due to two causes primarily:—

a. The inherent inability of man at this juncture to attain the causal level and the consciousness of the causal level.

b. The absence of a Master in personal presence, able and equipped to teach the true scientific development which is the aim of true meditation.

The troubled condition of the world at present is sufficient barrier to any general acceptation of training, and of the scientific development of the vehicles.

These premises are laid down here as a starting point. That some individuals here and there achieve the goal, that some people do master the system of Occult Meditation and make the desired progress is undeniable, but they are only few in number and those numbers are inappreciable when set against the vast bulk of human beings in incarnation at the same time. They achieve by right of age-long effort, and because in previous lives they trod the Path or neared the portal of initiation. But even the average man of intelligence of today—the product, for instance, of western civilisation—is far from being ready for occult training. Experiments are being made now, unknown oft to the subjects themselves, to see how quickly a man may be pushed through experience and a general hastening of the evolutionary process into a position where it will be safe to train him further. People in many civilised countries are under supervision, and a method of stimulation and intensification is being applied which will bring to the knowledge of the Great Ones Themselves a mass of information that may serve as a guide to Their future efforts for the race. Especially are people in America, Australia, India, Russia, Scotland and Greece being dealt with. A few in Belgium, Sweden, and Austria are likewise under observation, and should the response be as hoped they will form a nucleus for further expansion.

Future Schools of Meditation

In handling this matter we might, as is our usual custom, divide the subject matter under different heads:—

1. The one fundamental School.
2. Its national subdivisions.
3. The location, personnel, and buildings of the School.
4. The grades and classes.

Now I would emphatically point out to you the fact that all that I now impart is a portion of a tentative plan, which has in view the hastening of the evolution of the higher mind, and the bringing under control of the bodies of men, through the power of the God within. This plan has been drawn up in view of the crying need of a world in which the mental equipment of men is increasing out of all proportion to their emotional balance and to their physical equipment. The rapid advance of knowledge, the spreading of the educational system which brings the product of many minds into the environment of the very poor, the ability of all to read and write in such a country as America or among the other Anglo-Saxon races, has been the cause of a very real (I might almost say an unexpected) problem arising to confront the Great Ones.

Mental development when paralleled by emotional stability and a strong healthy body is the aim for all. But now you have mental development paralleled by an unstable astral and a weak, underfed, badly raised physical. Hence disorder, lack of balance, the clouding of the vision and disproportionate discussion. Lower mind, instead of being a means to an end and a weapon for use, is in fair way of being a ruler and a tyrant, preventing the play of the intuition and shutting out the abstract mind.

Hence the Masters, if it can in any way be accomplished, purpose a movement that has in view the harnessing of the lower mind through the instrumentality of the people themselves. With this object in view They plan to utilise the incoming Ray of Ceremonial Law or Organisation, and the period immediately co-incident or following the coming of the Great Lord, to start these schools (in a small inconspicuous way at first) and bring to the consciousness of men everywhere the following four fundamentals:—

    a. The evolutionary history of man *from the mental side*.

    b. The septenary constitution of the macrocosm and the microcosm.

    c. The laws governing man's being.

    d. The method of occult development.

A beginning has already been made........through the various schools at present extant.......All these are the beginnings of the plan. When they are firmly grounded, when they are working smoothly and with public recognition, and when the world of men is being somewhat coloured by them and their *subjective* emphasis, when they are producing scholars and workers, politicians and scientists and educational leaders who make their impress on their environment, then mayhap will come the time for the founding in exoteric fashion of the true occult school. By that I mean that if the earlier schools and colleges do their work satisfactorily they will have demonstrated to the world of men that the subjective is the true reality and that the lower is but the stepping stone to the higher. This subjective reality being universally admitted will, therefore, permit of the founding of a chain of inner schools

... that will be publicly recognised. This will never at any time obviate the necessity for always having an esoteric and secret section, for always there will be certain truths and facts of dangerous import to the uninitiated; but what I seek to point out is that the mysteries will eventually be admitted as facts for universal recognition and for universal aim and goal. They will be prepared for and entered from schools that definitely undertake, under expert guidance, to train novitiates for the mysteries.

Such schools have existed before and in the turning of the wheel again they will be in manifestation.

You ask, when? That depends on humanity itself and on all of you who work with faith and aspiration at the beginnings of the plan.

H. P. B. laid the foundation stone of the first school in this particular lesser cycle (which is nevertheless a relatively important one, being an outgrowth of the fifth root-race, the efflorescence of the fifth principle). This is the keystone. The work proceeds in the founding, as aforesaid, of the various schools, and mental science also has its place. It will go forward as desired if each one who is now under occult training strains every nerve and bends every effort to the work in hand. If all that is possible is done, when the Great Lord comes with His Masters the work will receive a still further impetus, and will gradually expand and grow till it becomes a power in the world. Then will come the day of the occult schools that will definitely train men for initiation.

September 27th, 1920.

We must today take up our first point for it is only as we lay the foundation aright that the superstructure measures up to requirements.

1. *The one fundamental School.*

It is therefore very essential that the emphasis is laid on the fact that no matter what the offshoots, the basic school of occultism is that one which has its root in the sacred centre of the planet, *Shamballa*. At that place, directly under the eyes of the One Initiator Himself, Who is—as is seldom realised—the highest expression of the Teaching Ray upon the earth, is found what might be termed the central office for the educational disciplinary training work of the Hierarchy. There will be found the Chohan Who is directly responsible for the various endeavours, and to Whom the Masters Who take pupils, and the Heads of the various occult schools are directly responsible. All proceeds under law and order.

One point that it will here be necessary to emphasise is that the Brotherhood of Light, as represented by the Himalayan Masters, has its other representatives elsewhere who all carry out specific work under proper and adequate supervision. Too apt are the Theosophists to think that they alone are the repositories of the wisdom religion. Not so is the fact. At this particular moment (with the aim in view of the development and tendering of opportunity to the fifth subrace) the Himalayan Brotherhood is the main channel of effort, power and light. But the work with other races proceeds simultaneously and numerous other projects, all emanating from the central office at *Shamballa,* are paralleling the Himalayan work. Get this clearly in mind, for the point is important. The Himalayan School and Lodge is the one that principally concerns the occident and *the only school without any exception* that should control the work and output of the occult students in the West. It brooks no rival nor contemporary work with its pupils, not for the sake of its own teachers but to ensure the safety of its pupils. Danger lurks in the path of the occult student and the Himalayan adepts know adequately how to protect their pupils, provided those pupils stay within the periphery of Their united auras, and wander not out to other schools. All true occult schools demand this of their pupils, and all true Masters expect Their pupils to refrain from taking other occult instructions at the same time as they are receiving it from Them. They say not: "Our method is the only right and true method." They say: "When receiving instructions from Us it is the part of wisdom and the line of safety to refrain from occult training in another school or under another Master." Should a pupil desire so to do he is perfectly free to seek out other schools and teachers, but he must first break his connection with the old.

The one fundamental school may be recognised by certain outstanding characteristics:—

By the basic character of the truths taught as embodied in the following postulates:—

a. The unity of all life.
b. The graded steps of development as recognised in man, and by the graded steps of its curriculum, which lead a man from one expansion of consciousness to another until he has reached that which we call perfection.
c. The relationship between the microcosm and the macrocosm and its sevenfold application.
d. The method of this development and the place of the microcosm within the macrocosm as revealed through the study of the periodicity of all manifestation and the basic law of cause and effect.

By the emphasis laid on character building and spiritual development as a foundation for the development of all the faculties inherent in the microcosm.

By the requirement, demanded of all affiliated pupils without exception, that the life of inner unfoldment and development should be paralleled by a life of exoteric service.

By the graded expansions of consciousness that are the result of the imparted training; these lead a man on from step to step till he contacts his higher self, his Master, his egoic group, the First Initiator, the One Paramount Initiator, until he has contacted the Lord of his Ray and has entered into the bosom of his "Father Which is in Heaven".

These are the outstanding features that are descriptive of the one true fundamental School.

This fundamental school has three main branches and a fourth that is in process of forming and which will make the four branches of this fourth round. These branches are as follows:—

1. The trans-Himalayan Branch.
2. The Southern India Branch.
   (these are Aryan Branches)
3. A Branch that works with the fourth root-race and has two fourth root-race adepts at its head.
4. A Branch in process of forming that will have its headquarters in the occident at some place not yet disclosed. It has for its main object the instructing of those connected with the coming sixth root-race.

These branches are and will be closely inter-allied and will work in the closest co-operation, being all focused and under the control of the Chohan at *Shamballa*. The heads of each of the four branches communicate with each other frequently and are really like the faculty of one stupendous university, the four schools being like the various major departments of the foundations—like subsidiary colleges. The aim of all is the evolution of the race, the object of all is to lead all to the point of standing before the One Initiator, the methods employed are fundamentally the same, though varying in detail, due to the racial characteristics of the races and types dealt with, and the fact that certain schools work paramountly with one ray and others with another.

The trans-Himalayan school has its adepts as known to you, and others Whose Names are not known.

The southern Indian school has special work with the deva evolution, and with the second and third sub-races of the Aryan race.

The Himalayan school works with the first, fourth and fifth sub-races.

The fourth root-race branch works under the Manu of that race and his brother of the Teaching Ray. Their headquarters are in China.

The Master R.—and one of the English Masters are concerning Themselves with the gradual founding of the fourth branch of the school, with the assistance of the Master Hilarion. Ponder on these imparted facts, for the significance is of profound importance.

Tomorrow we will deal with the future. Today I have but imparted facts in present manifestation.

September 28th, 1920.

Today our second point comes up for consideration, and we shall in the elucidation of it enter into the realms of prophecy. I would here point out to you that the thing which is indicated as existing in the future may not always work out in detail as foreseen. I but seek to lay before you the big general plan in its outline. The working out in the future will depend upon the intuition or high perception of the thinkers of the race and upon the ability of the incarnating jivas to seize upon the opportunities and fulfil their destiny.

We touched yesterday upon the one fundamental school with its four branches. Today I would take up:—

2. *The National subdivisions of the one school.*

At the outset I would point out to you that not every nation in the world will have its occult school. Only as the causal body of the national group has reached a certain rate of vibration will it be possible to found and institute these schools. Only as the educational work of the nation has reached a certain height will it be possible to use the mental equipment of the nation as a stepping stone for further expansion, and to use it as a basis for the occult school. And, curiously enough, only those nations which originally had a training school for the mysteries (with three exceptions) will be again, during the earlier stages, permitted national schools. The exceptions are:—

1. Great Britain.
2. Canada and the United States.
3. Australia.

And even these exceptions might be considered only one, the case of Australia, for the other two in Atlantean days had their occult foundations when they formed part of the earlier continent. In the turning of the wheel, earth itself reincarnates; places pass into pralaya and emerge into manifestation, holding within them the seeds that will eventuate in similar vibration, and bring into being again similar modes of expression, and similar *forms*.

It will be found later on, when the Occult Schools are founded, that they will be situated where some of the old magnetism yet lingers, and where in some cases certain old talismans have been kept by the Brotherhood with just this aim in view.

Branches, affiliated with one of the four central divisions of the one occult foundation, will be found in the following countries:

1. *Egypt*. This will be one of the later schools founded and will be profoundly occult and an advanced school in direct communication with the inner grades. This will be touched upon later.

2. *The United States* will have a preparatory school somewhere in the southern part of the Middle West, and an extensive occult college in California in a place later to be revealed. This school will be one of the first started when the Great Lord begins His earthly career, and during the next five years the seeds of it may be laid if students rightly apprehend the work to be done.

3. There will be one school for the Latin countries, probably in *Italy or Southern France,* but much depends on the political and educational work of the next ten years.

4. *Great Britain.* At one of the magnetised spots in either Scotland or Wales, a branch for occult training will be begun before so very long, which will lay the foundation and embrace the curriculum for the earlier grades. After it has been in existence for a few years and has proved the effectiveness of its training, and after troubled Ireland has adjusted her internal problems, a school for the more advanced grades, and for definite preparation for the mysteries will be started in Ireland at one of the magnetised spots there to be found. This school will be very definitely a school where preparation for a major initiation may be taken, and will be under the eye of the Bodhisattva, preparing the pupil for initiation upon the second ray. The first school in *Egypt* will be for those who take initiation on the first ray in the occident.

Those who take initiation on the line of the Mahacho-han, or on the third ray, will take it at the advanced occult school in *Italy*. In this way the occident will have its centre where active instruction may be given according to the three lines of approach, and which will give preparation in the inner mysteries.

5. A preparatory occult school will be found, too, in *Sweden*, for those of the northern and German races who seek the Path, and when it has been extant for some time *Russia* may then be in a position to house the headquarters for the more advanced school affiliated to the preparatory one in Sweden. In connection with the Egyptian advanced school will be a preparatory one in *Greece* or in *Syria*.

You have, therefore, the following schools as planned, and must bear in mind that the schools wherein the preparatory work and earlier grades are found will be first in order of time, and are in process of founding now, or will be founded during the period immediately preceding the Coming of the Great Lord. The founding of others will be definitely the outcome of His work, and that of His Masters, and will depend upon Their decision as to the success of the earlier endeavour.

Preparatory Grades	*Advanced School*
1. Greece or Syria leading to	Egypt
2. Middle West, U. S. A.	California
3. Southern France	Italy
4. Scotland or Wales	Ireland
5. Sweden	Russia
6. New Zealand	Australia

There is also planned a preparatory school for the advanced egos of the fourth root-race. This will be under the Manu of that race and will be situated in *Japan*, with its most esoteric branch in western *China*. This makes the seventh in the group of schools outlined.

It is not purposed as yet to have branches in Southern Africa or Southern America. Their day is not yet, but comes in the next cycle.

Now, I would earnestly call to your attention that the schools will make but small beginnings and will be launched in a way that will appear at first as too unimportant to be noticeable. A beginning will be made with members of the different occult schools, such as the esoteric sections of the Theosophical movement, and others. The work in Britain, America and Australia is already in process of inception, whilst that in Sweden will shortly be on foot. The others will follow at slightly later dates.

This much of the plan has been permitted publication as an incentive to all of you to study with greater aspiration and to work with more strenuous application. Each and all has his place in the plan would he but qualify by doing the necessary work. That work should be:—

An endeavour to recognise the Divine within each one. In this manner the true occult obedience, which is an essential in all occult training, will be fostered and developed, being not based, as is so oft seen, on personality, but on that instinctive realisation of a Master, and the willing following that comes from the recognition of His powers, the purity of His life and aims, and the profundity of His knowledge.

An endeavour to think in group terms and clearly for oneself, not depending upon the word of others for clarification.

An endeavour to purify and refine all the bodies and make them more reliable servants.

An endeavour to equip throughout the mental vehicle and to store within it the facts upon which extended knowledge may be based.

If these things are done great will be the day of opportunity.

October 2nd, 1920.

In the rigid disciplining of yourself comes eventual perfection. To the disciple nought is too small to undertake, for in the rigid adjustment of the details of the lower world life comes, at the end, attainment of the goal. The life of the disciple becomes not easier as the Gate is neared, but ever the watch must be more thorough, ever right action must be taken with no regard to result, and ever each body in all its aggregate of detail must be wrestled with and subjugated. Only in the thorough comprehension of the axiom "Know thyself" will come that understanding that enables man to wield the law and know the inner working of the system from the centre to the periphery. Struggle, strive, discipline, and rejoicingly serve with no reward save the misunderstanding and the abuse of those who follow *after*—this is the role of the disciple.

Today we will deal with our third point.

3. *The Location, personnel, and building of the occult school.*

Here at the outset I would remind you that much which might be said by me on this matter must remain unsaid for lack of the ability to comprehend. I might lay down certain approximate rules, and make certain fundamental suggestions that may find their place in the final working out. I can lay down no rule that *must* be kept. Such is not the occult law. In the establishment of these occult schools in their two divisions, preparatory and advanced, in the different designated centres under one of the four branches of the one fundamental School of Occultism, the work will begin in an inconspicuous manner, and those pupils and advanced egos whose work it is to make the necessary beginning must find out for themselves the method, place and manner. All must be wrought out in the furnace of endeavour and experiment, and the price paid will be high, but only that which is thus wrought out provides the residue or nucleus upon which the further work may be based. Mistakes matter not; nought but the fleeting personalities suffer. What does matter is lack of aspiration, inability to attempt, and incapacity to learn the lesson that failure teaches. When failures are regarded as valuable lessons, when a mistake is deemed but a warning signal that averts from disaster, and when no time is ever lost by a disciple in vain despair and useless self depreciation, then the watching Teachers of the race know that the work the Ego seeks to do through each expression on the lower plane goes forward as desired, and that success must inevitably eventuate. We will here take each detail of our subject, as enumerated above, by itself.

The Location. This is a matter of very real importance but differs according to the need of finding a situation whereon to found a preparatory or an advanced school. Generally speaking (for national requirements vary much), the school for the preparatory work will be situated within reasonable distance of some big centre or city, whilst the school for the advanced grades will be more isolated, and not so easily accessible.

Let us look into this for a moment. One of the fundamental things that the novitiate has to learn is to find his centre within himself, independent of surrounding circumstances, and preferably in spite of surrounding circumstances. The centre *must* be found to a considerable degree before he can pass on to the more advanced grades and work in the second school. The preparatory school above all things concentrates on the development of the threefold lower man, and his training in service. The advanced school definitely prepares for Initiation, and is concerned with occult lore, with the impartation of cosmic truth, with the abstract development of the pupil, and with work on causal levels. One can be best accomplished in the world of men and through contact with the world; the other demands necessarily an environment of comparative seclusion and freedom from interruption. We might express it thus:—the preparatory grades deal with the kingdom of God within, whilst the advanced school expands that training into one which includes the kingdom of God without. Therefore the first will be situated amongst the working sons of men, so that by his reactions and interactions in association with them, in service and struggle, the pupil may learn to know himself. The other will be for those who have somewhat mastered these things, and are ready to learn more of other evolutions and of the cosmos. Until a man is master of himself to a considerable degree he may not safely work, for instance, with the deva or angel evolution. In the preparatory school he learns this mastery; in the more advanced school he can thus be trusted to make other contacts than the human. In both these schools, the basic instruction is meditation in all its grades. Why? Because in occult schools information, clear instructions, or a conglomerate of facts are never given, nor are the exoteric textbook methods ever employed. The whole aim is only to put the student in the way of finding out for himself the needed knowl-

edge. How? By developing the intuition through meditation, and by the attainment of that measure of mental control that will permit the wisdom of the Triad to pour
down into the physical brain, via the causal. Therefore, in
the preparatory school emphasis will be laid on the meditation that concerns the mind, and the teaching embodied
in this book will be applied. This necessitates an environment wherein many and varied human contacts will be
made, and where the concrete knowledge of the world of
men will be easily available (music, libraries, and lectures), for in the preparation of true occult training the
astral and mental equipping of the student will be one of
the first considerations. When this has been somewhat
accomplished, and when the clairvoyant head of the
school sees that the rounding out of the lower auric egg
approaches the desired point, then the pupil will pass into
the more advanced school, and will be taught how from his
stable centre to contact the cosmic centre, and from the
point within himself to expand his consciousness till it
touches the periphery of the system macrocosmic, and embraces all that lives—lives in an occult sense. This necessitates, during the period of training, comparative seclusion, and this the advanced school will provide. Therefore
the preparatory school will be located near some large
city, preferably near the sea or some large expanse of
water, but never within the city; it will be on the confines
of the centres of learning within the city and will be readily accessible. The advanced school will be far from the
crowded places of the earth and preferably in a mountain-
ous region, for the mountains have a direct effect on the
occultist and impart to him that quality of strength and
steadfastness that is their predominant characteristic
and must be that too of the occultist. The sea or expanse
of water close to a preparatory school will convey to his

mind a constant reminder of the purification which is his paramount work, whilst the mountains will imbue the advanced student with cosmic strength and will hold steadily before him the thought of the Mount of Initiation which he aims soon to tread.

Tomorrow we will take the important factor of the personnel and faculty of the school and the types of building.

October 7th, 1920.

We deal today with that portion of our third point in the letter on "Future Schools of Meditation," which deals with the *Personnel of the School.*

This term includes both those who supervise and those who are under supervision, and the subject is necessarily large. As said in the earlier parts of this letter, the schools will be in two divisions wherever situated:—

a. A preparatory school for the earlier grades in occult instruction, and situated preferably near some large expanse of water and near some central city.

b. An advanced school for the later grades, which will definitely prepare the way for initiation, and train pupils in occult lore.

As you will consequently see, the personnel of both schools will necessarily differ, as will the curriculum. We will deal with each type of school separately, and lay down certain fundamentals which must be looked for in instructors and instructed.

The Preparatory Occult School. This—to the outer world—may appear not so different from an ordinary college. The differences will not be recognisable at first to the man of the world, though the differences will be there, and will demonstrate themselves in the school work, to the pupils, and on the inner planes. The fundamentals as regards the instructors are as follows:—

The Head of the school will be an accepted disciple; it is essential that the Master, Who is back of the work of any particular school, should be able at all times to tap the consciousness of that school as focussed through the disciple. This Head will be able to act as a medium of communication between the students and the Master and as a focal point for His force to flow through to them. He must be consciously able to function on the astral plane at night and to bring the knowledge through to the physical brain, for part of his work will be with students on the astral plane, guiding them to the Master's ashram at certain intervals for specialized work. He will have to train them too in this conscious functioning.

Under him will work six instructors, of whom one at least must be a conscious clairvoyant, and able to assist the Head with his information as to the auric development of the students; he must be able to gauge the colors and expansion of the students' vehicles, and co-operate with the Head in the work of expanding and attuning those vehicles. These instructors must be on the Probationary Path and earnestly devoted to the work of assisting evolution and devoted to the service of some one Master. They must and will be carefully chosen so as to supplement and complement each other, and in the school will form a miniature hierarchy, showing on the physical plane a tiny replica of the occult prototype. As their work will be largely to develop the lower mind of the pupil and to link it up with the higher consciousness, and as the focal point of their endeavour will be the rapid building-in the causal body, they will be men of erudition, and of knowledge, grounded in the knowledge of the Hall of Learning, and able to teach and to compete with the trained teachers of the world universities.

In every college the work of these trained seven men will be aided by that of three women chosen for their capacity to teach, for their intuitive development and for the spiritual and devotional touch they will bring to the lives of the students. To these ten teachers will be entrusted the work of grounding the students in the important essentials, in superintending the acquirement of the rudiments of occult lore and science, and their development in the higher psychism. These ten must be profound students of meditation, and able to superintend and teach the pupils the rudiment of occult meditation, as taught, for instance, in this book. Occult facts will be imparted to these pupils by them and the basic laws that—in the advanced school—will be the subject of definite practice by the would-be initiate. Exercises in telepathy, causal communication, reminiscence of work undertaken during the hours of sleep, and the recovering of the memory of past lives, through certain mental processes, will be taught by them,—themselves proficient in these arts.

As you will see here, all these teachers will be devoted to the definite training and inner development of the threefold man.

Under these will work various other teachers, who will superintend other departments of the pupils' lives. Exoteric science will be taught and practised by proficient teachers, and the lower mind will be developed as much as possible, and kept in check by the other ten teachers who watch over the proportional development, and the aptitude for correct meditation of the student.

Along with all this will be the life of world-service, rigidly demanded of each and every pupil. This life of service will be carefully watched and recorded. One thing to be noted here is that in this there will be no compulsion. The pupil will know what is expected of him and what he must do if he is to pass on to the more advanced schools, and the school's charts (recording the condition of his vehicles, and his progress and his capacity to serve) will all be available for his personal inspection, though to no one else. He will know clearly where he stands, what he must do and what remains to be done, and it rests then with him to aid the work by the closest co-operation. A certain amount of care will be taken in the admittance of pupils to the school, and this will obviate the necessity of later removal for inability or lack of interest, but this I will deal with later, when taking up the grades and classes.

You have, therefore, ten superintending teachers, composed of seven men and three women, including a Head who is an accepted disciple. Under them will work a set of instructors who will deal largely with the lower mind and in the emotional, physical and mental equipping of the pupil, and his passing into the advanced school in a condition to profit by the instructions there to be imparted. Here I would point out that I have planned out the ideal, and pictured for you the school as it is hoped it will eventually be. But as in all occult development, the beginning will be small and of little apparent importance. Tomorrow we will take up the rules governing the admission of students and the personnel of the more advanced school.

October 16th, 1920.

......Today we will take up:—

The personnel of the advanced school, and the rules of admission to both the preparatory and advanced. This latter part will be largely technical.

The first point I seek to make here is that these advanced schools will be numerically small, and this for a very long time to come, and the personnel will be correspondingly small. . . . At the head of the school will always be found an Initiate of the first or second degree, the aim of the school being to prepare pupils for the first initiation. This necessarily requires an Initiate head. This Initiate head will be definitely appointed by the Master Who has the school in charge, and he will be—within the confines of the school—sole judge and autocrat. The risks of occult training are too great to permit of trifling, and what the Head demands must be obeyed. *But* this obedience will not be compulsory but voluntary, for each pupil will realise the necessity and will render obedience from spiritual recognition. As aforesaid, these different occult schools will be practically *ray* schools, and will have for their personnel teachers on some one ray or its complementary ray, with pupils on the same ray or complementary ray. For instance, if the school is a second ray school —such as the one in Ireland is purposed to be—teachers and pupils on the second, fourth and sixth rays will be found in it. At least one fifth ray teacher will be found in every school of occultism. If a first ray school, the personnel and pupils will be first, third and seventh ray, with again a fifth ray teacher among the others.

Under the initiate Head will be two other teachers who will be accepted disciples, and every pupil under them must have passed through the preparatory school, and graduated from all the lower grades. Probably these three will comprise the entire teaching staff, for the pupils under them will be relatively few in number and the work of the teachers is supervisory more than didactic, for the occultist is always *esoterically self-taught*.

Much of the work done by these three will be on the inner planes, and they will work more in the seclusion of their own rooms than in class room with the students themselves. The pupils are—it will be presumed—ready to work for themselves and to find the way to the portal of initiation alone. The work of the teachers will be advisory, and they will be available to answer questions and to superintend work *initiated* by the pupil himself, and not compelled by the teacher. Stimulating vibration, aligning the bodies, superintending the work on inner planes, and the pouring in of force with the shielding from danger by occult methods, will be the work, in part, of the Teachers, added to the supervision of definite and strenuous meditation. At intervals they will conduct the pupils to the Master, advise as to their passing into the different grades of discipleship, report at intervals on the quality of their life service and assist them in building their buddhic vehicle, which has to be in an embryonic condition when the first initiation is taken. The teachers likewise superintend the working out in practice of the theories anent the other evolution, the deva evolution, laid down in the preparatory schools; they watch over the manipulation of matter by the pupil and his demonstration of the laws of construction; they safeguard him as far as may be in his contact with sub-human and super-human evolutions, and teach him to wield the law and to transcend karma. They enable him, through their instructions, to recover the knowledge of past lives and to read the akashic records, but as you will see, the pupil is the one in this school who initiates and does the work, superintended and guarded by the teachers, and his progress and the length of his residence within the school depend upon his own effort and initiatory powers.

The rules of admission into the preparatory school will be somewhat as follows, but I only indicate probabilities and not ascertained and fixed facts:—

1. The pupil must be free from obligatory karma and able to take the course without neglecting his other duties and family ties.

2. There will be no fees or money charged, and no money transaction. The pupil must be somewhat self-supporting and able to earn the means of livelihood whilst in the school. The schools in both their divisions will be supported through the voluntary contributions of people, and through a knowledge of the laws of supply and demand occultly interpreted.

3. The pupil must be able to measure up to the average educational standards of his day and generation and must show aptitude for some line of thought.

4. He must be seen clairvoyantly to have a certain amount of co-ordination and alignment and the causal body must be of a certain grade or quality before he is admitted. Teachers of occultism waste not time on those not ready. Only when the inner light shines forth, only when the causal body is of a certain capacity can the pupil profit by the curriculum. Therefore, with the Head of the school will the final verdict lie as to whether a pupil may enter or not. That word will be final, and will be passed after due inspection of the pupil by the Head of the school through clairvoyant and causal vision, and after reference to the man's own Master.

5. He must have demonstrated, by a previous period of service, his ability to work in group formation and to think in terms of others.

6. His past incarnations must be somewhat looked up, and the indications given through their study will guide the Head in his final decision.

7. The pupil must be over twenty-one and under forty-two years of age.

8. His etheric body must be in good condition and be a good transmitter of prana, and there must be no physical disease or handicapping physical deformity.

These are the fundamental rules which it is at present possible to give. There will be others and the problem of selection may pass through some vicissitudes in solving.

The rules for admission into the advanced school are far more esoteric and fewer in number. The pupils will be chosen from out of the preparatory school, after having passed through the graded courses. But selection will depend not on the mental development and the assimilation of concrete knowledge, but upon the inner comprehension and the occult understanding of the student, upon the quality of the *tone* of his life as it sounds forth in the inner world, upon the brilliance of the indwelling light, and upon his power in service.

This suffices for today; tomorrow we will deal with the final division of this third point, the buildings of the school.

October 17th, 1920.

In dealing today with the subject of the buildings of the two types of occult schools, little can be said and only a general outline can be given. Climatic conditions and the desired size of the schools will greatly vary and the consequent plant will vary likewise......

The buildings for the preparatory school will differ not so much from those of an ordinary college in the exoteric world. One rule only will be laid down—each student must of necessity have his own separated chamber. The type of building matters not, provided these conditions are fulfilled. Each room must be non-communicating, save with the central corridor, and must be in three divisions, necessarily small yet distinct. One division will be given up to the student's life and study; another to the bath and the third will be the place for meditation containing the pictures of the Great Ones duly curtained. This third division is kept for the sole purpose of meditation and will contain little save the mat on which the student sits, a couch on which he will repose his physical vehicle during certain stated exercises and a small stool in front of the Master's pictures, on which will be found the incensor and a vase for floral tributes.

The resident teachers will reside with the students, the women taking charge of the women students, and the men residing with the male students. The Head of the school will reside alone in a detached house which will contain—besides the rooms in which he will live his private life—a reception room of small proportions for his work with individuals, and a larger room for joint concourses, besides a shrine room for the meeting of the united body of pupils.

The buildings for the advanced schools, even though they concern us not intimately as yet, provide in their construction much of occult significance for those who have eyes to see. The main feature in the occult advanced school will be the central temple of circular shape providing for each of the pupils (and you must remember that numerically they will not be large), a private shrine entered from the rear by a closed door and having a curtain between it and the large central shrine where the group meetings will be held.

This large central shrine will have a pavement whereon will be traced the triangle, and within the triangle the group will sit, the three spaces outside the triangle having tables whereon will be found various symbols and a few of the fundamental books on symbols and some large parchments whereon the cosmic symbols will be portrayed.

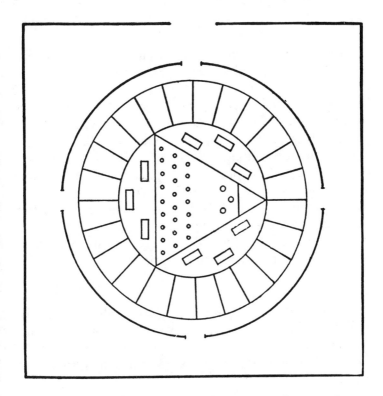

The colour of this shrine will be dependent on the ray which it represents. The curtains which separate will be in the ray colour also and each individual shrine curtain will carry the sign of the pupil's nativity—his sign, rising sign, and controlling planets. These curtains will be the property of the pupil, as will the mat within the shrine which will carry the symbol of his ray, egoic and personality.

On the wall of the great circular passage will be found the signs of the zodiac, the four entrances standing for the four Maharajas.

A square wall will surround the whole, enclosing a garden which will be the care of the pupils themselves. There will be but one entrance through this wall on the north side. Outside will be small buildings to house not more than three pupils, and a house wherein will reside the three instructors. The Initiate Head will likewise have his private residence distinguished by a domed tower at one side. This domed tower serves two purposes:—It is the place for astronomical and astrological instruction and will have the latest appliances of science for the study of the planets and of microcosmic life, and will also serve as a secure shelter for those pupils who can consciously leave their physical bodies and function elsewhere on the physical plane.

This is all I can give as yet. Record, watch and await the hour when the ideal will materialize.

October 29th, 1920.

Our fourth point comes up for consideration today, and in its discussion I will give you somewhat concerning the preparatory occult school but little concerning the advanced. This fourth point is one anent the grades and classes.

4. *The Grades and Classes.*

We have, in an earlier letter, touched upon the curriculum of the preparatory schools and have seen that that curriculum deals much with the development of lower mind, with the laying of the foundations upon which to build the later work, and with the formulation, the study, and the memorising of the theories and occult laws upon which the true occultist will later base his practical work. We saw also that much that was taught was necessarily closely allied with the exoteric teaching of the world, and necessitated the school being in close touch with the centres of modern thought. Today I seek to point out certain things that will be seen in the scheme of the student's work and to show the method whereby he is gradually led on until he is fit to pass on into the more advanced college. We will as usual divide our subject into three heads:—

a. The times of study.
b. The types of work.
c. The transformation of potential faculty into active powers through practice.

a. *The times of study.*

All the work of the school will be based upon an occult knowledge of times and seasons, and two things will be carefully adhered to:—1. The school year will be divided into two halves, one half wherein the pupils are strenuously acquiring knowledge, that period being that in which the sun moves northward or the earlier half of the year, and a second half—separated from the earlier by an interval of six weeks—wherein he assimilates and puts into practice that which earlier was imparted. During the earlier months of the year he goes through a drastic system of reception, of learning, of hard study, of accumulation of facts and of concrete knowledge. He attends lectures, he wades through many books, he studies in the laboratory, and with the aid of the microscope and of the telescope he widens the range of his vision, and builds into his mental body a vast store of scientific data.

During the six weeks' vacation he is recommended to rest entirely from all mental effort save that associated with the practice of the imparted occult meditation. He mentally follows the cycle and goes into pralaya temporarily. At the end of six weeks he returns to his work with the object in view of systematising the mass of information, of perfecting his comprehension of the facts earlier studied, of practicing that part of the occult lore permissible, with the object in view of becoming proficient and to discover his weak points. He writes during the "dark period" of the year the themes and essays, the books and pamphlets that will embody the product of the assimilated information. The best of these books will be published yearly by the college, for the use of the public. In this way he serves his time and generation and educates the race in the higher knowledge. 2. In exactly the same way his studies each month will be so arranged that the harder part (dealing with the higher mind) will be undertaken during the part of the month which is called the bright half, whilst the work of the dark half will be more given over to the things concerning lower mind and to an effort to hold the gain of the earlier weeks. Each day will be likewise divided into set times, the earlier hours being those in which the more abstract and occult data will be given, the latter part of the day being given over to a more practical type of work.

The basis of all occult growth is meditation, or those periods of silent gestation in which the soul grows in the silence. Therefore, during the day there will be for every pupil in the school three periods of meditation—at sunrise, at midday, and at sunset. During the earlier part of the pupil's attendance at the school these periods will be for thirty minutes each. Later he will give one hour to the practice of occult meditation three times a day, and during his final year he will be expected to give five hours a day to meditation. When he can do this and get results he will be able to pass on into the advanced school. It is the great test and mark of readiness.

The hours of the school will begin with sunrise and end with sunset. After the sun sets, and for one hour after each of the other two periods of meditation, the pupil is permitted to relax, take his meals and recreate himself. All pupils will be required to retire to rest at night by ten o'clock, after thirty minutes of careful revision of the day's work and the filling in of certain charts that go to the completion of his record.

The length of a pupil's stay in the school depends entirely upon the progress made, the inner powers of assimilation and the outer life of service. It depends therefore upon the point in evolution at which he enters the school. Those just entering the Path of Probation will be there for five to seven years and on occasion even longer; those who are old disciples and those who have taken initiation in earlier lives will be there but a brief time, pushing rapidly through the curriculum and simply learning to produce for use the knowledge earlier stored. The period of their stay will be anywhere from one to five years, usually about three. Their innate knowledge will be developed by encouraging them to teach the younger brethren. A pupil passes out of the school, not as a result of an exoteric examination but simply on the notification of the Head of the School, who bases his decision upon esoteric results in the bodies of the pupil, upon the clarity of his auric colours and upon the tone of his life and the key of his vibration.

b. *Types of Work.*

First and foremost, the practice of meditation as laid down in these letters and as may be apportioned by the Head of the school. Once or twice a year the initiate Head of the school to which the preparatory school is allied will pass the pupils in review and in conference with the Head of the school will apportion specific meditation adjusted to the pupil's need. Once a year the Master responsible for both schools will likewise pass them in review and communicate to the Head any necessary adjustments. (I would here remind you that the relationship of a Master to a disciple is a private one and though He may be in constant touch with His pupil *privately,* this affects not His official review of the united auras of the school group.)

Secondly, a graded scientific study of the microcosm, including the following subjects, using the microscope when needed:—

The Microcosm.

    a. Elementary anatomy, physiology, biology.
    b. Ethnology.
    c. Study of the etheric body and its allied subjects of vitality and magnetism.
    d. Study of geology; of the vegetable kingdom, or botany; and of the animal kingdom.
    e. Study of the history of man and the development of science.
    f. Study of the laws of the microcosmic body.

The Macrocosm.

    a. Study of the laws of electricity, of fohat, of prana, and of the astral light.

    b. Study of astronomy and of astrology.
    c. Study of occult cosmogony.
    d. Study of the human hierarchy.
    e. Study of the deva evolution.
    f. Study of the laws of the solar system.
    g. Study of telepathy, mental creation, psychometry.

The Mind.

    a. The study of the mental plane.
    b. The study of the laws of fire.
    c. The study of the causal body.
    d. The study of the fifth principle.
    e. The study of colour and of sound.

Synthesis.

    a. The study of spirit-matter-mind.
    b. Study of numbers and of symbology.
    c. Study of higher mathematics.
    d. Study of the laws of union.
    e. Study of the laws of sex.

Psychic Development.

    a. Study of practical occultism.
    b. Study of psychism.
    c. Study of the astral light and the akashic records.
    d. Study of mediumship and inspiration.
    e. Study of past lives.
    f. Study of the macrocosmic and microcosmic centres.

Practical Work.

    a. Service to the race.
    b. Study of *group work*.
    c. Review work.

    d. Work on the subtler bodies with the view to producing continuity of consciousness.

    e. Study of magic.

    f. Study of the seventh ray.

You will see for yourself that when the pupil has completed the above curriculum he will be a potential magician, and will be a member of the Brotherhood of Light in embryo. He will be equipped and ready to pass into the advanced school, where he will be trained in using the knowledge already acquired, where his centres will be scientifically developed so that he will become a conscious psychic of the mental type, where he will be trained to contact and control the lesser evolutions and to co-operate with the other evolutions such as the deva, and where all his bodies will be so aligned and adjusted that he can at the end of a period—varying from two to three years—be ready to stand before the Initiator.

c. *Potencies becoming powers.*

This third type of work is based on the preceding curriculum and deals directly with individual development. It covers the following matters:—

    a. The aligning of the bodies with a view to egoic contact.

    b. The building of the antahkarana, and the development of the higher mind.

    c. The development of the intuition, and the definite spiritual awakening of the pupil.

    d. The study of the pupil's vibration, ray, color and tone.

    e. The conscious refining of all the bodies beginning with the physical.

When these matters are duly studied and all acquired knowledge put into practice, the inherent powers of the soul will become conscious powers. Above all, will the emphasis be laid upon the fact that the white magician is he who utilises all power and knowledge in the service of the race. His inner development must be expressed in terms of service before he is permitted to pass on into the advanced school.

I have indicated enough to provide much room for interested speculation.

LETTER X.

THE PURIFICATION OF THE VEHICLES.

1. The physical body.
2. The emotional body.
3. The mental body.

LETTER X.

THE PURIFICATION OF THE VEHICLES.

November 7th, 1920.

The need arises these days for tested instruments. When Those Who guide human evolution at this period cast Their eyes over the race in the search for such instruments They see few as yet ready for the service required. But likewise They see some who, with a certain amount of training, will fill the need fairly adequately.

As evolution proceeds the polarisation of the race changes. Men are polarised now principally in their emotional bodies,—the feelings, desires, the concerns of the personality sway them. The emotional body is the focal point for the personality. It acts as the clearing house for all that concerns it, and as the junction of the lower and the higher. It is like a busy railroad terminus, that receives cargo from all directions and empties it into the great city of the personal physical plane life. Then, as progress is made, the scene shifts higher, and the mental body becomes the focal point. Later the causal body becomes the important unit, and later still comes the ultimate sacrifice of even that, until the man stands bereft of all that vibrates to the three worlds, and all is over as regards the personal life,—nought remains but the life of the Spirit, and the voluntary giving of that life for the helping of the world.

In the speeding up of evolution, certain things have to be brought about before the man can be used as a reliable instrument, true as tempered steel, for the helping of his race. Forget not that, as a rule, a man (when tested and tried) forms the best tool, because he comprehends utterly the race consciousness, and because he enters into the problems of the day in a manner more thorough than an Ego from an earlier period. Hence the Masters desire to use those of you who live now to heal the wounds of the present suffering generation. What then has to be done? The matter I now give contains nothing very unusual, but it does hold thought for consideration by any who may desire to help.......In preparing a soul for service the Guides of the race have to deal with each of the bodies:—

The training of the Physical Body.

This involves certain definite requirements:—

The building in of matter of the higher subplanes and the elimination of the lower and coarser matter. This is needed because it is impossible for those with coarse bodies to contact high vibration. It is impossible for the Ego to transmit the higher knowledge and guidance through a coarse physical body. It is impossible for the loftier currents of thought to impact the little evolved physical brain. Hence the refinement of the physical body is an essential. It is effected in various ways, all of them reasonable and utilitarian.

> *By pure food.* This involves a vegetarian diet, chosen with wise discrimination; it requires the eating of only those vegetables and fruits that vitalise. Careful judgment shown in the choice of food, wise refraining from too heavy eating, and a little pure good food perfectly assimilated are all that a disciple requires. You ask what foods? Milk, honey, whole wheat bread, all the vegetables that contact the sun, oranges (above all, oranges), bananas, raisins, nuts, some potatoes, unpolished rice, and may I again reiterate,

just as much of all the above as to insure activity.

By cleanliness. Much use of water, externally and internally, is vitally required.

By sleep. This should be always between the hours of ten in the evening and five in the morning, and as much as possible out of doors.

By sunshine. Contact with the sun should be much sought after, and the vitalisation that comes through its rays. The sun kills all germs and frees from disease.

When these four requirements are attended to adequately a definite process of elimination proceeds, and in the course of a few years the whole physical body shifts its polarisation gradually up until ultimately you will have a body composed of atomic subplane matter......
This may take several incarnations, but it should be borne in mind that at each fresh incarnation a body is taken of the exact quality (if I may so put it) as the one previously discarded at death. Hence time is never lost in building. Eventually two other methods will be available by which more rapid refining may be effected:—

The use of coloured lights. These lights are played on the body of the disciple and effect a shaking-out process and a simultaneous stimulation of the atoms. This cannot be done till further information is given anent the Rays; when a man's ray is known, stimulation will come from the use of his own colour, a building-in will be brought about by the use of his complementary colour, and disintegration of unwanted matter will be brought about by the use of an antagonistic colour. This knowledge will later on be communicated to the great bodies that hold custody of the Mysteries, the Church and the Masons. Wait, for the time is not yet. When the Mysteries are restored some of this information will be in the hands of the two bodies I refer to.

The stimulation of music. Certain sounds shatter and break. Certain other sounds stimulate and attract. When the key of a man's life is known, when the sound he responds to is recognised, then comes the possibility of the utilisation of sound in refinement. All that is at present possible to those of you who seek to serve is to attend to the above essentials and to seek contact with high vibration.

One more point I would like to give, and that is, that in the manipulation of electricity lies hid much that concerns the vivification of the bodies, especially just now of the etheric. The principal use the sun has is the vitalising of the etheric. The heat of the sun is electrical force adapted to the need of the great average majority in all the kingdoms of nature. As progress is made an intensification of this force will be possible in individual cases. Herein lies one of the secrets of initiation. In the old days the Rod of Initiation acted actually as a conductor of this force to the centres of the initiate; it was so constructed that it answered this purpose. Now, on a higher turn of the spiral, just the same need and purpose are served, though the method of application necessarily differs, owing to the change in the polarisation of the race. The polarisation is now no longer physical, but is either emotional or mental. The method of application differs in all three, and hence the safeguarding of the secret. It holds the mystery hid.

The refining of the etheric.

This coincides with that of the physical body. The method consists principally of living in the sunlight, in protection from cold, and in the assimilation of certain definite combinations of vitamins which before long will be given to the race. A combination of these vitamins will be formulated and made into tabloid form, with direct effect upon the etheric body. This will not be until that etheric vehicle is recognised by science, and definitely included in the training offered by the faculty of medicine. The study of etheric diseases—congestion and atrophy— will ere long be a recognised study, and will lead to definite treatments and formulas. As before said, all that you can now do in sensitising the dual physical is to attend to the above rules, and allow time to bring about the remainder of the work.

The refining of the emotional body.

Here the method of procedure is different. The emotional body is simply a great reflector. It takes colour and movement from its surroundings. It receives the impress of every passing desire. It contacts every whim and fancy in its environment; every current sets it in motion; every sound causes it to vibrate unless the aspirant inhibits such a state of affairs and trains it to receive and register only those impressions which come from the intuitional level via the Higher Self, and therefore via the atomic subplane. The aim of the aspirant should be to so train the emotional body that it will become still and clear as a mirror, so that it may reflect perfectly. His aim should be to make it reflect only the causal body, to take on colour only in line with the great Law, and to move under definite direction and not just as blow the winds of thought, or rise the tides of desire. What words should describe the emotional body? the words: still, serene, unruffled, quiet, at rest, limpid and clear, of a quality mirror-like, of surface even, a limpid reflector,—one that accurately transmits the wishes, the desires, the aspirations of the Ego and not of the personality. How should this be accomplished? In several ways, some at the direction of the aspirant, and some at the direction of the Master.

a. By the constant watching of all desires, motives and wishes that cross the horizon daily, and by the subsequent emphasising of all those that are of a high order, and by the inhibition of the lower.

b. By a constant daily attempt to contact the Higher Self, and to reflect His wishes in the life. At first mistakes will be made, but little by little the building-in process proceeds, and the polarisation in the emotional body gradually shifts up each subplane until the atomic is reached.

c. By definite periods daily directed to the stilling of the emotional body. So much emphasis is laid in meditation on the stilling of the mind, but it should be remembered that the stilling of the emotional nature is a step preliminary to the quieting of the mental; one succeeds the other and it is wise to begin at the bottom of the ladder. Each aspirant must discover for himself wherein he yields most easily to violent vibrations, such as fear, worry, personality desire of any kind, personality love of anything or anyone, discouragement, over-sensitiveness to public opinion; then he must overcome that vibration, by imposing on it a new rhythm, definitely eliminating and constructing.

d. By work done on the emotional body at night under the direction of more advanced egos, working
under the guidance of a Master. Stimulation of
vibration or the deadening of vibration follows on
the application of certain colours and sounds. At
this particular time two colours are being applied
to many people for the specific purpose of keying
up the throat and foremost head centre, namely,
violet and gold.

Remember that the work is gradual, and as the polarisation shifts up, the moment of transition from one subplane to another is marked by certain tests applied at
night, what one might term a series of small initiations
that eventually will be consummated in the second great
initiation, that marks the perfection of the control of the
body of the emotions.

Four small initiations find their culmination in the
initiation proper. These are the initiations on the emotional plane, called respectively the initiations of earth,
fire, water and air, culminating in initiation the second.
The first initiation marks the same point of attainment on
the physical plane. Each initiation marks the attainment
of a certain proportion of atomic matter in the bodies.
The four initiations, prior to that of the Adept, mark respectively the attainment of a proportionate amount, as
for instance:—At the first initiation one-fourth atomic
matter, at the second one-half atomic matter, and so on to
the consummation. The intuition (or buddhi) being the
unifying principle and thus welding all, at the fourth
initiation the lower vehicles go, and the adept stands in
his intuitional body, and creates from thence his body of
manifestation.

The refinement of the mental body.

This is the result of hard work and discrimination. It necessitates three things before the plane of the mental unit is achieved, and before the causal consciousness (the full consciousness of the higher Self) is reached:—

Clear thinking, not just on subjects wherein interest is aroused, but on all matters affecting the race. It involves the formulation of thought matter, and the capacity to define. It means the ability to make thought forms out of thought matter, and to utilise those thought forms for the helping of the public. He who does not think clearly, and who has an inchoate mental body, lives in a fog, and a man in a fog is but a blind leader of the blind.

The ability to still the mental body so that thoughts from abstract levels and from the intuitional planes can find a receptive sheet whereon they may inscribe themselves. This thought has been made clear in many books on concentration and meditation, and needs not my elucidation. It is the result of hard practice carried over many years.

A definite process brought about by the Master with the acquiescence of the disciple which welds into a permanent shape the hard won efforts and results of many years. At each initiation, the electrical or magnetic force applied has a stabilising effect. It renders durable the results achieved by the disciple. Like as a potter moulds and shapes the clay and then applies the fire that solidifies, so the aspirant shapes and moulds and builds, and prepares for the solidifying fire. Initiation marks a permanent attainment and the beginning of a new cycle of endeavour.

Above all two things should be emphasised:—

1. A steady, unshaken perseverance, that recks not

of time nor hindrance, but goes on. This capacity to persevere explains why the non-spectacular man so frequently attains initiation before the genius, and before the man who attracts more notice. The capacity to plod is much to be desired.

2. A progress that is made without undue self-analysis. Pull not yourselves up by the roots to see if there is growth. It takes precious time. Forget your own progress in conforming to the rules and in the helping of others. When this is so, sudden illumination may come, and the realisation break upon you that the point has been reached when the Hierophant can demand your presence and bestow initiation upon you. You have, by hard work and sheer endeavour to conform to the Law and to love all, built into your bodies the material that makes it possible for you to stand in His Presence. The great Law of Attraction draws you to Him and nought can withstand the Law.

LETTER XI.

THE RESULTANT LIFE OF SERVICE.

1. Motives for service.
2. Methods of service.
3. Attitude following action.

LETTER XI.

THE RESULTANT LIFE OF SERVICE.

September 16th, 1920.

I seek to give you today, in closing this series, something of general use. I wish to speak to you anent service and its perfect rendering. What I give you in this connection may be of vital use. Remember always that material gain in knowledge for the individual causes stagnation, obstruction, indigestion and pain, if not passed on with wise discrimination. Food absorbed by the human body, if not assimilated and passed through the system, causes just the above conditions. The analogy is correct. Much tuition comes to many these days, but it is for the use of a needy world, and not for their own exclusive benefit.

In rendering service three things are of moment:—

1. The motive.
2. The method.
3. The attitude following action.

With wrong motives and methods I deal not. To you they are known. I indicate the right, and by adjustment of the life of service to my indications comes correction and inspiration. A life of much service opens up to many these days; see, all of you, that it commences right. A right beginning is liable to eventuate in continuous correctness, and helps much in the endeavour. Where failure follows in such a case, all that is needed is readjustment. In failure where the beginning has been at fault (an inevitable failure), the need is for the renewal of the inner springs of action.

1. *The motives for service.*

These motives are threefold in the order of their importance:—

a. A realisation of God's plan of evolution, a sensing of the world's dire need, an apprehension of the immediate point of world attainment, and a consequent throwing of the total of one's resources into the furtherance of that end.

b. A definite personal goal of achievement, some great ideal—such as holiness of character—that calls forth the soul's best endeavour; or a realisation of the reality of the Masters of the Wisdom, and a strong inner determination to love, serve, and reach Them at all costs. When you have this intellectual grip of God's plan, coupled with the strong desire to serve the Great Ones, in physical plane activities will come the working out.

c. A realisation next of one's innate or acquired capacities and a fitting of those capacities to the need appreciated. Service is of many kinds, and he who wisely renders it, who seeks to find his particular sphere, and who, finding it, gives effort gladly for the benefit of the whole, is the man whose own development proceeds steadily. But nevertheless the aim of personal progress remains secondary.

2. *The methods of service.*

These are many and varied. I can but indicate the ones of paramount importance.

First and foremost comes, as I have often inculcated, the faculty of *discrimination*. He who considers that he can attempt all things, who balks not at aught that happens his way, who rushes wildly in where wiser ones refrain, who considers he has capacity for that which arises, who brings zeal but no brains to bear on this problem of service, but dissipates force; he renders oft destructive action, he wastes the time of wiser and greater ones in the correcting of his well meant mistakes, and he serves no end but his own desires. The reward of good intention may be his, but it is frequently offset by the results of foolish action. He serves with discrimination who realises wisely his own niche, great or small, in the general scheme; who calculates soberly his mental and intellectual capacity, his emotional calibre and his physical assets and then with the sum of the whole applies himself to fill the niche.

He serves with discrimination who judges with the aid of his Higher Self and the Master what is the nature and the measure of the problem to be solved, and is not guided by the well meant though often ill-judged suggestions, requests and demands of his fellow-servers.

He serves with discrimination who brings a realisation of *time* into action, and comprehending that each day contains but twenty-four hours and that his capacity contains but the expenditure of just so much force and no more, wisely adjusts his capacity and the time available to each other.

Next follows *a wise control of the physical vehicle*. A good server causes the Master no anxiety from physical causes, and may be trusted so to guard and husband his physical strength that he is always available for the carrying out of the Master's requests. He does not fail from physical disability. He sees that his lower vehicle gets sufficient rest, and adequate sleep. He rises early and retires at a seemly hour. He relaxes whenever possible; he eats wholesome and suitable food and refrains from heavy eating. A little food, well chosen and well masticated, is far better than a heavy meal. The human race

eats these days, as a rule, four times as much as is
required. He ceases from work when (through accident
or the recurrence of inherited physical disability) his
body reacts against action and cries out for attention. He
then seeks rest, sleep, dietary precautions and necessary
medical attention. He obeys all wise instruction, giving
time for his recovery.

The next step is a steady *care and control of the
emotional body.* This is the most difficult of the vehicles
to tend, as is well known. No excessive emotion is permitted, though strong currents of love for all that breathe
are allowed to sweep through. Love, being the law of the
system, is constructive and stabilising, and carries all on
in line with the law. No fear or worry or care shake the
emotional body of the aspiring servant of all. He cultivates serenity, stability, and a sense of secure dependence
on God's law. A joyous confidence characterises his ha-
bitual attitude. He harbours no jealousy, no cloudy grey
depression, and no greed or self-pity, but—realising that
all men are brothers and that all that is exists for all—
he proceeds calmly on his way.

Then ensues *the development of his mental vehicle.*
In the control of the emotional body the server takes the
attitude of elimination. His aim is so to train the emotional body that it becomes devoid of colour, has a still
vibration, and is clear and white, limpid as a pool on a
still summer's day. In fitting the mental body for service
the worker strives at the opposite of elimination; he seeks
to build in information, to supply knowledge and facts,
to train it intellectually and scientifically so that it may
prove as time goes on a stable foundation for the divine
wisdom. Wisdom supersedes knowledge, yet requires
knowledge as a preliminary step. You must remember
that the server passes through the Hall of Learning prior

to entering the Hall of Wisdom. In training the mind body he seeks therefore orderly acquisition of knowledge, a supply of that which may be lacking, a sequential grasp of the innate mental faculty accumulated in previous lives, and lastly, a steadying of the lower mind so that the higher may dominate and the creative faculty of thought may be projected through the stillness. From the Silence of the Absolute was projected the universe. From darkness issued light, from the subjective emanated the objective. The negative stillness of the emotional body makes it receptive to impression from above. The positive stillness of the mental body leads to the higher inspiration.

Having sought to control and wisely use his personality in its three departments, the lover of humanity seeks *perfection in action*. No magnificent dreams of martyrdom and the glorious yet ephemeral chimeras of spectacular service engross his attention, but the instant application of all his powers to the next duty is the line of his endeavour. He knows that perfection in the foreground of his life and in the details of his environing work will cause accuracy in the background too, and result in a whole picture of rare beauty. Life progresses by small steps, but each step, taken at the right time, and each moment wisely occupied, leads to long distance covered and a life well spent. Those Who guide the human family test out all applicants for service in the small detail of everyday life, and he who shews a record of faithful action in the apparently non-essential will be moved into a sphere of greater moment. How, in an emergency or crisis, can They depend on someone who in everyday matters does slovenly and ill-judged work?

A further method of service shews itself in *adaptability*. This involves a readiness to retire when other or more important people are sent to fill the niche he may be occupying, or (inversely) an ability to step out of office into work of greater importance, when some less competent worker can do his work with equal facility and good judgment. It is the part of wisdom in all who serve neither to rate themselves too highly nor to underrate themselves. Bad work results when the non-efficient fill a post, but it is equally a loss of time and power when skilled workers hold positions where their skill has not full scope and where less well equipped men and women would do as well. Be ready, therefore, all ye who serve, to stay a lifetime in office non-spectacular and seemingly unimportant, for such may be your destiny and the place you best may serve; but be equally ready to step on to work of more apparent value when the Master's word goes forth, and when circumstances—and not the server's planning—indicate that the time is come. Ponder this last sentence.

3. *The attitude following action.*

What should this attitude be? Utter dispassion, utter self-forgetfulness, and utter occupation with the next step to be taken. The perfect server is he who does to the utmost of his ability what he believes to be the Master's will, and the work to be done by him in co-operation with God's plan. Then, having done his part, he passes on to a continuance of the work, and cares not for the result of his action. He knows that wiser eyes than his see the end from the beginning; that insight, deeper and more loving than his, is weighing up the fruit of his service; and that judgment, more profound than his, is testing the force and extent of the vibration set up, and is adjusting that force according to the motive. He does not suffer from pride over what he has done, nor from undue depression over lack of accomplishment. At all times he does his very best, and wastes not time in backward contemplation, but steadily presses forward to the accomplishment of the next duty. Brooding over past deeds, and casting the mind back over old achievement, is in the nature of involution, and the servant seeks to work with the law of evolution. This is an important thing to note. The wise server, after action, pays no attention to what his fellow servants say, provided his superiors (either incarnating men and women, or the Great Ones Themselves) prove content or silent; he cares not if the result is not that which he anticipated, provided that he faithfully did the highest thing he knew; he cares not if reproach and reproof assail him, provided his inner self remains calm and non-accusing; he cares not if he loses friends, relatives, children, the popularity once enjoyed, and the approbation of his environing associates, provided his inner sense of contact with Those Who guide and lead remains unbroken; he cares not if he seem to work in the dark and is conscious of little result from his labours, provided the inner light increases and his conscience has nought to say.

To sum it all up:—

The motive may be epitomised in these few words:— The sacrifice of the personal self for the good of the One Self.

The method may also be shortly put:—Wise control of the personality, and discrimination in work and time.

The resultant attitude will be:—Complete dispassion, and a growing love of the unseen and the real.

All this will be consummated through steady application to occult Meditation.

THE GREAT INVOCATION

From the point of Light within the Mind of God
   Let light stream forth into the minds of men.
   Let Light descend on Earth.

From the point of Love within the Heart of God
   Let love stream forth into the hearts of men.
   May Christ return to Earth.

From the centre where the Will of God is known
   Let purpose guide the little wills of men —
   The purpose which the Masters know and serve.

From the centre which we call the race of men
   Let the Plan of Love and Light work out
   And may it seal the door where evil dwells.

Let Light and Love and Power restore the Plan on Earth.

"The above Invocation or Prayer does not belong to any person or group but to all Humanity. The beauty and the strength of this Invocation lies in its simplicity, and in its expression of certain central truths which all men, innately and normally, accept — the truth of the existence of a basic Intelligence to Whom we vaguely give the name of God; the truth that behind all outer seeming, the motivating power of the universe is Love; the truth that a great Individuality came to earth, called by Christians, the Christ, and embodied that love so that we could understand; the truth that both love and intelligence are effects of what is called the Will of God; and finally the self-evident truth that only through *humanity* itself can the Divine Plan work out."

ALICE A. BAILEY

Training for new age
discipleship is provided
by the *Arcane School.*
The principles of the
Ageless Wisdom are
presented through esoteric
meditation, study and
service as a *way of life.*

*Write to the publishers
for information.*

GLOSSARY

Adept. A Master, or human being who, having traversed the path of evolution and entered upon the final stage of that path, the Path of Initiation, has taken five of the Initiations, and has therefore passed into the Fifth, or Spiritual kingdom, having but two more Initiations to take.

Adi. The First; the primeval; the atomic plane of the solar system; the highest of the seven planes.

Agni. The Lord of Fire in the Vedas. The oldest and most revered of the Gods in India. One of the three great deities Agni, Vayu and Surya, and also all the three, as he is the triple aspect of fire; fire is the essence of the solar system. The Bible says: "Our God is a consuming fire." It is also the symbol of the mental plane of which Agni is paramountly lord.

Agnichaitans. A group of fire devas.

Atlantis. The continent that was submerged in the Atlantic Ocean, according to the occult teaching and Plato. Atlantis was the home of the Fourth Root Race, whom we now call the Atlanteans.

Antahkarana. The path, or bridge, between higher and lower mind, serving as a medium of communication between the two. It is built by the aspirant himself in mental matter.

Ashram. The centre to which the Master gathers the disciples and aspirants for personal instruction.

Atma. The Universal Spirit; the divine Monad; the seventh Principle; so called in the septenary constitution of man. (See diagram in Introduction.)

Atomic subplane. The matter of the solar system is divided by the occultists into seven planes or states, the highest of which is the atomic plane. Similarly, each of the seven planes is divided into seven subplanes, of which the highest is called the atomic subplane. There are therefore forty-nine subplanes, and seven of these are atomic.

Aura. A subtle invisible essence or fluid which emanates from human and animal bodies, and even from things. It is a psychic effluvium, partaking of both mind and body. It is electro-vital, and also electro-mental.

Auric egg. An appellation that has been given to the causal body owing to its form.

Bodhisattva. Literally, he whose consciousness has become intelligence, or buddhi. Those who need but one more incarnation to become perfect buddhas. As used in these letters the Bodhisattva is the name of the office which is at present occupied by the Lord Maitreya, Who is known in the occident as the Christ. This office might be translated as that of World Teacher. The Bodhisattva is the Head of all the religions of the world, and the Master of the Masters and the Teacher of angels and of men.

Buddha (The). The name given to Gautama. Born in India about B.C. 621, he became a full buddha in B.C. 592. The Buddha is one who is the "Enlightened", and has attained the highest degree of knowledge possible for man in this solar system.

Buddhi. The Universal Soul or Mind. It is the spiritual soul in man (the Sixth Principle) and therefore the vehicle of Atma, the Spirit, which is the Seventh Principle.

Causal Body. This body is, from the standpoint of the physical plane, no body, either subjective or objective. It is, nevertheless, the centre of the egoic consciousness, and is formed of the conjunction of buddhi and manas. It is relatively permanent and lasts throughout the long cycle of incarnations, and is only dissipated after the fourth initiation, when the need for further rebirth on the part of a human being no longer exists.

Chohan. Lord, Master, a Chief. In this book it refers to those Adepts who have gone on and taken the sixth initiation.

Deva (or Angel). A god. In Sanskrit a resplendent deity. A Deva is a celestial being, whether good, bad, or indifferent. Devas are divided into many groups, and are called not only angels and archangels, but lesser and greater builders.

Egoic Groups. On the third subplane of the fifth plane, the mental, are found the causal bodies of the individual men and women. These bodies, which are the expression of the Ego, or of the individualised self-consciousness, are gathered together into groups according to the ray or quality of the particular Ego involved.

Elementals. The Spirits of the Elements; the creatures involved in the four kingdoms, or elements, Earth, Air, Fire, and Water. Except a few of the higher kinds and their rulers they are forces of nature more than ethereal men and women.

Etheric body. (Etheric double.) The physical body of a human being is, according to occult teaching, formed of two parts, the dense physical body, and the etheric body. The dense physical body is formed of matter of the lowest three subplanes of the physical plane. The etheric body is formed of the four highest or etheric subplanes of the physical plane.

Fifth Principle. The principle of mind; that faculty in man which is the intelligent thinking principle, and which differentiates man from the animals.

Fohat. Cosmic electricity; primordial light; the ever-present electrical energy; the universal propelling vital force; the ceaseless destructive and formative power; the synthesis of the many forms of electrical phenomena.

Guru. Spiritual Teacher. A Master in metaphysical and ethical doctrines.

Hierarchy. That group of spiritual beings on the inner planes of the solar system who are the intelligent forces of nature, and who control the evolutionary processes. They are themselves divided into twelve Hierarchies. Within our planetary scheme, the earth scheme, there is a reflection of this Hierarchy which is called by the occultist the Occult Hierarchy. This Hierarchy is formed of chohans, adepts, and initiates working through their disciples, and, by this means, in the world. (See diagram, page 254.)

Initiate. From the Latin root meaning the first principles of any science. One who is penetrating into the mysteries of the science of the Self and of the one self in all selves. The Path of Initiation is the final stage of the path of evolution trodden by man, and is divided into five stages, called the Five Initiations.

Jiva. A separated unit of consciousness.

Kali yuga. "Yuga" is an age or cycle. According to the Indian philosophy our evolution is divided into four yugas or cycles. The Kali-yuga is the present age. It means the "Black Age", a period of 432,000 years.

Karma. Physical action. Metaphysically, the law of ret-
ribution; the law of cause and effect, or ethical
causation. There is the karma of merit and the
karma of demerit. It is the power that controls all
things, the resultant of moral action, or the moral
effect of an act committed for the attainment of
something which gratifies a personal desire.

Kumaras. The highest seven self-conscious beings in the
solar system. These seven Kumaras manifest
through the medium of a planetary scheme in the
same way as a human being manifests through the
medium of a physical body. They are called by the
Hindu ''the mind-born sons of Brahma'' amongst
other names. They are the sum total of intelligence
and of wisdom. Within the planetary scheme the
reflection of the systemic order is also seen. At the
head of our world evolution stands the first Kumara,
aided by six other Kumaras, three exoteric and
three esoteric, Who are the focal points for the dis-
tribution of the force of the systemic Kumaras.

Kundalini. The power of Life: one of the forces of nature. It is a power known only to those who prac-
tise concentration in yoga, and is centred within the
spine.

Lemuria. A modern term first used by some naturalists
and now adopted by Theosophists to indicate a continent that, according to the Secret Doctrine of the
East, preceded Atlantis. It was the home of the
third root race.

Logos. The deity manifested through every nation and
people. The outward expression, or the effect of the
cause which is ever concealed. Thus, speech is the

Logos of thought, hence it is aptly translated by the "verbum" and the "word" in its metaphysical sense. (See John I:1-3.)

Lord of Civilisation. (See Mahachohan.)

Lords of the Flame. One of the great Hierarchies of spiritual beings who guide the solar system. They took control of the evolution of humanity upon this planet about 18 million years ago, during the middle of the Lemurian, or third root race.

Macrocosm. The great universe, literally; or God manifesting, through His body, the solar system.

Mahachohan. The Head of the third great department of the Hierarchy. This great being is the Lord of Civilisation, and the flowering forth of the principle of intelligence. He is the embodiment on the planet of the third, or intelligence, aspect of deity in its five activities.

Mahamanvantara. The great period of time of an entire solar system. This term is applied to the greater solar cycles. It implies a period of universal activity.

Manas, or Manasic Principle. Literally, the Mind, the mental faculty; that which distinguishes man from the mere animal. It is the individualising principle; that which enables man to know that he exists, feels, and knows. It is divided in some schools into two parts, higher or abstract mind, and lower or concrete mind.

Mantrams. Verses from the Vedas. In the exoteric sense a mantram (or that psychic faculty or power that conveys perception or thought) is the older portion of the Vedas, the second part of which is composed of the Brahmanas. In esoteric phraseology mantram is the word made flesh, or rendered objective through divine magic. A form of words or syllables rhythmically arranged, so that when sounded certain vibrations are generated.

Manu. The representative name of the great Being Who is the Ruler, primal progenitor and chief of the human race. It comes from the Sanskrit root "man" —to think.

Manvantara. A period of activity as opposed to a period of rest, without reference to any specific length of cycle. Frequently used to express a period of planetary activity and its seven races.

Maya. Sanskrit, "Illusion." Of the principle of form or limitation. The result of manifestation. Generally used in a relative sense for phenomena or objective appearances that are created by the mind.

Mayavi Rupa. Sanskrit, "Illusive Form." It is the body of manifestation created by the adept by an act of will for use in the three worlds. It has no material connection with the physical body. It is spiritual and ethereal and passes everywhere without let or hindrance. It is built by the power of the lower mind, of the highest type of astral matter.

Microcosm. The little universe, or man manifesting through his body, the physical body.

Monad. The One. The threefold spirit on its own plane. In occultism it often means the unified triad—Atma, Buddhi, Manas, Spiritual Will, Intuition and Higher mind,—or the immortal part of man which reincarnates in the lower kingdoms and gradually progresses through them to man and thence to the final goal.

Nirmanakaya. Those perfected beings who renounce Nirvana (the highest state of spiritual bliss) and choose a life of self-sacrifice, becoming members of that invisible host which ever protects humanity within karmic limits.

Permanent atom. Those five atoms, with the mental unit, one on each of the five planes of human evolution (the mental unit being also on the mental plane) which the monad appropriates for purposes of manifestation. They form a stable centre and are relatively permanent. Around them the various sheaths or bodies are built. They are literally small force centres.

Planetary Logos. This term is generally applied to the seven highest spirits corresponding to the seven archangels of the Christian. They have all passed through the human stage and are now manifesting through a planet and its evolutions, in the same way that man manifests through his physical body. The highest planetary spirit working through any particular globe is, in reality, the personal God of the planet.

Prakriti. Derives its name from its function as the material cause of the first evolution of the universe. It may be said to be composed of two roots, "pra" to manifest, and "krita" to make; meaning, that which caused the universe to manifest itself.

Prana. The Life Principle, the breath of Life. The occultist believes the following statement: "Life we look upon as the one form of existence, manifesting in what is called matter, or what, incorrectly separating them, we name Spirit, Soul, and Matter in man. Matter is the vehicle for the manifestation of Soul on this plane of existence; soul is the vehicle for the manifestation of spirit, and these three as a trinity are synthesised by Life, which pervades them all."

Purusha. The spiritual self. The embodied self. The word literally means "The dweller in the city"— that is, in the body. It is derived from the Sanskrit "pura" which means city or body, and "usha," a derivative of the verb "vas," to dwell.

Quaternary. The fourfold lower self, or man, in the three worlds. There are various divisions of this, but perhaps for our purpose the best is to enumerate the four as follows:
1. Lower mind.
2. Emotional or kamic body.
3. Prana, or the Life Principle.
4. The etheric body, or the highest division of the twofold physical body.

Raja Lord. The word "Raja" simply means King or Prince; the word has been applied to those great angels or entities who ensoul the seven planes. These are great devas who are the sum total and the controlling intelligence of a plane.

Raja Yoga. The true system of developing psychic and spiritual powers and union with one's higher self or the Ego. It involves the exercise, regulation, and concentration of thought.

Ray. One of the seven streams of force of the Logos; the seven great lights. Each of them is the embodiment of a great cosmic entity. The seven Rays can be divided into the three Rays of Aspect and the four Rays of Attribute, as follows:

Rays of Aspect

1. The Ray of Will, or Power.
2. The Ray of Love-Wisdom.
3. The Ray of Activity or Adaptability.

Rays of Attribute

4. The Ray of Harmony, Beauty, Art, or Unity.
5. The Ray of Concrete Knowledge or Science.
6. The Ray of Abstract Idealism or Devotion.
7. The Ray of Ceremonial Magic, or Law.

The above names are simply some chosen from among many, and embody the different aspects of force by means of which the Logos manifests.

Ring-pass-not. This is at the circumference of the manifested solar system, and is the periphery of the influence of the sun, both esoterically and exoterically understood. The limit of the field of activity of the central life force.

Root Race. One of the seven races of man which evolve upon a planet during the great cycle of planetary existence. This cycle is called a world period. The Aryan root race, to which the Hindu, European, and modern American races belong, is the fifth, the Chinese and Japanese belonging to the fourth race.

Sensa, or Senzar. The name for the secret sacerdotal language, or the "mystery speech" of the initiated adepts all over the world. It is a universal language, and largely a hieroglyphic cypher.

Shamballa. The City of the Gods, which is in the West to some nations, in the East to others, in the North or South to yet others. It is the sacred island in the Gobi Desert. It is the home of mysticism and the Secret Doctrine.

Triad. The Spiritual Man; the expression of the monad. It is the germinal spirit containing the potentialities of divinity. These potentialities will be unfolded during the course of evolution. This Triad forms the individualised or separated self, or Ego.

Viveka. The Sanskrit "discrimination". The very first step in the path of occultism......is the discrimination between the real and the unreal, between substance and phenomenon, between the Self and the Not-self, between spirit and matter.

Wesak. A festival which takes place in the Himalayas at the full moon of May (Taurus). It is said that at this festival, at which all the members of the Hierarchy are present, the Buddha, for a brief period, renews his touch and association with the work of our planet.

Yoga. 1. One of the six schools of India, said to be founded by Patanjali, but really of much earlier origin. 2. The practice of Meditation, as a means of leading to spiritual liberation.

Note: This glossary does not undertake fully to explain all the above terms. It is simply an attempt to render into English certain words used in this book, so that the reader may understand their connotation. The majority of the definitions have been culled from the Theosophical Glossary, The Secret Doctrine, and the Voice of the Silence.

INDEX